BIRCHBARK CHRONICLES

An Adirondack Journal

Pat Garber

Cover Design by Pat Garber
Author photo by Michele White

ISBN 9781707676576

******

Also by Pat Garber

Ocracoke Wild; A Naturalist's Year on an Outer Banks Island 1995

Ocracoke Odyssey; A Naturalist's Reflections on her Home by the Sea 1999

Little Sea Horse and the Story of the Ocracoke Ponies 2005

Heart Like a River; the Story of Confederate Sgt-Major Newsom Edward Jenkins 2011

Paws and Tales 2014

Little Matey; a make-believe legend of Blackbeard the Pirate's cat, set on Ocracoke Island 2018

The View from the Back of a Whale; Poems and Selected Prose 2018

Westward Bound with the Bloxtons; Settling the Arizona Territory; One family's amazing journey west 2019

Glenmore Farm; An intimate look at life on a 19th-century Virginia farm 2019

******

for my family

With gratitude to my sister Betsy Miller and my friends, Denny Dobbin, Jeannie Griffiths, Connie Leinbach, and Carol Pahl for their help in preparing this book

Table of Contents

Preface

When I moved into a one-room log cabin in the Adirondack Mountains of New York in August of 2002, I had no idea of writing this book. I wasn't exactly sure why I was coming back, but I felt that I needed a place to sit alone; to reflect; to try to glean some understanding about the twists and turns of my life and where it might go now.

Soon after I arrived, I pulled some bark off a paper birch log near my cabin, peeled it into layers, and began recording journal entries of my daily life upon it, using a ballpoint pen. Finally it became impossible to write everything I wanted to say on the bark, so I put it away and took out paper and word processor. Deciding to write down stories from my past came later, and even then it was years before I thought of publishing them.

I recorded these stories for three reasons. The first was to preserve them; they are, after all, who I am, and may be all that will be left when I am gone. The second was to escape them. By putting them down on paper, for all to see, for all to judge, they might no longer be swirling around my subconscious, sneaking up and blackmailing me at every corner of my life. The third reason was to try and do as John Steinbeck wrote in his book, *The Pastures of Heaven*; "to make something, all in one piece, that has a meaning, instead of all these trailing ends..." A meaning, not just for myself, but for others, so that they might learn and profit from my failures and my triumphs.

My mother said to me, when I was still a child, "You should have been more than one person." I guess she was right. I have tried, in the more than sixty years of my life, to be many people and to live many lives. If it was out there to try, I wanted to try it. I wanted to be an anthropologist, a cowboy, a hobo, a singer, a fisherman, a teacher, a barmaid. I wanted to live like the rich and famous and I wanted to hang with the down and out; to make a home in the farthest wilderness and in an inner city. I wanted to go every place I saw on the map and live in most of them. I still want to be every one of those people, living every one of those lives, in every one of those places.

I can't. In writing down these stories of those past lives, I hope to escape their pull. To be able to say, that's enough. To move forward without longing to move backward. To stop feeling torn in so many pieces. That is what I hope.

Birchbark Chronicles is also an account of my life in the Adirondacks Mountains, written day by day on the pages of my journal, recording my experiences while living in the wilderness and interacting with the community of Long Lake. It is based not on memories, but on events and emotions as they occurred. I have altered certain parts of it for this publication, changing names of those who did not wish to be identified, omitting pieces that were redundant, irrelevant, or in some cases unnecessarily aspersious. I have not, to my knowledge, written anything that did not happen, that was not true as I saw it.

Recently, as I began compiling these stories for this manuscript, I realized that there were far too many for one book. I decided to include those leading up to 1984, a momentous time when my life changed direction, and to publish the rest in some future book or books.

The stories are true, as best I can remember them. I have used journals that I kept and letters that I wrote to substantiate my recollections, and when possible I have compared what I recall with the memories of others who were there. But nothing can guarantee that what I remember is what really occurred. Memory can play tricks.

On the other hand, what and how I remember it is the truth as I see it, and that may be, in the end, the only truth that matters for each of us. Those who profess to know ultimate truths, pedantic scientists and academicians, may live in the falsest world of all.

Each of us is alone in the world we have created around us. Only we can know that world intimately. These pages represent my world.

I've never had time to think...If I could live...there for a little, why, I'd think over all the things that ever happened to me, and maybe I could make something out of them, something all in one piece that had a meaning, instead of all these trailing ends, these raw and dragging tails.

The Pastures of Heaven
John Steinbeck 1932

Pat Garber

.

August 2002

11:30 pm August 12, 2002

Translucent in the pale light of my campfire, the layers of bark peel away beneath my fingers, producing sheets as fine and fragile as letters from my grandmother. I reach down and pick up another log, one of several pieces of birch which are stacked nearby. Large flakes of the white bark cling in patches to the wood, and as I strip another sheet away, words form in my mind. As I often do, I pretend that I am writing, this time on the papyrus-like sheets I have stripped from the logs. I place the pieces of wood on the coals and prod them into flames as the words tumble onto the pages of my imagined birchbark journal:

Self-doubt gave way to fear as I turned onto Rt. 30, the road that leads into the heart of New York's Adirondack Mountains. Flashing lights blinded me, and I hit the brakes. "What the heck?" I wondered as a flashlight targeted my side window. Opening it, I peered up at the officer's face. "Road's closed!" he told me. "You'll have to go around." He did not seem inclined to elaborate, so I asked what was wrong. "Been a big storm. Trees, lines are down in the road. Electricity's out all the way to Blue Mountain." I didn't know how to "go around" so he directed me; take the next dirt road to the left, all the way to the end, turn when you see a light and follow it out.

The night was dark as pitch and heavy with rain; the unpaved road narrow and tortuous. It was spooky, and I was glad to have Huck, my doberman pinscher companion, beside me. We finally reached the light he'd mentioned, a flashlight held by another policeman, and turned. I drove the next hour in darkness, wondering what this strange arrival back in the Adirondack Mountains might portend.

Now I am camped in the lean-to down by Buttermilk Falls, my sleeping bag spread out on a few cedar branches beside me. The wood around camp was too wet to burn, but there were a few logs, marginally dry, tucked in a corner of the lean-to. I tore up some newspaper and managed to start a fire, then heated a can of franks and beans, which I shared with Huck. I'm sitting on a tree stump and Huck is trotting through the woods, sniffing for deer or chipmunks. I can hear the purr of the falls, where the Raquette River pirouettes over giant boulders in its path from Forked Lake to Long Lake. Once known as Phantom Falls, it is here that the ghost of an Indian maiden purportedly searches in the mist for her lost lover, and the famous (or perhaps infamous) preacher/writer William Murray took an accidental but successful ride down the falls in his canoe.

Sitting here, wrapped in a blanket, I try to make out the call of a distant owl, and I wonder what tomorrow will hold. I plan to try and find a place to live and a job here in Long Lake, the little hamlet which lies in the center of this ancient lake-strewn northern mountain range. I left behind me, in Buffalo, a perfectly good job teaching Head Start, a nice home with my sister, friends, a lover. Why? They wanted to know. I ask myself the same question.

7:00 pm August 14, 2002

Home! I have a home! I spent most of today moving into my new cabin. I'm tired but thrilled. I asked Margaret and Carl, from whom I'd rented a small apartment when I lived here before, if they had anything available. I had no idea they'd rent me their cabin, so when Margaret mentioned it I jumped at the chance. "Let me look at it again and think about it," I said. It took about ten minutes for Huck and me to hike up the hill, sit down on the futon, and return. "I'll take it!" I told her.

This log cabin, built on a great slab of stone near the top of Mt. Sabattis, is as close to heaven as I expect to get any time soon. It sits up here alone, one large room with a sleeping loft upstairs and a deck on the back which overlooks a small meadow. Looking out the front window, I can see the lake in the distance, framed by the branches of birch trees and white cedars. Balsam fir and hemlock trees surround the cabin. Wood ferns and lichens emerge from the cracks in the rock. Blackberries ramble along the deck, almost hiding the stairs that lead down to the meadow. A great pile of logs, cut years before, waits for me to get at them with the splitting maul and wedge that Carl, my landlord, has loaned me. All manner of brightly colored and oddly shaped fungi protrude from the rotting bark. There are even some pieces of birch bark lying nearby, which I brought in and am using to write on. They work just as well as paper. Better in a way, since you can wipe the smudges off.

Carl built this cabin three years ago, using logs and leftover bits and pieces from other jobs. He furnished it with everything you need to live up here: sheets and blankets, dishes, even CDs for the stereo. For me, showing up here with next to nothing, it's perfect. I do want to bring some of my own stuff, though, so that it feels like home.

The biggest challenge in living here is going to be getting up and down this hill, especially when it's covered in snow and ice. Carl doesn't want me to try driving up the steep part, and I'm not sure I want to either. In warm weather I can park below his house, but in winter I'll have to snowshoe all the way up from the road. I guess I'll get my exercise!

Mitchell Sabattis, the man for whom this mountain is named, was an Abanaki Indian guide who lived near here around the turn of the century. He was famous for his skills in leading visitors to wonderful secret places where they would find white-tailed deer and huge brown trout, fulfilling their fondest dreams. Perhaps it was his spirit that guided me though the darkness on the night I arrived and brought me here.

8:30 am August 15, 2002

I woke with a start this morning, listening to a softly undulating, plaintive cry which I recognized as the wail of a loon. Only then did I remember where I was. I had a good night's sleep, though I spent it on the futon downstairs instead of in the bed in the loft. Huck can't manage the metal spiral staircase, and he whined so pitifully when I started to go up to bed that I brought down a pillow and sheet and slept on the futon with him curled at my feet.

There is nothing that I have to do today, so I'm having my coffee on the deck and luxuriating in the peace that surrounds me. Some of the land here is privately owned, but much of it is part of the Adirondack Park. Established in 1892, it is the largest state park in the country, covering nearly six million acres. It is unique in that it includes towns and logging camps and other private land within its boundaries. The regulations imposed by the park on private lands cause the biggest political issue up here. Much as I hate rules, though, I sure like living where there are no fast food restaurants or strip malls.

In a little while I'll take Huck for a walk on the snowmobile trail that passes behind the cabin. Yesterday I turned left, following the trail to Sabattis Park, where the town holds dances, auctions, and other community events. I picked a few blueberries along the way and saw a big pile of what I'm sure is bear scat, full of berries. Today I want to go the other way, see what lies over there. Huck is having a great time running free up here. He goes nuts when he gets on a deer trail, which I don't much like; but he comes back before too long. I've used up the birchbark paper I've been writing on, so I hope to pick up some more along the way.

11 am August 16, 2002

Guilt assails me as I ignore Huck's somber gaze. He is yearning to go for a walk, or better yet a run, up some nearby mountainside. I am tempted to succumb to his wishes, but I am even more determined to get at this mess. I have this pressing feeling that it may be my last chance.

Strewn around me like pieces of a puzzle are the pieces of my life. I have pulled them from the tangled maze of my mind in much the same way one would reach into a jigsaw puzzle box and clasp, without looking, handfuls of the jagged-edged pieces to dump helter-skelter on a table. I have cloistered myself here today for this express purpose. I need to fit these mismatched pieces into a picture that makes sense; that gives some tangible meaning to my life.

Outside, the sky is the crisp blue of a robin's egg and the tall pines and cedars that surround my cabin are astir with warblers taking a brief rest on their journey south. The raspberries are heavy on the bushes that line both sides of the trail, and the blackberries are starting to ripen. Later I will attach Huck's leash to his collar, hike over the hill to the Post Office, and gather the berries on the way back. Maybe make a cobbler. But not yet. I need to attend to this business first.

*****

I reach across the distance and select a random piece of the puzzle. The year is 1983. I see an old wooden fishing boat, twenty-four feet long, riding an ocean swell. On the boat are two people, a man and a woman. The man, wearing a green oilskin coat, is steering the boat, trying to keep a straight course amid three-foot waves. The woman wears a heavy sweater pulled down over worn jeans. Her hair is pulled back and stuffed into a wool hat, but a few long tendrils have escaped and swirl around her face. She is turning a huge winch, from which heavy fishing lines extend far behind the boat, sinking beneath the churning waters.

I study her face, furrowed with concentration as she reels in the lines. She is 33 years old, momentarily distracted from the fog of despair which has engulfed her since she filed for divorce three weeks before. Waiting for the paperwork to go through, she has exiled herself to Neah Bay, a tiny point of land extending from the rocky coast of northwest Washington into the Pacific Ocean. She has gone over in her mind, time and again, the crooked, rocky path that led to this final impasse in her marriage, wondering if, had she done just one thing differently, it could have been averted. Now, out of money, she has gotten a job on a long-liner, fishing for giant Pacific halibut. I remember...

Long Lining in the North Pacific

"Coffee's done."

I pushed myself up from the pallet where I sprawled, rubbing my eyes and shoving the hair back from my face. The smell of the coffee, just perked on the propane stove, roused me. I stumbled across the deck, my sea legs not yet in place, and reached for the bucket, tied with a rope and hanging over the gunwale. Crouching down out of sight of the galley (if you could call it that,) I relieved myself, recalling the social rule my southern-bred mother had recited when I was young; "Ladies do not pee, they wee-wee." "Hah!" I said to myself. "Some lady I am!"

Ron handed me a mug of steaming black coffee as I stepped back into the cabin. I wrapped my hands around it, warming them, and sat down in the one and only chair. Shivering, I raised the mug to my lips and sipped it with appreciation. He held out a package of Oreos, half empty now, and offered me one. I took it slowly, dunked it into the coffee, and took a small bite. I couldn't remember anything ever tasting as good as these coffee-dipped Oreos we shared twice a day. He looked at me for the first time that morning.

"Maybe we'll throw out a short line and catch some salmon for lunch. There's nothing much left in the larder." I nodded eagerly. I hadn't had much to eat since we'd left the dock three days before, and most of what I had eaten had been spewed across the gunwales into the turbulent waters below. Even now I felt my stomach roll uneasily and I took a deep breath, trying to steady myself. I had a hard day's work ahead of me--I couldn't afford to get seasick again. I was determined to stick this job out for as long as the captain wanted.

We had set sail out of Neah Bay, a tiny harbor on the Makah Indian Reservation at the very northwest tip of the continental United States. We were long-lining for Pacific halibut, large flounder-like flatfish which lived in the frigid waters of the Strait de San Juan de Fuca and the Pacific Ocean. I had been eager to come, walking up and down the docks looking for a job, asking at every fishing boat. When Ron said that I could be his mate I accepted eagerly, and slept on the dock so as not to miss his 5:00 AM departure. His boat, the "Albatross," was small--24 feet--and old. It lacked the simplest of amenities--a refrigerator, a head (or bathroom), comfortable berths for sleeping. I knew it was no luxury yacht and I knew the seas here were rough and cold. But I didn't know how hard it would be.

The jacket I wore did little to ward off the icy spray that regularly washed across the bow, soaking me to the skin, or the cold north wind that never seemed to stop blowing. The heavy gloves that Ron loaned me kept my hands warm for only a short while as I continually reached into the ice chest to pull out bait for the huge multiple hooks that were attached to the fishing lines. The lines were wrapped around winches. It was my job to turn the winches and set out the thousands of feet of line we pulled behind the boat; then to haul them back in, along with the 800-pound fish that would be Ron's livelihood and my week's pay. Except that there weren't any. The halibut were nowhere to be found in the cold gray waters we plied for five long days and nights.

My hands grew sore and blistered as I set the lines and winched them back in, always empty. The mood of Ron, the captain, grew dour. Worst of all were the constant, never-ending swells of the North Pacific seas. My stomach heaved when the boat heeled over, dipping into the waves, and even on the calmest days I felt a sickness upon me.

What, I wondered, had Ron expected of me when he took me on? That I would bring good luck? I certainly hadn't brought it yet. He seemed like a man to whom Luck had never been a friend. In the past he'd have been called a half-breed, part Makah and part who-knew-what? Maybe French, maybe English. A man caught between two cultures, or maybe lost between two cultures is a better way to put it. Eyes the color of the sea, thin, crooked nose with dark skin and pale lips, his was an unremarkable face; a face which, were one to notice it at all, would soon be forgotten. He seldom spoke, and when he did there was a taste of defiant bitterness which seemed to cling to each word. Which hinted at some incomprehensible unforgivable betrayal. Having given his life to the sea, the sea refused to give back. Defeat sat upon his shoulders; a heavy coat that kept out no cold. Hope was his last defense.

Day after day he stared ahead, scanning the horizon, and it seemed to me that he was searching for something more than fish. As with Ernest Hemingway's old man and the sea, Ron had somehow sailed into forbidden waters. A man on the verge of desperation, perhaps he had sensed a similar desperation in me. Perhaps that is what had drawn us together, two strangers clinging to empty lines in an old wooden boat on an unforgiving ocean.

We saw gray whales, also known as devilfish, making their way north from California and Baja Mexico to Alaska, a journey of 5000 miles. They sometimes passed within a hundred feet of us, seeming to pay us no mind. I worried that they might become entangled in our lines, but Ron was unconcerned. The spectacular flash of black and white orcas, or killer whales, caught my eye several times, thrilling me with a surge of wonder. Storm petrels hovered over the waves and arctic terns did headlong dives into the swells. Long-tailed jaegers flew overhead, scanning the waters below for fish, and once I thought I saw an albatross, namesake of the little boat we clung to. But the halibut were not there.

Each morning I said a silent prayer that Ron would decide to give up and return to Neah Bay, but I said not a word. Once, as evening approached, he steered the "Albatross" close to a deserted beach where great black Neolithic rocks reared up out of the water. He looked for a place where we might go ashore. Oh, how I longed to put my feet on that solid ground! But the waves crashed upon the rocky ledges and treacherous currents swirled around the rocks. There was no place to land, so we anchored for the night, in sight of the tempting shore but totally out of its reach.

One day, when we were miles from land, I heard Ron's voice: "Get the net!" I hurried to obey his command and he pointed to a spot a few yards away from the boat. I stared, seeing nothing at first. Then there appeared what looked like a blue-green, iridescent bubble, about four inches across. It bobbed upon the waves, sucked in and then spit out by each swell. Ron steered the boat close to it, reached out and, encircling it with the net, pulled it in.

He held it in his hand for a moment, studying it, then handed it to me. It was a glass float, washed across the seas from a distant land and a distant time; from a Japanese fishing boat that might have been much like the one I now stood on. It seemed incredibly fragile to have survived the journey it must have made, and I held it with a kind of awe. When I started to give it back, he shook his head. "I have enough of 'em," he said gruffly. I wrapped it carefully in a shirt and stashed it in my backpack.

We continued to fish and the halibut continued to elude us. Finally Ron shook his head in disgust. "They're not here, and I'm gonna run out of fuel." He turned the bow of the "Albatross" landward, and we started back. We didn't talk on the way, but then we never had wasted any words between us. I was secretly overjoyed at the prospect of standing on dry land again and getting warm, but I knew that this trip had been an expensive failure for him. We arrived back at Neah Bay at sunset, after five days at sea, and we tied up at the dock. He pulled a ten-dollar bill out of his wallet and handed it to me, not much pay for five days work but more than the percentage I had agreed to. More too, I knew, than he had made.

Stuffing it into my pocket, I walked away down the dock, lurching a little on the unfamiliar stability of solid ground, not knowing where I was going next. I didn't look back. Didn't turn to see if he was watching me, or was already preparing for his next fishing trip. I still have the glass float. It sits up on the shelf in my house, and sometimes when I gaze at it I find myself back on the "Albatross," cold and seasick, watching gray whales and orcas, hunting for halibut and an elusive dream with a grim, silent man who couldn't bring himself to accept defeat.

*****

9:30 pm August 18, 2002

I have a job! Starting tomorrow, I'll be waiting tables at the Long Lake Diner.

I spent yesterday wandering around Long Lake, revisiting familiar places and renewing old memories. At the bottom of the hill I walked past Harry's house, where I had lived before. I had met Harry when I stopped here for a hamburger and a beer on my way north from North Carolina to Canada. We fell head over heels and, as long as I lived down south in Ocracoke, it worked great. Things fell apart pretty quickly when I, along with Huck and my three cats, came to Long Lake and moved in with him. Harry was the Long Lake building inspector, but he also tended bar at the Diner, which is where I'd met him. I guess having us at home was too much for him, because he spent more and more time at the bar. I worked at a museum down the road but, as our relationship disintegrated, I spent most of my free time alone, hiking and kayaking with Huck or cuddling up with a book and my cats.

Finally I left, moving into Dawn's (a friend from the museum) ancient travel trailer in Minerva. Here I cooked on a campfire, read by oil lamp, and visited an outhouse when the need arose (which sounds kind of fun, but since it rained buckets the whole time I was there, got pretty cold and miserable.) I stayed there till Carl and Margaret had an apartment open; then came back to Long Lake and finished out the season at the museum.

I then moved to Buffalo and began a new life. But I didn't feel like I was finished with Long Lake. I'd become very fond of this little hamlet and now I want to try living here on my own.

Long Lake is not very big--just 800 people live here full time, but it is spread out, with houses and camps tucked into hillsides and along lakes and ponds well away from town. It's located about half way between the villages of Blue Mountain Lake and Newcomb. The main part of the hamlet wraps around the lake it's named for. With its quaint country churches, stately town hall, rustic shops, and turn-of-the-century hotel, all set against a backdrop of verdant mountains, it is quite pretty. Huck and I walked through town to a causeway which leads to a small island in the lake. I dangled my feet in the water and watched Huck bound about, sniffing for minks and otters. On the way back I stopped at the Diner and asked to speak with Jim.

Jim, who manages the Diner, had had a sparring friendship with Harry when I lived here before. He and I got along well enough, so when I applied for a job he hired me right off. I start tomorrow.

4:15 pm August 19, 2002

I just got home from my first day of work and I'm beat! Huck wants to go for a walk, but I don't think I can move from this futon. Eight hours of running back and forth from kitchen to dining room, table to table, my head full of a dozen different orders. Make more coffee. Would you mind heating up this donut? Someone wants a straw for her beer, of all things! The sunny-side-up eggs are too sunny! I swore ten years ago that I'd never wait tables again, and here I am working full time at the Long Lake Diner, the busiest damn restaurant I ever saw. Breakfast and lunch provided free, but I never found one spare minute to sit down, much less take a bite of food. I brought a sandwich home with me, and I'll eat it soon. Right now I'm too tired to take it out of the bag. I'm not complaining, though. I wanted a job and a place to live, and I got them.

After work, we waitresses and cooks sat down for a free after-work drink in the Owls Head Pub, located in the back and named after Long Lake's biggest mountain. They gave me the lowdown on my new place of employment. The restaurant, formerly known as the Village Inn, is a century-old, rambling, white, two-story clapboard affair, resembling an old farmhouse and overlooking Jennings Park Pond. It has changed hands at least a dozen times, it sounds like.

The present owner, Tom O'Conally, is a logger. Originally from Maine, he came here 21 years ago, established a small logging business, and then bought the Diner a few years back. From what everyone says, he's a real nice guy, and he sure as hell is good-looking; attached though.

I brought home a menu to study. I'm going to look it over after Huck and I get back from our walk, then hit the sack. I'm tired.

9:15 pm August 21, 2002

Today was my birthday. I had the day off, so I spent it on Long Lake. The lake is actually a widening of the Raquette River, which flows north into the St. Lawrence Seaway. It is fourteen miles long, about a mile wide, and an average of thirteen feet deep. The Indian name for Long Lake was In-ca-pah-co, which referred to the basswood trees which grew along its banks. Allen, a local bird-carver whom I met last year, uses the wood for his carvings.

I can walk down the lane from my cabin, cross the highway, and clamber my way through a little wooded lot to the lake in about five minutes. There's no one around, and there's a big rock for sunning on and, when the water's high enough, diving. I had brought my kayak with me to Long Lake, strapped to the top of my pickup truck. Now I put on my bathing suit, called Huck, and hauled it down the hill to the water's edge.

Huck loves kayaking. He knows how to get in, position himself between my knees, and sit quietly as I paddle. ("Knows how" doesn't always mean he does it. He got real antsy when we approached a pair of mergansers. I had to cover his eyes to keep him still.) I paddled north, toward town, passing under the bridge and following the shoreline to Northern Borne, a country store that carries a bit of everything. I pulled the kayak up on the town beach, tied Huck near the store, and bought some bananas.

Then we walked up the hill to the library. I still have my card, so I stopped in. It's a great little library with a big moose head on the wall, a stone fireplace, and friendly librarians. I checked out Barbara Kingsolver's new book of essays and a book on Adirondack history, then walked back to the beach. I paddled a little farther up the lake, past homes and camps built on its steep banks, before returning home. Tired now and wet (Huck always manages to splash water on me when he jumps out,) I tied the kayak to a tree on the shore near my cabin. I don't know who the land actually belongs to, but I don't figure my boat will do it any harm. Then Huck and I hiked back up the hill to the cabin.

Later, I walked to the century-old Adirondack Hotel for a beer and a pizza to go. I chatted with my landlord, Carl, and several other old acquaintances, all of us seated on bar stools beneath the sightlessly staring eyes of a fisher, a short-tailed weasel, a bobcat, and a moose. I told no one that it was my birthday.

Now I've been sitting on the futon with Huck at my feet, a belly full of pizza (shared with Huck), a glass (actually an empty peanut butter jar) of red wine on the table beside me, and my guitar on my lap. Working on a new song.

Not a bad birthday, but I dread going back to work at the diner tomorrow. I am too old for this waitress job; too old, too slow, too scatter-brained. I'm going to start working part-time at the Adirondack Museum, where I'd been before, but it's seasonal work, and I need a job for the entire long, cold, dark Adirondack winter. I'm determined to stick this out, if I can.

8:30 pm August 22, 2002

I survived another day of work. I'm getting to know the people I work with. There are three full-time waitresses, two cooks, a dishwasher, and Jim, the manager, plus a lot of part-time and seasonal staff. Evy, a tall redhead who moved here from Massachusetts twenty years ago, has waited tables at the Diner for so long it should be called Evy's Diner (that's what one of the customers told me, anyway.) Eve, petite with long dark hair, grew up here, moved to Colorado, and came back with her husband in 1980. She's been at the diner for four years. Julie, young, sexy, and Irish, is fairly new. Joey, from Long Island, and Sheryl, a Long Lake native, are the cooks. They both put out some dynamite food. Rodger, the dishwasher, was an army officer at one time, but moved here to get away. Jim is here from Rochester, where he was a college soccer and baseball star. He fell in love with an Adirondack girl, moved to Long Lake, and has been managing the Diner for six years.

When I got home I started on my wood pile, splitting the whole logs into pieces that would fit into the wood stove. Boy, am I out of practice! I think I pounded the ground with my maul about as much as I hit the wedge. I did manage to get a few logs split, but if I don't improve I'll never be ready for winter.

The logs have been sitting up here for a couple years at least, and they've developed a real personality of their own. Each one is a work of art; a wood sculpture designed by Mother Nature; each a different shape and size, some decorated with mosses or lichens, others in fungi. I carried a particularly interesting piece inside and, using a hammer and nails that I found in the cabin, affixed it to the wall, making it into a shelf for a picture of my parents. I'll be depending on these logs to keep Huck and me warm this winter, so I hope they are as utilitarian as they are artistic!

Building the shelf reminds me of another time when I worked with wood, as a child with my father.

*****

My mind drifts far back, across forty-some years. Now I am thinking about my new, self-assigned project: reconstructing the puzzle pieces of my past. If I am going to make sense of it, maybe I should start at the beginning. I was five years old when my family (Momma, Daddy, and five kids) moved to a fourteen-acre farm in Short Pump, just west of Richmond, Virginia, where my parents had teaching jobs. I was called Patsy back in those days.

The piece I pick up now shows a young girl, six years old, standing in front of a white, Williamsburg-style house. The yard, surrounded by fields, is shaded in part by two magnolias and a graceful old elm tree, but then it stretches out in sunlight to the road. A long drive follows along it, flanked by forsythia bushes and colorful irises. Patsy has short, dark blonde hair, with bangs hanging over serious blue-gray eyes. Dirty knees protrude beneath worn shorts and mud splotches adorn her white tee-shirt. Her feet are bare. On her head, almost hiding her face, is a wide-brimmed, felt cowboy hat. Leaning against her, almost as tall as she is, is a tan and white St. Bernard dog named Tiny. She is talking to a pretty woman with dark curly hair who is picking peas from the garden.

Tornado or Daddy's Workshop

"Where's Daddy?"

How many times I must have asked that question of my mother as I was growing up. An incorrigible tomboy, I guessed that whatever he was doing outside was more exciting than anything going on in the house. If she answered that he was out in the workshop, as was often the case, out I would go. It was one of my favorite places, growing up in Short Pump, Virginia; that old workshop of my father's. It was here that Daddy and I conjured up and brought to life "Tornado," my stick horse.

27

Pat Garber

The workshop was a long wooden building, painted white, that marked the boundary between the well-manicured safety of our back yard and the exciting but sometimes frightening wildness of the gardens, fields, and woods below. The workshop had paint peeling off some of its boards and a window broken out at the back. The walls and rafters were draped with the leavings of my father's collecting--old bicycle tires, broken can-openers, a used horse harness, baling twine, secondhand carpeting, parts of old toys. The shop was never neat and tidy, not even after Daddy spent an afternoon cleaning it up. It contained just about everything you could imagine.

Daddy's workshop was a place of enchantment, a place where my father could take ordinary pieces of wood and other odds and ends, and with the help of a hammer and nails, create marvelous inventions. He always preferred to build or fix something we needed rather than buy a new one. The hinges on our outbuildings were fashioned out of old shoe soles. Flies were killed, not with an ordinary fly swatter, but with a fly snitcher he made from a fountain pen, a child's pop gun, and a clothespin. He repaired the holes in his socks, much to my mother's consternation, with swimming pool caulking.

Little scraps of wood, left over from his carpentry, he saved for me. While he built shelves and magazine racks from big pieces of wood, I would hammer together the leavings into cars, rockets, and doll beds. Sometimes he would interrupt his work to help me with some particularly ambitious project.

Of all the things I made with my father in his workshop, my favorite was Tornado, my wooden stick horse. He was made in the image of Zorro's fiery black stallion, his namesake, and he was far superior to all the stick horses sold in toy stores.

Daddy helped me draw the outline for his head on a piece of leftover wood. The body was an old broom handle whose bristles had worn out long before. We found a can of black paint on a workshop shelf and painted him the color of darkest night. Other odd bits of paint were used to create his eyes and nostrils. I held the stick body tightly while Daddy drilled holes along the top of his neck and forehead. Momma found some black yarn in her cedar chest and helped me thread it through the holes and tie it to make Tornado's mane and forelock. A hole was positioned where a bridle bit should be, and a rope run through it to make the reins.

Tornado came to life then. I rode him galloping all over our yard and fields and woods, at least as far as I dared. I stabled him in my bedroom

28

at night, where I would give him one last pat on the head before I closed my eyes.

That was a long time ago. I never knew what happened to that old stick horse. I put him aside when Momma and Daddy bought me Blaze, a true flesh and blood horse. Tornado was, after all, just a toy, and I was growing up into a big girl. I didn't even wonder until now.

But something has brought him to mind. Somehow, through all these years, he has managed to survive, hidden away in a little corner of my memory. No longer made of wood and yarn, he is nonetheless still real. I can see him now, in my mind's eye, galloping across the front yard with a small tow-headed girl holding on tightly. And I can feel again the wonder and excitement I felt on the day my father and I made him, all those years ago, in Daddy's workshop.

★ ★ ★ ★ ★

3:00 am August 25, 2002

I woke up a little while back when Huck began barking. He is restless tonight and, now that I'm awake, so am I. I stepped outside for a few minutes, listening to the night sounds of the woods, wondering whether fox, coyote, or deer was stirring the leaves beside the cabin. There is a bear, a two-year-old that regularly traverses this ridge looking for berries. I've been told this by several folks, though I haven't seen it yet. Maybe that is what Huck was barking at.

I'm back inside now but I still can't sleep. I feel ghosts lurking. Not Adirondack ghosts, but my own personal haunts that I never seem able to leave behind. I wonder what I am doing, embarking on a new life for the umpteenth time, alone, with only my dog to talk to, the deer and birds to listen. I miss my cats, still back in Buffalo with my sister. The euphoria I felt when I arrived has given way to self-doubt. The telephone company says the cabin is too far up the mountain for them to install a line, so I feel terribly isolated. Un-needed...purposeless...lost...How did I get here, a fifty-two-year-old woman alone with a nine-year-old dog, high on this Adirondack landscape with an eternity between her and her nearest neighbor? What am I running from, or toward? How did I end up with this jumbled mess of a life in such desperate need of sorting out?

This kind of thinking is pointless, I tell myself; I'd better get back to sleep. I have to be up in just three hours to get ready for work.

8:30 pm August 26, 2002

After work I stopped by the library for a while, and I checked out a book on lichens and mosses. Then Huck and I walked down to the causeway that separates Long Lake from Jennings Pond. There was a pair of loons diving and surfacing close by, so I sat down on the bank and watched them for a while. Loons, also known as great northern divers, are kind of iconic here. The shops sell all kinds of items decorated with loons, and I must admit I bought a few myself when I was here last year.

11:30 am August 27, 2002

I do not have to work today, so I slept in, getting up at 8:15 and luxuriating with a cup of coffee, listening to Peter, Paul, and Mary on the CD player. Then Huck and I took a leisurely stroll down the snowmobile trail, me humming the tune of "Puff the Magic Dragon."

When I first came to the Adirondacks, two years ago, I had the strange feeling that I had come home. It took me a while to realize why. I grew up, not only on a farm in Virginia, but in the pages of a series of books my parents read to me, and which I read to myself as soon as I was old enough.

Written by naturalist Thornton Burgess, they took place in the woodlands and fields of New England, at such places as the Smiling Pool, the Green Meadow, the Laughing Brook, and the Great Forest. The main characters were the wild animals that lived there, and they were the same as those who live around me here. Blacky the Crow, Prickly Porcupine, Hooty the Owl, Reddy Fox; these were some of my earliest friends, along with the myriad other animals that Burgess wrote about. Over the years I acquired dozens of these books, and I still own and treasure them.

So, on our stroll this morning Huck and I stopped by the Smiling Pool, as I have named it, and peered in, looking for tadpoles, small fish, and water striders. We listened to the jolly gurgles of the Laughing Brook, farther down the trail, and gazed into the dark recesses of the Great Forest that grows alongside. Once back at the cabin, we stopped at the Green Meadow to pick some daisies. It's no wonder I feel so at home here!

Birchbark Chronicles

5:00 pm August 28, 2002

There's a big pile of birch bark sitting on my table. I picked it up on my walk with Huck, finding it on the ground and stripping it from dead trees. I've been finding all sorts of things to do with it, not just writing this journal. Yesterday I peeled the layers apart and wrote a letter to my sister on one of the thin, paper-like sheets. Furniture, mirrors, and picture frames were made with it in the old days, and there is a revived, lucrative market for these items today. Folks up here love to put them in their Adirondack camps. The Indians that once traversed these mountains stretched it across frames of northern white cedar to make canoes. They sewed them with threads made from tamarack trees and caulked the seams with balsam fir or pine resin.

Dozens of paper birch trees surround my cabin, mixed in with white cedar, tamaracks, balsam fir, and white pine. I could make a canoe without leaving this acre if I knew how!

Trudging back home with Huck, I located the turnoff to the cabin by finding the glistening white arch formed by a tall birch tree bent low across the trail. Seeing it, the words of Robert Frost resounded in my mind:

> *When I see birches bend to left and right*
> *Across the line of straighter darker trees,*
> *I like to think some boy's been swinging them.*
> *But swinging doesn't bend them down to stay.*
> *Ice storms do that.*

I feel sure that it was ice that bent this particular tree, since there are no boys living nearby and it's most definitely bent down to stay. But I rejoice in the words of Frost's poem; his belief that climbing a birch tree is like climbing toward Heaven, and that *one could do worse than be a swinger of birches.*

Things are rough at the Diner. I'm so darned pokey, compared to the other waitresses. I don't see how they work so fast, and they take cigarette breaks to boot. They always give me the slow section, which means less money, but I'd never be able to keep up with the busy stations. I can tell they get irritated with me sometimes.

I'm feeling like a failure, and I need to get back to my past. Maybe there I will find the self-assurance I need.

Pat Garber

*****

Taking out one of my sheets of birchbark paper, I sit back on the futon, close my eyes, and watch a young girl, maybe nine years old now, working at another job--very different from the one I now have. She is small for her age, with spindly arms and legs, a serious face, and heavy, dark blonde hair, cut short and held out of her face with a barrette. She is waiting impatiently for her father. I begin writing.

Digging for Gold in Short Pump

"Are you ready, Patsy?" Daddy stepped out the workshop door, armed with a shovel and a burlap feed sack. I stood quietly, trying to contain my impatience, and nodded with a little smile. He handed me the sack and headed out toward the bottom field. I trotted after him, and we were soon joined by our brown and white St. Bernard, Tiny. We stopped briefly to open the gate (which I thought was a waste of time, but he insisted that climbing on gates ruined the hinges, and there was no other way around.) The horses were in the front field, so we really didn't need to close it back, but that was another one of his rules, so once we were all in he slipped the cross-board back through.

We began our trek across the big back field, following the fence line. Blackberry bushes and honeysuckle vines hid the fence itself, climbing over and through the wire strands. They made great hiding places for bobwhites, and somewhere ahead of us we could hear one's plaintive two-syllable whistle. We stopped beside the persimmon tree and studied the branches to see if the small orange fruits were getting near ripe. "Not for another week or two," Daddy concluded.

Farther along we scared up a cottontail rabbit and watched it scurry across the field. Tiny started to trot after it but changed her mind. She was not big on chasing anything except the horses, and then she always stayed on the safe side of the fence. You couldn't see the bottom field yet; there was a bit of a rise to the field we were in and you had to get over it first. Near the top was a haystack, most of the hay old and dusty now. We passed close by it, which was fine with me since I was with Daddy; but I kept my distance other times. I had this uneasy feeling that something scary might live inside. I figured I was too old now to take that kind of thing seriously, but it didn't hurt to be careful.

Now we could see the bottom field. It was surrounded on three sides by woods, held back by a barbwire fence. Sometimes you'd see a deer

32

down here, but this evening there were just the birds. You could hear them all around--the cawing of crows, sounding like they were arguing about something; a constant rustle in the bushes which betrayed the presence of some kind of little birds, what Momma called warblers most likely. I figured they were eating berries. Once my brother and I saw a gray fox down here, and we guessed that it was probably the one that got our duck.

The part of the field we came to first had been planted in corn this summer. Daddy and my brother Sandy had picked it earlier, but there were still some stalks left standing. They made a clattering sound when the breeze blew through them. I looked to see if there were any ears they'd missed. I was making a corn-husk doll, and I needed some nice brown tassels to use for its hair. I found a couple and slipped them into the sack.

We were there now. This part of the field was covered with low-growing plants, spindly-looking, and caramel-brown as they dried in the autumn sun. Daddy stopped at one end and turned around, looking at me expectantly. "Okay, Patsy. Are you ready? We're gonna dig some gold now!"

I was ready; in fact, I'd been waiting for this moment all week. I knew what to do, what my job was. Daddy sank the shovel blade deep into the ground, lifting out a shovelful of dirt. I crouched down and peered expectantly into the hole he'd made. Nothing. He scooped down again, and this time I cried out. "Wait!" I reached down and picked up a piece of golden treasure. This is what we had come to search for. It was an inch and a half long, curved and the color of wheat. Daddy and I called it a piece of gold, but it was, in fact, a peanut.

I reached for another one and handed it to Daddy, then cracked mine open and popped the two green nuggets into my mouth. "Mmmmm." Daddy dug some more and I searched eagerly, running my fingers through the cool dry soil and scooping up all the peanuts I could find. We worked for about an hour. The sky turned a soft purple as the sun crept toward the horizon. The sack grew heavy as I dragged it from hole to hole, filling it with our precious treasure. Finally Daddy stood up straight, twisting the kinks out of his back and shoulders, and looked down at me.

"Shall we take these to your mother?" He took the sack this time, tossing it over his shoulder, and I carried the unwieldy shovel. We were tired now, and dragged our feet as we headed for home. Tiny had lost

interest earlier and had already gone back, hoping, no doubt, that Momma would have her dinner ready.

Daddy carried the peanuts into the basement, and I ran up the back steps into the house to tell Momma about our great "haul." Momma loved raw peanuts, I knew, and she would be happy. She was cooking supper when I burst into the kitchen.

"Did you find any treasure?" she asked. "Come and see for yourself!" I replied, bubbling over with excitement and an air of importance. "We brought back a whole sack of gold!"

I wonder now, looking back, if my parents realized what a wonderful gift, and what a terrible obligation, they left me with. Finding gold in a rural Virginia field, turning a backbreaking task into an exciting treasure hunt. Momma and Daddy made childhood into a wondrous, magical adventure, but left adulthood an oh-so-hard-to-accept reality.

Those days were not always wonderful. Momma had her "moods," and in such times we all tiptoed around the house. I did not understand why such minor things as the goat eating her roses, or Daddy forgetting to pick her up after her teachers' meeting, or buying me a horse when he was supposed to be buying pigs, seemed so important to her. But at such times all good things were put on hold until she returned to normal. She never yelled, but her silence felt devastating. The sound of her whistling some nameless tune meant that all was right with the world again.

It is that state of "all's right with the world" that I am constantly pining for, but that I never seem able to reach.

*****

8:00 pm August 29, 2002

A yellow-bellied sapsucker is moving up and down one of the white pines, drilling holes and gorging itself on insects and sap. I'm watching it from my deck, also watching the evening sky turn a soft mauve, and listening to the songbirds in the trees. Not far from the cabin, hidden in the branches of a striped maple, is an ovenbird. I caught a glimpse of the plump, rust-colored warbler when I was picking raspberries, and I can hear his sharp song--"teacher teacher"--as I sit here. I wonder if it has its nest (a Dutch-oven-like affair built on the ground, according to my book) nearby. It's probably empty by now, if it does.

I started my job working as exhibit attendant at the Adirondack Museum today. It's located in the hamlet of Blue Mountain Lake, a ten-mile drive from my cabin. The museum, which was founded in 1955, occupies the site of an old hotel, the Blue Mountain House, built in the late 1800s. One of the hotel buildings still exists, and is now part of the museum. There are twenty-three other exhibits, located on a beautiful mountainside and landscaped with native flora, overlooking the waters and islands of Blue Mountain Lake. The New York Times described the museum as "the best of its kind in the world." It is indeed a wonderful museum.

I had worked there two years before, and it was wonderful to see my friends again today, to sit at our break table drinking coffee and sharing the cookies Joanne brought in. Their ancestors are the people the museum is really about! Talk about stories! It was also good to wander through the exhibits, refreshing my memories of Adirondack history.

3:30 pm August 30, 2002

I almost quit my job at the Diner today. Actually, I did quit, but Evy talked me out of it. All the tables were full, lines of tourists waiting to get in. I ran into the kitchen, repeating in my head the order I'd just taken but hadn't had time to write down. I grabbed the club sandwich I'd asked for and ran it out to the customer sitting at the counter. He took a bite. Turned out it wasn't his; he'd ordered beef and this was turkey. When Evy, the waitress who'd ordered the turkey club, went to get hers, well...everyone got mad, the cook, Evy...Then I was so upset that I made the next pot of coffee without remembering to put the pot under the spigot...Coffee went everywhere! All over the floor and the dishes on the shelf underneath, which meant the dishes had to be taken out and washed again. So now the dishwasher got mad at me too.

I burst out in tears, right in front of the whole restaurant. Evy told me to go sit down (something I never have time to do) and count to ten. She said things would slow down soon, when school started back, to hang in until then. I said I'd try. And I will. There is no other work up here at this time of year, and I need to work if I'm going to stay the winter. I'm lucky to have this job, I know that.

7:00 am August 31, 2002

I opened the kitchen drawer this morning to get a dish towel, and when I reached in I found myself grasping not terrycloth but a handful of dog food. I was baffled for a moment, since I knew that I had not put Huck's food in there. When I pulled the drawer out, however, I realized that Huck and I had a new housemate. He (or she) had fashioned a little round door in the back panel, and had made a cozy little bed using shredded bits of paper towel. "Oh no," I said, in case he was listening, "You can't spend the winter here. I'm bringing my cat Miss Kelley from Buffalo soon, and she'll eat you for breakfast! You'd better forget this plan right now!" So saying, I cleaned the drawer out and dumped the food into Huck's bowl.

I'm heading to the Diner now for another day of work.

September 2002

9:15 pm September 1, 2002

Great day! I was off work, so I took Mrs. Hosley up on her offer to let me launch my kayak at her camp on South Pond. I had to leave Huck at home, which nearly broke his heart, but I wanted to paddle out to some of the islands, and I was afraid to go that far offshore with him. South Pond is a beautiful, isolated lake a few miles west of here. I took a picnic lunch and sat on a huge rock on a little island to eat my tuna fish sandwich. I finished it off with wild blueberries, which grew along the crevasses in the rock.

Later I followed the creek that feeds into the pond, passing a beaver lodge and a freshwater marsh. I stopped for a while to watch a pair of river otters dive and play. On the way back I passed the spot where, near as I could tell, Long Lake's first sawmill was built in 1836. There wasn't much to it back then, but then there wasn't much to the hamlet of Long Lake back then either. Settled just a few years before, Long Lake had been a smattering of families trying to eke out a meager living in a tough land. There is almost nothing left of the sawmill today.

I stopped and walked along the north shore of the pond, admiring the colorful witch hobble shrubs. As their sap slowly dries up, Mother Nature paints intricate red and gold designs on the leaves; elaborate scripts forewarning us of cold weather to come. Winter will come early, I know, here in the Adirondacks.

It was nearly dark when I got back. I gave Huck a rawhide chew to make up for leaving him, but that hasn't quite wiped the hurt expression off his face.

*****

Sitting on the rock at South Pond today, I began thinking about Momma. Not the mother who is back in Richmond now, descending slowly into dementia and helplessness; but the mother she was when I was growing up. A pretty, gracious Southern lady who also managed to be funny, smart, and strong-minded. Tough, even. I go back in my mind to the momentous occasion of a shopping trip with her. I begin writing.

Shopping with Momma

Going downtown on a shopping trip was a big occasion for a little girl living in the rural community of Short Pump, Virginia, in the 1950s.

38

Birchbark Chronicles

On ordinary days my father, Nancy, and I might stop by Stone's Grocery, a little corner store just down the road, for staples, such as sugar or flour, which Momma might have run out of. Daddy would treat my sister and me to a bottled drink--Brownies and Truades were my favorites--and a handful of penny candy. Most vegetables and fruits Momma and Daddy grew themselves in their big garden out back. The bread man delivered Nolde's bread (including miniature loaves for my sister and me) and the milk man brought our milk.

Once a month or so we'd go to the shopping center, Willow Lawn, a twenty-minute drive from where we lived. I remember when Willow Lawn was built, and how wonderful it seemed. There was a Penney's, a shoe store, and two dime stores: Woolworth's and Murphy's. Woolworth's had a counter where we would get root beer sodas or sometimes a grilled cheese sandwich. Both dime stores had all manner of things to buy, most for prices we could afford. We usually accompanied our trip to Willow Lawn with a visit to my Uncle Bill's house, only a few blocks away, where my cousin Ellen lived. That made it an extra treat.

Twice a year we took a big shopping trip, all the way into downtown Richmond. To where, on dark, narrow city streets surrounded by tall, ominous gray buildings, the amazing, many-windowed Miller & Rhoads and Thalhimers Stores towered. These trips were marvelous occasions that we planned for weeks ahead. Momma told stories about going shopping at Miller & Rhodes when she was a little girl, driving up from Littleton, North Carolina, in her aunt's huge open Pierce Arrow. They would shop for shoes and dresses and later have lunch at the Tea Room; then make the four-hour return trip to Littleton.

When the day came for us to go shopping Momma would dress me up in one of my best dresses, making sure I had my white gloves. Daddy would drive us down and drop us off at a special spot between the two stores. Then he would leave and do I'm not sure what for the hours we spent shopping. Sometimes one of my other sisters, Sally or Betsy or Nancy, would come, but I liked it best when it was just Momma and me.

The buildings soared high above our heads, filled with floors and floors of everything imaginable. Both stores had huge windows filled with elaborate displays showing off their newest merchandise, and we would pass all those wonderful windows as we walked to the big double doors at the entrance. On our annual Christmas shopping trip the windows of the stores would be filled with holiday scenes that made it a veritable wonderland. There would be snow and Santa's workshop with moving elves that made toys and packed the sleigh and a Christmas tree and even a real Santa Claus, waving as we walked by.

On our summer trip the windows would have mannequins showing off the newest styles of clothing. Momma would always buy us a new dress for school.

One year, too long ago for me to actually recall, Daddy's photographer friend Marion Morton, a tall big-boned woman whose visits I vaguely remember, had entered a photograph of me in the Miller & Rhoads annual photography contest. I was taking a bath in a wooden tub outside of our Beechwood Farm house when she snapped the photograph. It won, and was enlarged and placed in one of those huge windows for everyone in Richmond to see. I still have a copy of that picture.

After passing the windows, Momma and I and whoever else was along would enter the big glass doors and find ourselves surrounded by all manner of wondrous things. Momma always had a list of things to buy. Some of them would be for me, especially at Christmas time. Whenever she bought something she would pay for it and leave it to be delivered, so we did not have to carry everything with us. That way we had an additional treat on Monday or Tuesday, when the deliverymen would come to our house with all the packages.

After we had walked and shopped and bought and bought and were exhausted, we would put on our white gloves and go to the Miller & Rhoads Tea Room for deviled crabs. Then, at the appointed time, we would go back to the corner where Daddy had left us off. Sometimes it would be dark now, and quite scary. But Daddy would always be there waiting for us or drive up soon in his big old De Soto, painted tractor green with left-over paint. Almost always, that is. One time he fell asleep and forgot all about us and we stood on the curb for what seemed like hours. Momma never let him forget about that time!

Miller & Rhoads and Thalhimers are gone now, as is Stone's Grocery. Willow Lawn is still there, though remodeled and vastly different. Shopping malls have replaced the old stores, and going shopping is no big deal anymore. Still, it's fun to think back and remember how it was then; the anticipation and excitement of preparation, the thrill of the tall buildings, the elegance of the tea room, the scary wait on the dark street curb, and finally the over-joying sight of Daddy, coming to pick us up and carry us back home again, me snuggled up safe and sound asleep in the back seat of the car.

*****

7:00 pm September 2, 2002

I worked at the museum today. In the logging building, which depicts the long colorful history of harvesting, or annihilating (whichever way you want to look at it) the great forests of the Adirondacks. The tunes of the old logging songs, played incessantly on the tape deck, still ring in my head; "Ye mighty sons of freedom, that round the mountains roam; come all you gallant lumber boys and listen to my song..."

Tom, the owner of the Diner, has photos of his small lumber mill on the walls, as well as pictures of some old loggers, not too different from those at the museum. Janet, one of the women I work with, said her grandfather drowned trying to break up a log jam on the Hudson River one long ago spring day. Windy, another one of the exhibit attendants, walks with a limp from a logging accident he had years ago. Knowing the Adirondacks means knowing the stories of its loggers.

They used to cut the trees in winter, using great crosscut saws, one man on each end. The logs were loaded onto bobsleds and pulled by horses or oxen to a "skidway," where they were placed on skids with runners and hauled along treacherous roads encrusted with snow, the loggers sitting on top. Sometimes the skids, carrying several tons of logs, would get to moving too fast on downhill roads. The loggers would jump to safety, if they could, but the skids would run over and crush the luckless horses. The logs were hauled to rivers and stored in banking grounds, held together by "booms" of logs strung together. When the ice melted in the spring, the logs were floated down the rivers by "drivers" to lumber towns. Breaking up the jams that sometimes formed was a dangerous job, as Janet can attest to; but then, no logging job was a safe job. Most of the logs cut in this area were driven down the Hudson River to Glens Falls.

Upon arriving home I checked the kitchen drawer and found it once again full of dog food. This time my mouse friend had made a bed by shredding a dishcloth. I cleaned it out again and patched the hole in the back with duct tape. "You'd best give up and find a home outside," I said.

I've finished supper, leftover chicken soup I brought home from the Diner yesterday, and am going to hit the sack early.

6:30 pm September 3, 2002

Carl signaled for me to stop my truck as I drove home from work today, and through the open window he told me that that his friend, Jerry, a retired telephone man, was coming over in a little while. He was

41

bringing some line and they were going to try to hook up a phone for me. Sure enough, they showed up an hour later and we walked the line up the hill, draping it over bushes and tree branches, and then slipped it under a window screen. I had my doubts about the whole thing, but it works. Hoorah! Now we'll see how long it lasts!

My first call was to my sister Nancy, in Richmond, to see how Mom's doctor appointment had gone. Okay, Nancy said, but she's still losing weight, down to ninety pounds now. When the doctor asked Mom how she was doing, she told him she was fine, which is ridiculous of course. She's not fine; she can't even hold a spoon to eat, or remember that she is supposed to. I just wish they could figure out what is wrong with her. I guess it doesn't matter a lot, though, if they can't fix it. She hasn't seemed to care about anything since Daddy died three years ago.

After Nancy and I hung up I called the rest of my family to let them know that I would no longer be incommunicado.

8 pm September 4, 2002

Huck and I walked along a deer trail this evening, following it over a few downed branches and through a muddy hollow up to a long ridge. I picked up a few rocks along the way and, after examining them, slipped them into a pocket. I have them here on the deck with me.

I worked today in the museum's Main building, as they call it, which houses an introduction to the Adirondack Park and its geology. I browsed through the exhibits, renewing my knowledge of how this intriguing place had come to be. The Adirondacks were known as "Couch Sacrage" to the early Indians who hunted and fished here (an approximate spelling since the language was not written.) They are made of some of the oldest rock in the world, pushed up around five million years ago in an uplift of molten magma, and gradually worn into their present form by weather, water, and glaciers. Some of the rock, anorthosite, can be found above-ground. I wonder if these pieces I picked up might be remnants of that ancient, once molten rock.

7:30 pm September 6, 2002

After work today I put on my bathing suit and, calling Huck to join me, headed down the hill to the lake. The water was, as always, icy cold, but the air was still warm enough to enjoy a short swim. I have a feeling it won't be for long. I watched Huck splash about for a while and then, calling him back, I headed up the hill, stopping to admire the shimmering leaves of what I have learned are quaking aspen. They are, I read, related to eastern cottonwoods, and are among the most widespread trees in the United States. I don't remember noticing them at other places, but since I've been here I've been intrigued by them. I love the way they respond to the slightest breeze, dancing with what seems like exuberant joy, all together in syncopation, when the leaves of other trees are still or barely moving.

As we hiked up to the cabin I saw what I thought was a large black dog on the deck. "Here boy," I called. "Here boy." He must have been abused, I thought to myself with dismay, as I saw the look of distrust on his face. I started to approach him, but then realized that it was not a dog at all, but a bear! A small, thin black bear, maybe a yearling. It had been a dry summer, the locals tell me, and the berries have been sparse. The bears are hungry. Maybe this one was looking for something to eat.

Huck had not yet noticed him, and I didn't relish an encounter between the two, so I hurried him back down the hill and locked him in my truck. Then I walked back up to where the bear sat, literally sat! near the cabin. "Git!" I yelled at him; "Git out of here!" He just looked at me. Afraid to go too close, I banged a couple boards together and yelled till he finally disappeared into the woods. I went back and retrieved Huck, who now caught his scent and went nuts. "Too late, Huck, he's gone!"

Black bears are probably the most famous residents of the Adirondacks, and they're becoming some of the most populous. Biologists estimate that there are about 5,000 living in the park today. They are protected except during hunting season. Most adults weigh somewhere between 160 and 350 pounds, with the males being much larger than females, but one bear killed not too far from Long Lake weighed 750 pounds. There's not always enough for them to eat, and when pickings get scarce they start getting in trouble with people. Last year a bear broke through the door of the museum cafe and trashed the place. Irene, an Adirondack native who works at the museum and lives nearby, has frequent visits from hungry bears.

7:00 am September 7, 2002

I lay in bed for a long time this morning, just at dawn, listening to the call of a loon. I tried to imagine what it was saying, what it was thinking. I have read that they have four different calls, identified in human terms as the wail, the tremolo, the yodel and the hoot. I have heard at least three of them. I'm thinking that the one I heard this morning was the wail, often used to locate another loon.

10:30 pm September 8, 2002

I'm exhausted! I thought things were supposed to slow down at the diner after Labor Day. What I didn't know was that the college kids would leave, meaning fewer waitresses on the floor. I'm busier than ever, and I don't seem to ever get a day off. I'm working Prime Rib Night and the Fish Fry now, both of them in the evening. It's easier than lunch in a way, since the menu is smaller, but on a busy night like this it's insane. I can't seem to keep up, no matter how hard I try.

I stayed after for a while and had my shift beer in the pub. Got to talking to Cathie Parker, a native Long Laker whom I had met the year before. Her mother has lots of stories to tell about growing up here, she said. I told her I'd like to hear some of them.

The phone was ringing when I got home. It was my sister Sally, calling from Virginia to see how I was. Sally has had a rough life, but she is doing better now, and has remarried. She still has drinking binges, but things are going smoother, thank God. We talked for a long time. Now I'm ready to hit the sack with a copy of Lee Smith's "Saving Grace."

4:30 pm September 9, 2002

After work today I stopped by Hoss's, a store that carries just about everything, and asked if they would carry my books "Ocracoke Wild" and "Ocracoke Odyssey." They agreed, so I'll take a few copies by there tomorrow and see what happens.

Our new house guest/trespasser has not given up. The duct tape didn't work. The drawer was full of dog food again this morning, and I got a brief glimpse of him, scooting across the floor. Big ears, large luminous brown eyes, luxurious gray-brown fur above and white below, with a long furry tail. I figured it was either a deer mouse or a white-footed mouse, known also as wood mouse, so I looked them up in "Adirondack Mammals." Both species belong to the genus Peromyscus "and are hard to tell apart. Deer mice often move into houses in autumn, it says, so I'm guessing that's what it is. But either way, it needs to find another home. I emptied the drawer out again and stuffed a cloth in the hole.

The stories keep coming. It takes too long to write down everything by hand, so I have given up writing on birch bark. I put my handmade journal aside, storing it carefully.

*****

I now sit with my word processor and a stack of typing paper, thinking back to a quirky, pre-adolescent girl trying to find her way.

Pirates and Tomboys

"Ahoy mates! Draw your swords and prepare for battle! The Queen's ship is in sight!" I looked around at my crew, straightening my eye patch and pulling my bandana tighter so that it covered my blonde hair. I watched my motley crew of boys with a stern eye as they donned their pirate hats and lifted their swords. "Over here, Don, I need you at my side!" A petite girl with long dark hair pulled back in a ponytail stalked over, pulling a cardboard dagger out of her belt. "Aye, aye, Captain."

Just then a bell rang loudly overhead. "Flee, boys!" I yelled. "There's a British warship coming! Put on your disguises!" We quickly dispersed and, putting away our pirate gear, resumed the appearance of sixth-grade students. We then returned to our classroom.

I had made up my mind a couple weeks before. Being a girl was just too boring. I wanted to be an explorer, an adventurer, a seeker of great things. None of my heroes were women, and my dreams were not the dreams dreamt by other girls. I would, as of now, the fall of 1961, become a boy.

First off, I changed my name. Patsy became Pat. My hair, already short, would need to be cut shorter. There would be no more dresses, no more frilly clothes. Dungarees became my preferred wardrobe. My best friend Donna would be included in this transformation. She changed her name to Don. "We're boys now," we announced emphatically. To prove it, we started a "Boys Only Pirate Club" at school. We made cardboard pirate hats, swords, and eye patches. I declared myself president, Don vice-president, and then opened the membership to boys only. Almost all the boys in our sixth grade class joined. We had meetings at lunchtime, plotting attacks on treasure-laden ships and raids on the holdings of tyrants. We were a Robin Hood-like crew, planning to give our loot to the poor. One Saturday I invited the whole club to my family's fourteen-acre farm, where we could really plot some mischief. Ignoring the physiological differences between the sexes, I pretended, at least for a while, that I had outsmarted Mother Nature and the expectations of society and had turned into a boy.

Turning into a boy was not my first attempt at changing identities. Much earlier, when I was six or seven, I had been a horse. I had galloped around the yard, eaten grass and oats, neighing an answer to my mother's questions. My cousin Ellen had joined me. Sometimes my little sister Nancy came along, but I don't think she was ever a true believer.

Later, when I had a horse of my own, I did my best to emulate my cowboy heroes. I got my first horse, Blaze, a brown and white pinto stallion, at the age of seven, and later, a more docile black and white gelding, Domino. Riding bareback, by the age of ten I could perform all of Zorro's most daring riding feats--a running jump from behind to mount, a leap from the branches of a tree onto Domino's back as Donna would gallop him beneath me.

How long Don's and my "boys only" club lasted I don't recall. I do know that my biggest disappointment was that Steve Whitten, the class-mate I'd had a crush on for years, refused to join. Sometime during the school year the notion seemed to dissipate. Don, whose parents had never approved of any of it, became Donna again, and before I knew it she was dating.

I too was developing an interest in boys, but it seemed like a terrible betrayal of my long-proclaimed values, so I kept it hidden. I kept my crushes secret and read love stories by flashlight after my parents were in bed. Besides, I became convinced that I was so unattractive that no boy would ever like me anyway, so what was the sense in giving them the chance to reject me? Commanding pirate of a whole crew of boys in sixth grade, by seventh grade I refused to even look a boy in the face.

Long after I gave up the notion that I could wish myself into being a boy; after I had begun dating and even after I had fallen in love and married; I still believed that I had been born the wrong sex. The things I longed to do were not things normally done by women. I wanted to be a commercial fisherman, a cowboy (No, NOT a cowgirl!), a hobo, an explorer of the wilderness. I scorned the things women were supposed to value--makeup, hairdressers, new couches, love stories, and soap operas. I abhorred my own desires for these things and tried to deny them. I always identified with Peter Pan, never with Wendy.

Though just a small piece of my life, my attempt at being a pirate boy represents a dilemma that has affected my relationships, my self-esteem, my whole life. At some point I realized that, while it might be more difficult for a girl, I could do many of the things I wanted, and I have.

My life might have been easier had I been a lesbian, or had I simply had no interest in love or romance. Trying to conform my desire to be an attractive, feminine, and yes, even sexy woman with my longing to lead the life of an adventurer has been confusing not only to me but to the men in my life.

I have come to realize several things. Most men do NOT long to be pirates or fishermen or cowboys, especially not at this age, so my oddities cannot be blamed strictly on gender. Besides, I know now that many women share my interests and values, if not my proclivity for insane adventures. I have accepted those traits in myself which are generally considered womanly. I love little children and cuddly kittens. I like my house and I enjoy house-keeping. I love dressing up for a party, I like nice jewelry and slinky negligees, and I'm delighted when some strange man tells me that he loves my hair.

Still, I became aware of something vaguely disturbing last time I was at Ocracoke. I found myself feeling like an outsider, somehow left out of the camaraderie I longed for. I watched the fishermen as they worked and joked together, and I realized that I was longing to be included by them, not by their wives and girlfriends. I liked the women, but I wanted to be talking about setting crab pots and outrunning a nor'easter, not getting my hair done or baking a pecan pie. All these years later, I guess I still have some of that pirate boy inside me.

*****

5:30 pm September 10, 2002

I decided to ignore the gray clouds which blanketed the sky today so, after coming home from work and walking Huck, I climbed down the hill to go kayaking. I ignored the big drops that began to fall just a few minutes after I left, looking with hope at a stretch of blue sky ahead. I set my course for the bridge that crosses a narrowing in the lake, leading to the village, and I smiled when the drops stopped. I was feeling a little guilty about leaving Huck behind, but I wanted to get some good exercise, which I can't do when he is balanced between my knees.

I paddled hard, and before long I was past the bridge and scooting by the town beach. Just as I passed the back side of Northern Borne Grocery, a wind seemed to blow up out of no-where, and before I knew it rain began to fall. Not just the occasional drops of earlier, this was a real downpour. Between the wind and the rain it was hard to see and harder to paddle, but I turned around and made for the bridge, figuring I could take shelter under it until the torrent ended. I was sopping wet by the time I reached it.

There was a small motor boat under there already, so I waved to the young father and (presumably) two sons, who smiled and waved back. Between the sound of the log trucks thundering overhead and the pounding rain, conversation was impossible, but it felt quite sociable, hovering there with them under the bridge, curtains of water falling on each side. The rain finally slowed, and I studied the sky, delighted to see that beyond the restless clouds a small patch of blue was growing larger. As the blue expanded, the raindrops lessened, and I heard the young boys yell to their father "Let's go! Let's go!" I left at the same time they did, each of us heading in different directions, waving goodbye.

The sun came out and dried me off, but I found myself shivering as I climbed back up the hill to the cabin, so I have put on warm pajamas and wrapped myself in a blanket. Huck is snuggled close.

8:00 pm September 11, 2002

There was an aura of sadness hanging over the diner today. The radio rehashed the events of this day last year over and over, and you could tell it was on everyone's mind. They say that, as with John Kennedy's assassination, we'll always remember what we were doing when we heard that the Twin Towers had been struck.

I well remember that day. I was carrying a load of garbage to the Long Lake Dump, trash I had collected while cleaning up the tiny apartment I had moved into after leaving Harry. "Nice day," I said to Gene, the man who oversees the landfill. "Yeah," he said, "you wouldn't think something so horrible could happen on a day like this."

He told me the news then, and I drove 22 miles to Tupper Lake to buy a radio. Having broken up with Harry, the man I'd moved to Long Lake to live with, I had almost nothing of my own, not even a radio or telephone. I was already feeling about as low as you could get, but now I felt even worse. At least I hadn't lost friends or family in the attack, like some people I know up here.

I turned on the radio and I got down on my hands and knees with a scrub brush and a bucket, and I spent the day scrubbing the floor. I worked harder than I needed to, as images of the towers flashed before my eyes. Finally, exhausted, I pulled out a bottle of beer and sat down and cried like a baby.

6:00 pm September 12, 2002

I'm sitting on the bluff beside my cabin in my very own Adirondack chair, watching as a pileated woodpecker searches through a pile of logs for insects. I asked Windy, a part-time exhibit attendant at the museum who also makes Adirondack chairs there, if he would make two for me. He fashions them from white pine milled in his own sawmill at North River. He brought mine to the museum today and followed me home after work. He helped carry them up my hill, which he agreed, panting when we reached the top, is one killer hill. We put one chair on my deck, one on this bluff. Then he stayed for a cup of tea.

Windy is a native Adirondacker, descended from the Abanaki Indians who used to live here. He is a great story teller and he has some great stories to tell. He used to be a logger, but he'd had an accident which almost killed him thirty years before, leaving him "maimed," as he calls it, with a bad leg. He'd gone up the trunk to top a big maple, when the vibrations of his saw caused it to crack in half down near the base. He and the tree had gone down together, and he'd spent two years in the hospital. But he was one of the lucky ones. An experienced logger in nearby Indian Lake had been killed, just the week before, when a tree fell on him. In the logging business, Windy said, you don't ask if you're gonna get hurt, but when. He still walks with a limp, but he doesn't let it slow him down any.

After Windy left I came out here to try out my chair. The Adirondack chair is one of the things this mountain range is best known for. It evolved from a chair invented in 1903 by a man staying on the shores of Lake Champlain, not too far from here. It was known as the Westport Chair. Thomas Lee never made a nickel from his invention; but a lot of woodworkers have done so since then, including Windy.

Pileated woodpeckers are among the most remarkable birds I know, both for their size and for their exotic scarlet crests, topping off their black and white feathered tuxedos. I always catch my breath when I spot one. My bird guide says that they feed mostly on carpenter ants found in fallen logs, and maybe that is what this one is feasting on. I am thrilled to have it right here at my doorstep, but seeing it makes me sad, too. I am reminded of its close kin, the ivory-billed woodpecker, an even larger bird, driven to the brink of extinction by the destruction of the old-growth river forests it depended on. I can only hope that occasional reported sightings in some southern states are valid, and that a few still remain.

8:00 pm September 13, 2002

A tragedy occurred here last night; a small tragedy, I suppose you'd say, with a small mouse. Yet even as I write this, I question whether tragedy can be measured on any scale. I was sleeping soundly when I heard a tiny splash. I listened to the gurgle of water, which lasted a few seconds, wondering, in my half awake state, if the bathroom plumbing was messing up. Then I drifted back to sleep. When I went to put the coffee on the next morning I started at the sight of Huck's water bowl. The deer mouse, my month-long adversary, floated there, lifeless. The bowl was not big, the water not deep, but the stainless steel sides were too slick to climb and the water, obviously, deep enough. Our long battle, our contest of wills, was over. I had won, but I felt no sense of victory. I am reminded of Robert Burns' poem, "To a Mouse." I pull out my worn book of poetry, inherited from my mother.

> *"The best laid schemes of mice and men gang aft a-gley,*
> *an' lea'e us nought but grief an' pain, for promised joy."*

I think of John Steinbeck's classic novel, its title derived from Burns' poetic phrase, "Of Mice And Men." I remember George and Lennie's dream: to have a little farm, work for themselves, and harvest their own food--not so different from the dream of this drowned deer mouse, each ended by an unfair twist of fate.

My mammal guide says that deer mice are good swimmers. I wonder how long he paddled, trying to keep afloat. If I had only gotten up and checked...I wonder about my own plans, and whether they will end in a similar way. Burns says to his mouse, evicted from his home in a field by the plough,

> *"Still thou art blest, compared wi' me!*
> *The present only toucheth thee: But Och!*
> *I backward cast my e'e on prospects drear!"*

What wouldn't I give to be able to relinquish the guilt and regret I carry from my past--and now I must add to it this mouse's death.

I cleaned out the kitchen drawer for the last time, sadly throwing the scraps of his bed into the trash, the dog food into Huck's bowl. I buried the mouse (I never had given him a name) under the carpet of evergreen needles outside the cabin. Now I can bring my cat, Miss Kelley, here without worry, I tell myself. It is, however, an empty consolation. I will miss our daily battles of the will. I will miss the fleeting glimpses I had of him, streaking across the floor, nimble and petite, with his big, dark, deer-like eyes.

6:30 pm September 16, 2002

I'm sitting out on the deck enjoying my Adirondack chair. The colors this evening are breathtaking; golden layers of birch, magenta-toned moosewood and crimson leaves of sugar maple. A black-and-white, or possibly a black-polled, warbler is scratching around in the browning blackberry bushes, and a downy woodpecker is tapping a rhythm on the dying hemlock across from the cabin.

6:00 pm September 19, 2002

Well, I quit my job at the diner! Left a note for Jim, my boss, in the cash register, telling him that I would finish out this week if he needed me, but that's all. Told him that I don't fit in there, and can't seem to no matter how hard I try. Didn't mention any names, but he'll probably hear I had a run-in with one of the other staff. He can't stand it because, to quote him, I "do everything ass-fucking-backwards from everybody else!!" Well, I'm sure he's right, I always have, but I don't understand why it bothers him so much. I actually like him, except for the way he gives me hell. I was hoping we could be friends. But I guess not. It's not just him though. I'm just not cut out for this job. At least I'm free now, though how I'll pay my rent I don't know...

When I got home I called my friend Sandy, back in Virginia. She has been my best friend forever, and I miss seeing her. I like a lot of the people here, but I don't have any close friends to talk to when I am upset.

1:30 pm September 20, 2002

My "freedom" did not last long. Jim called last night and said he wanted to talk to me. He even volunteered to climb up this hill if I didn't want to come down! But I told him I would come into town today to talk to him, and I did. He says he doesn't want me to quit. Says he talked to everyone at the diner and they don't want me to quit either; that things will be better if I come back. I agreed to give it another try. He is a cool boss, I must admit. He does a damned good job of running the diner, I think, and bends over backwards for his employees.

Afterwards I took a long walk with Huck, following the snowmobile trail across a bridge and deep into the forest.

Spending the afternoon outdoors in this glorious land makes me realize how glad I am for its status as "Forever Wild," protected as a state park from over-development, supposedly forever. Such has not been true of other places I have lived and loved.

*****

I recall an adolescent girl sitting bareback on the back of a black and white horse. She is fifteen years old, unsure of herself and even less sure of the world around her. Formerly a petite child--the shortest in her class--she has shot up to a gawky, long-legged 5'7" and is taller than most of the boys. She hates the shape of her nose and is ashamed of the large, square hands she inherited from her father, hiding them in her pockets whenever possible. Shy and awkward, she avoids the boys in her class and is uncomfortable with all but a few of the girls. Her Latin teacher has announced to the class that her project for the year is to "bring Patsy out," much to Patsy's humiliation.

She no longer likes going to school and escapes more and more into her private Shangri-La, fleeing to the horse pasture as soon as she gets home each afternoon. With her long legs wrapped around the back of Blaze or Domino, she follows the trails and explores the woods for miles. She ignores "No Trespassing" signs, remembering Woodie Guthrie's song, positive that they are not meant for her.

She knows every creek, every swamp. She knows where the whiskey stills are hidden behind curtains of honeysuckle and Virginia creeper (she's been shot at for riding too close.) She knows where the lady-slippers emerge, as if by magic, in the spring; which rocks hide fat green crayfish in the creeks; and where to find delightfully big and ugly mudpuppies buried in the swamps. She could tell the hunters, if she chose to, where the deer fed; the trappers where the muskrats dug their burrows. Sometimes she rides by an empty, derelict house where Ku Klux Klan meetings are held on dark nights. Often she stops at some of the colored houses and gives rides to the children who stand by the roadside, watching for her. Out here, in the woods and fields, she feels competent and accepted.

Midnight Ride

It was midnight. I had just completed my report on artist John Constable, due the next day in English class. I sat still in my bed, listening for any sound that might suggest that someone was still awake. All was silent. My parents were asleep in their bedroom downstairs, my younger sister in the dormer room next to my own. I gently pushed my cat Tiger off my lap and stood up. Mister Trouble, our wire-haired terrier, was stretched out on the foot of my bed. I patted him on the head as I slipped past him and out of my room. Down the stairs and through the kitchen, where I took a fat carrot from the refrigerator, and out the back door. Now I was free.

I stopped by the big double-door garage, designed for a bootlegging operation years before, and slipped one of the bridles off its hook. I went into Daddy's workshop, where I had stashed a can of black paint and a paintbrush. I placed them in the canvas bag which I used for these occasions and set it on a fence post. Then I trotted down past the garden and climbed the fence next to the gate which led into the back pasture.

I could see the horses in the distance. Caprice, a dark sorrel, was invisible at night, but Blaze and Domino were both pintos, and the white splotches in their coats were easy to spot. They were near the woods, not far from the bottom field where Daddy grew corn and peanuts. I often came out on late nights like this to visit them, so they were not surprised to see me. They looked up as I approached, and Blaze nickered a soft greeting. I broke the carrot into thirds and, holding a piece in the palm of my hand, felt his soft lips as he gently took it. I gave the next piece to Caprice, who snorted and eagerly searched my pockets for more. When I got to Domino, I slipped my arm around his neck as he crunched his carrot; then slipped the bridle reins over his head. I wasn't sure he would appreciate this midnight ride, and I didn't want him trotting off. "How about an adventure tonight, boy? Are you up for it?" He nuzzled my cheek, as if in answer.

Slipping the bit into his mouth, I grasped a handful of mane and swung up onto his back. "See ya'll later!" I called to Blaze and Caprice, and then nudged Domino in the ribs and cantered off.

Securing the gate behind us, I stopped to pick up the paint and, glancing at the house to make sure no lights had come on, turned onto Church Road. The moon was nearly full, so we could see clearly as we cantered past the Nugents' old farmhouse, following the whitewashed fence which bordered our place and the Boxleys' home. I was relieved that none of the neighborhood dogs heard us and sounded an alarm. Up at Proffits' Garage we slowed to a trot and bore left onto Pump Road. A half a mile more and we had reached our destination.

I had noticed it the week before, riding Blaze along this same road. Another woodland had been put on the market. Following the roadside, "For Sale" signs were posted intermittently for a quarter of a mile. I recognized the name printed on the bottom of the signs; a wealthy real estate developer. If this woodland were sold, I knew the trees would be cut down; the deer chased out of their safe haven, the wood turtles and moles bulldozed over and killed. This lovely natural place would be destroyed, replaced by a housing development or chain store. I had seen it happen before.

They were trying to destroy the place I loved most in the world, but I wouldn't take it lying down. Glancing both ways to look for approaching car lights, I pulled out my paint brush, dipped it into the paint, and proceeded to paint each sign an opaque black. When nothing more could be seen of those loathsome capitalistic words, "For Sale," I turned Domino towards home and gave him a quick kick in the ribs. We galloped down the road, me feeling like some sort of secret warrior in the fight against progress.

I lost, of course. My little acts of sedition could not have been more than mild irritants to the real estate companies. Looking back, I wonder why I did not simply pull the signs down instead of going to the trouble of painting them. In truth, my attempts at monkey wrenching were not acts of an intelligent, nearly grown woman (I was an honors student in high school) but desperate, hopeless attempts by a recalcitrant child to stop the progression of time. I had been devastated when, eight years earlier, my brother had gone away to college. My oldest sister's marriage and departure from home sent me reeling again. I did not want to grow up; I did not want my parents to grow old; I did not want anything to change.

I am still fighting the same battles, perhaps with the same chances of success. Within two years of my sign-painting exploits, a parking lot and a sprawling building had replaced the woods. Twenty-five years later, my beloved home is unrecognizable. The house where I grew up, the fields where the horses grazed, the woods where I played; all are gone.

Still, there is always another forest to save, somewhere; another dream, albeit hopeless, to cling to. One can't make time stand still. One can't go back. These things I have learned, though the path to this knowledge has been tortuous and wracked with pain. One can only move forward, plowing blindly through the dust of old memories toward an ambiguous, ephemeral hope, which maybe, just maybe, can save us.

*****

8:45 pm September 23, 2002

I had dinner tonight with Cathie Parker, the woman I had met at the Owls Head Pub, and her mother Avis. Cathie cooked a chicken and Avis told stories about growing up in Long Lake in an earlier time. She described two golf courses where she used to play golf (there are no golf courses here now.) She had caddied at one of the courses, owned by the Sagamore Hotel, now long gone.

My favorite story was about Noah John Rondeau, Long Lake's famous hermit, "Mayor of Cold River City, population one." One of the most popular exhibits at the museum is a replica of Rondeau's cabin, with a statue of the man himself. I bought a book about him, which includes excerpts of his diary and a few poems he wrote, and I hope one day to kayak to his "city" on Cold River. Noah Rondeau was a French Canadian who made himself famous by living like a real hermit on a little river north of Long Lake. During the 1940s he traveled by helicopter to New York City to put on shows, but he always came back to the Adirondacks. Avis knew him, and even has a picture of him holding Cathie's sister when she was a baby. Avis told me about a day Noah showed up at her door and had dinner with the family—"a pan of brook trout," she recalled.

6:30 pm September 25, 2002

Huck and I climbed Blue Mountain today. It's one of the higher peaks around here, 3,759 feet, though not considered one of the official "high peaks." When we got to the top Huck headed right up the fire tower by himself! I called him back, since there are big gaps between the stairs he might fall through. Then, with me holding his leash, we went up together. It was kind of cloudy so the view wasn't great, but it was exhilarating to be at the top of that tower. I imagined how it would have been, sitting up here every day, watching for a wisp of smoke that could turn this whole place into a hellish inferno. Frances, an older lady who grew up in Long Lake, used to have a job watching for fires. I heard her give a talk about it once.

In the later days of logging, railroads crisscrossed these mountains and trains hauled the logs out. Great piles of slash were left behind in the woods, and if a spark from one of the engines ignited them, they burned like wildfire. The whole landscape around me was shaped by fire, though you'd never guess it now.

A lot of the towers have been torn down, partly because they're not safe anymore and partly because the Park Agency wants the land returned to its natural state. They're not needed, since fire patrol is now done by airplanes with electronic equipment. There are a lot of people who want the towers preserved, though, as they are an important part of Adirondack history, and some are being renovated. Climbing fire towers is actually a hobby today, and people travel all over the country to do it, keeping records and writing books about it.

Huck and I took our time coming back down, and now we're settled in the cabin for the night.

8 pm September 26, 2002

I've about finished packing for my trip back to Buffalo. I plan to leave early tomorrow afternoon, in time to have dinner with my sister Betsy. Then, for two days, I'll conduct music programs at some of the Head Start centers where I used to work. I can't wait. I really miss the kids. I put new strings on my guitar, and I've been practicing my favorite children's songs.

I've also missed Buffalo, with her stately old downtown buildings; the Victorian neighborhood where my sister lives; the derelict grain mills we kayaked around on the Buffalo River. Also the coffee houses where I played my guitar, sang my folk songs, and read my poetry. I miss the soup kitchens where I volunteered, and even the inner city with its dilapidated tenements and shabby corner stores.

I miss my cats too, which Betsy has been keeping. I can't wait to bring Miss Kelley back with me—I hope she likes it here!

October 2002

7:30 pm October 2, 2002

I just got back from Buffalo, hiking up and down the hill twice as I lugged up Miss Kelley's crate, my guitar, and the groceries I had bought while there. I also brought my accordion, which I had left at Betsy's house earlier. I put the groceries away and now I'm beat! Miss Kelley is peeking into every nook and cranny she can find. I wish I could have brought my other cats, Squirt and Scamp, but they're older, and I'm afraid it will be too cold for them this winter. They seem happy at my sister's house.

Things went well while I was there. I saw my old boyfriend, Robb--a fellow musician and poet. I went with him to a poetry reading at a great old bookstore in Niagara Falls where I read a couple of my new poems. The Head Start music programs were a success; the kids enthusiastic. I've got to work at the diner tomorrow, so it's lights off.

5:30 pm October 3, 2002

Work seemed to go better today. That blow-up seems to have cleared the air. Business has slowed down, finally, so now there's time to talk to the customers, get to know people. Working the counter's my favorite; that's where the regulars usually sit. Since that's the easiest station, that's where I usually end up. So, if I'm not busy, there's time to talk.

There's Don "Juan," as Eve and Evy call him, tall and thin and something of a flirt, who most days orders a bowl of soup with a grilled roll. Kathleen is slender and pretty with multiple earrings and a diamond in the side of her nose. She comes in for coffee almost every morning, often joined by one of her four sons. Jimmy never misses a day. He's a native Long Laker with a passion for old Adirondack books, maps, and diner coffee. I'm getting to know what the counter customers like to order, and it's kind of fun. Good people, for the most part.

I just built my first fire of the season, curled up in front of it with my guitar, and played some old Joan Baez tunes. Now I'm staring into the flames, sipping on a glass of merlot. The wood stove sits in the middle of the room, propped up on bricks, and puts out a lot of heat. I hope it keeps us warm this winter. That reminds me that I'd better get busy splitting more wood!

7:00 pm October 6, 2002

The days are growing short. It is already dark outside, in spite of a million stars that sprinkle the skies tonight. I worked at the museum today, one of my last days before they close for the season. I was stationed up in Bull Cottage, one of the camps built on Merwin Hill when the original hotel was operating. The view is phenomenal, and I never get tired of the rustic Adirondack furniture displayed there, most of it designed for the great camps of the wealthy--Sagamore...Santanoni--built by craftsmen who were true Adirondackers.

We were not busy and I had plenty of time, so I worked on a poem that had been swirling around in my head since yesterday's walk on the snowmobile trail. The leaves were so gorgeous as the wind lifted them from the branches and floated them to the ground around me, laying a carpet of incredible hues. But I couldn't help thinking that this was their last hurrah, their final descent to death. I pondered over their mortality and my own as well. How much finer to go out in a blaze of glorious color than the way so many of us do, dying slow deaths as my father had done, as my mother was doing now.

5:30 am October 8, 2002

Autumn must be the most beautiful season in the Adirondacks; the air crisp, the sky blue, the mountains a hundred different nuances of color. I walked down Sagamore Road with Huck after work yesterday and stopped to visit my friend from the museum, Doris, and her husband Ed. Doris is the oldest employee at the museum, 74 years old. She's been working there forever, it seems, and knows everything about it there is to know. She has been sick though, with congestive heart failure, so she's missed the last few weeks. We talked a little about her meds and the oxygen tank she's using, meanwhile watching chickadees and mourning doves at the feeders that Ed fills religiously. They told me stories about riding a Harley Davidson motorcycle through the mountains together when they were first married, and Doris told me about stopping, as a teenager, to feed bottles of Coca Cola to a captive, tame black bear.

Then Huck and I continued on down the little dirt road. I saw a red fox, probably the one Ed said he's been seeing, but Huck didn't notice him, thank goodness. At the end of the road is a little town beach, not far from the site of what was once the Sagamore Hotel. It was built in the early 1900s and considered at one time among the largest and most modern hotels in the Adirondacks. It was where Cathy's mother, Avis, had played golf and caddied for the wealthy visitors. Gradually allowed to deteriorate, it was deliberately burned in the '50s, and Mother Nature has since reclaimed the land. Today there is no sign of the one-time opulence.

I am reminded of Percy Bysshe Shelley's poem, read in high school, "Ozymandias of Egypt"; *Round the decay of that colossal wreck, boundless and bare, the lone and level sands stretch far away...*

I took a bar of doggie soap along and gave Huck a bath, so he smells good now. A flock of Canada geese flew over, their voices drifting across the lake like an autumn melody; *"going south...going south...going south."* I went for a quick swim myself, but the water is cold now, and I shivered all the way home. Winter is coming...

*****

Now, after a hot shower, I am wrapped in a blanket and sitting before my word processor. The person I see before me is a young woman, nineteen years old. Tall and slender with long dark blonde hair, she has outgrown her adolescent gawkiness and is surprised to realize that young men find her attractive. She has withdrawn from college, a small Methodist school in North Carolina where she felt out-of-place and homesick. She returned home to Short Pump and got a job training horses on a nearby farm, but now she has gone to live with her older sister and brother-in-law in California. She finds herself in a world previously unknown to her, where she must make decisions that re-define who she is and how she sees herself.

Treasure Island's Hot Dog Girl

The San Francisco sky was hidden by a blanket of fog on this late September morning as I stretched my blue-jean-clad legs in front of me, adjusting my buttocks on the curb where I sat. Glancing up, I saw a stocky dark-haired man in a sailor suit approach. I smiled and stood up. "Hi! You want a hot dog?" He answered with a nod. "Yep, sure do. Sauerkraut and onions please." I stepped over to the metal box on wheels which was my hot dog cart and, using a wax paper, lifted a bun from one of three bins. Then with a set of tongs I grasped a slippery red dog from another and plopped it on the bun. From the third bin I scooped a spoonful of milky-white sauerkraut and smothered the hot dog. "Help yourself to onions and mustard," I told him, indicating two containers. I accepted the dollar bill he handed me and looked up to see another customer approach.

This young man had sun-bleached blonde hair and a mustache and wore jeans and a black tee shirt. My stomach lurched. I smiled at him and spoke, trying to keep the quiver out of my voice. "Hi, Bill. You're back again, huh? You must like hot dogs."

"They're not bad," he said. I'll take two plain. How are things going?" I stretched one arm up as I answered him, then scratched my head slowly. "Oh, not bad I guess." I tried to still the trembling in my hand as I reached for a bun, but then the hot dog was forgotten. Three men, dressed in ordinary clothes, were running toward my cart. Two circled around and grabbed Bill by the arms while another pulled out a gun. They grappled with him, dragging him toward a van; then pushed him against it, face forward. The one with the gun took out a set of handcuffs and secured his wrists behind his back. I saw Bill glance back toward me as they herded him into the van. Now I gave up on trying to hide my feelings. Sinking back onto the curb, I covered my face with my hands and began to sob.

This, my one and only encounter and collaboration with the U.S. Military Police, and my subsequent love affair with its suspect, had begun on a typically beautiful autumn San Francisco afternoon. I was living with my sister Sally and her husband Turner, a Lt. commander in the U.S. Navy, on the island of Yerba Buena. Yerba Buena (which means green goodness in the language of its Spanish conquerors) sits in the middle of San Francisco Bay. It provides a foothold for the trestles of the Bay Bridge, which connects the Golden City to her less glamorous neighbor, Oakland. As its name implies, Yerba Buena is a verdant oasis, rising like a garden from the dark bay waters. It is inhabited by the families of Navy officers. The homes are landscaped with flowers, and graceful trees and shrubs grow at becoming intervals. There is a guard at the entrance to Yerba Buena. He allows no "undesirables" to trespass there.

Nearby, connected by a different, low-lying bridge, is Treasure Island. Whereas Yerba Buena is hilly, green, and landscaped with gardens, Treasure Island is a dredge fill; flat, colorless, and covered with the gray asphalt of a Navy Base. At the time I was there, in 1969, it was teeming not only with Navy personnel (most of whom were "enlisted" non-officers,) but also with Marines (also enlisted) on their way to and from Vietnam. The air at Treasure Island was thick with all of the emotions--

fear, patriotism, anger, betrayal, and heartbreak--that the War in Vietnam evoked in its most involved players.

I lived on Yerba Buena Island but I worked on Treasure Island. Each morning I got up at 7:00 AM and drove across the bridge to the commissary, where I loaded a small metal cart with hot dogs, sauerkraut, buns, and mustard. I pushed it to a nearby street, where I sat on the curb and sold hot dogs to the sailors and marines. One of the sailors made a sign and attached it to my cart. It said "Pat: Treasure Island's Hot Dog Girl."

I was one of the only single women on the island, my long hair draped with braided flowers, the symbol of the '60's flower child. My hot dogs drew the lonely young servicemen in droves. My boss said I sold more hot dogs than any employee he had ever had.

I got to know many of my customers and listened to their stories: tales of horror from the front lines told by wounded men returning home on medical leave; tales of broken hearts told by men whose girls had opted not to wait for them; tales of terror from young boys, never before away from home, now bound for jungles of death. I enjoyed my job, but soon found myself immersed in the passions of the times.

One day a man bought a hot dog and introduced himself as Bill. We chatted for a few minutes. I found him rather interesting but thought no more about him after he left. The next day he came again, this time carrying a folder. Again, he bought a hot dog. But this time, he asked me if I would mind his leaving some literature he had with him on my cart. I said I supposed not. We talked for a few more minutes; then he took some flyers out of the folder and set them on my stand.

I glanced at the flyers after he left and saw the name "White Panthers." I didn't know much about them but I thought they were a leftist organization which advocated overthrowing the U.S. government. Reading a flyer, my impression was confirmed. "Kill the enemy," it said (meaning government officials) with an address for contact. Later that afternoon, when I closed up and pushed my cart back to the Commissary, I took the flyers with me and set them on the dresser in my bedroom.

I was off for the next two days, and the flyers sat innocuously on my dresser top. One morning my sister came in to talk to me about something and noticed them. She told her husband about them and he asked me where they'd come from. Before long I was being questioned by the military police. They told me more about the White Panthers, convincing me that they were a dangerous organization which believed in violence and killing to get their way. In spite of my own liberal, somewhat leftist views, I was reluctantly persuaded that it was my duty to help end this movement. Thus it was that I sat out there that September morning, surrounded by undercover police waiting for me to raise my arm and scratch my head, signaling them that this enemy of the American People had arrived.

Afterwards, I wondered how he was and whether I had done the right thing. Here in California I was being forced to confront some difficult issues that I had so far evaded thinking about. My father, whom I dearly loved and admired, held some political beliefs that I found harder and harder to agree with. He believed in the Vietnam War and was angered by those who acted, in his view, unpatriotic and cowardly by protesting against it. I also loved my brother-in-law, Turner, and did not want to find fault with his views, which were even more extreme and militaristic than my father's. I had no desire to rebel against my family's values, and turmoil and confusion wracked my peace of mind.

Turner did not approve of my dating enlisted men, but I had yet to meet an officer at Treasure Island that I was interested in. I found them stuffy and boring, and I disliked their pompous attitudes. More than that, I found that the Navy's class system of discrimination went against some of my deepest principles. Turner, son of a Naval officer and well indoctrinated in that system, did not forbid my dating the boys I liked, but he refused to meet or acknowledge them. My sister Sally had no such reservations, and she treated all my visitors with kindness.

Many of my new friends, just back from the jungles of Vietnam, were disillusioned with the War. They had the best of justifications for opposing it. The stories they told me or, even more moving, the stories they couldn't tell, breaking down instead into tears or stares of horror, convinced me that neither this war, nor any war, could be justified. I found myself growing more and more opposed to the military philosophy, and in doing so I questioned the words of the military police who had convinced me to turn Bill in.

Sally worried that if Bill escaped from the brig or was released, he would come after me. She asked the Navy police to let her know when he got out, and they promised that he would not be allowed back on the base. She warned me to watch out for him, and to run if I ever saw him.

But when I looked up from my hot dogs one day a month later and saw him standing in front of me, I simply stood there, speechless.

"I just want to know one thing," he said, "Why did you do it?"

63

I spoke slowly, trying to express my feelings, explaining that I had truly believed that what he was doing was wrong. To my surprise, he agreed. "I had a lot of time to think while I sat in the brig," he said, "and I realized that I don't believe in violence, whatever the reason. I still oppose what our government is doing, but I don't belong to the Panthers anymore. I'll try to find another way to change things. I'd really like to talk to you some more."

Ignoring my sister's warnings, I agreed to meet him after I got off work. Since he would not be allowed on Yerba Buena Island, and he certainly would not be welcome at my brother-in-law's house, I decided to meet him at the foot of the bridge. Thus began an illicit, illogical romance, all the more exciting because it was forbidden. I would tell Sally and Turner goodnight and retire to my room to "read." Then I would open the window, climb out, and hurry across the darkened island to where it met the Bay Bridge and watch for Bill's old blue Volkswagen bug. He would pull over to the side of the highway and I would run down the hill, fling open the passenger door, and collapse inside, laughing at my own temerity. Then we would head for the wild and wonderful Hait-Ashbury section of San Francisco.

Entering Hait-Ashbury was like slipping into the skin of Alice and visiting Wonderland. Having spent most of my life on a small farm in a little hamlet outside of staid and conservative Richmond, Virginia, where my mother had tried to instruct me in the ways of being a Southern lady, I was amazed and intrigued. The San Francisco I saw with my brother-in-law and my sister was unrecognizable on these back streets. Bill got me a fake ID which allowed me to enter nightclubs lit with flashing psychedelic colors, thick with the smoke of marijuana, and pulsing with the sounds of the Grateful Dead, the Rolling Stones, and Jimmy Hendrix. We visited tiny apartments where Bill's friends lived. I sat, intrigued, watching them hover around bongs and other strange, para-phernalia as they experimented with the various drugs of the '60s. I never partook, politely shaking my head and saying no thank you. I was not opposed to the use of drugs, but I was content to watch from the sidelines, a part of and yet separate from their underground culture. Nor did I engage in sexual activities with Bill. He never put undue pressure on me to do so.

After a few months I decided I was ready to return to Virginia. Christmas would be here soon, and I couldn't imagine spending it away from home. When I told Bill, he said that he had been thinking of visiting his parents, too, in Boston. Why didn't we go east together?

Why not? I made my plans to return home by bus. Turner took me to the bus station and dutifully watched me climb aboard, then waved goodbye and drove away. "Stop!" I hailed the bus driver as he started to pull out into the street. Clutching my bag, I ran to the front and exclaimed that I had forgotten something. He opened the door and I raced to the blue Volkswagen bug, parked nearby, and hopped inside. We were off!

Our trip across country took about a week. We saw elk and moose in Yellowstone Park, pronghorn antelope on the outskirts of the Grand Tetons, prairie dogs in the badlands of South Dakota. Bill said he wanted to visit some friends in Chicago, so we stopped there and spent the night.

After that Bill and I headed north into Canada and followed Canadian highways 'til we reached the southeast. We planned to cross the border back into the United States at Vermont, but we were in for a surprise. The border patrol decided that we looked suspicious and ordered us to pull over and get out of the car. During the next several hours they literally pulled our car and luggage apart searching, I presumed, for drugs. One of the policemen thought he had found something hot when he pulled a rose petal sachet--a gift from my mother--out of a side pocket of my bag. He seized it and rushed inside to have it tested, returning it to me with disappointment an hour later.

I found the whole scene incredibly amusing and sat on the grass in my tattered jeans laughing my head off. Bill kept frowning at me and telling me to hush but I paid no attention. Having searched all of our possessions and the car, the policeman next decided to remove the seats. Bill offered to help him and, reaching behind them, lifted them out. The man looked carefully around the floor, then finally signaled that he was done and that we could leave.

Bill drove across the border and continued for a few miles more. Then he pulled off onto a dirt road and said, "I have to show you something." He reached around behind my seat and pulled out a good-sized bag and opened it up. Inside was a stash of all kinds of illegal drugs--hashish, LSD, and speed, to name a few. "I picked these up at my friend's house in Chicago," he explained, "and I managed to keep the bag out of sight by holding it up behind the seat when I lifted it out!" He had outsmarted the border patrol!

He had also outsmarted himself, however, at least as far as I was concerned. I was aghast and furious that he had been smuggling drugs and putting me at risk without my knowledge. My parents would have been devastated had I been arrested. That was, in effect, the end of our relationship. I had planned to spend a few days visiting his family in Boston, but instead I asked him to put me on the first bus south that we could find. We spoke a few times afterwards and he wrote me a few letters, but I did not get over his last act of, as I saw it, betrayal. I moved back in with my parents in Short Pump and began taking classes in the English department at Virginia Commonwealth University. What became of Bill I never knew.

Looking back, I sometimes wonder if I had been right to follow my brother-in-law's advice and turn Bill in, though perhaps it was for the best. I also wonder what path my life would have taken had that bag of illegal drugs been discovered. In those days I almost certainly would have gone to jail, if not prison. It is amazing that it wasn't found, after all that searching. I guess the fairy godmother, whom my sister Sally swears keeps watch over me, was on duty that day. But who knows? Perhaps the resulting path would have led to a more sensible life, leaving me complacent and satisfied now. It is a question, I suppose, that has no answer.

*****

6:00 am October 10, 2002

Jack Frost climbed under the covers this morning, waking me up and letting me know that the fire had burned out. Now I feel like writing, in spite of the chill which has invaded the cabin. Evy was right when she said things would slow down at the diner. I didn't make much money yesterday, but I met an interesting man; a rattlesnake tamer! There were almost no other customers, so I listened, entranced, as he described his unusual livelihood. He travels around the country with a van full of rattlesnakes from Texas, putting on shows at schools and fairs. He gets the rattlesnakes from people who find them under their homes or trailers and want them removed. Rather than killing them, he catches them and uses them for education. He told me that he only keeps them for one season, then releases them.

I knew that snakes removed from their home territories seldom survive, but I didn't say anything, as it seems like a worthwhile enterprise anyway. Rattlesnake Man gave me one of his brochures before he left and asked me to write. I wonder if he thinks something might develop between us. He seems like a nice guy, but I'm not interested that way.

Rattlesnakes are not something I've had to think about recently. There are supposedly no rattlesnakes, or any other poisonous snakes, in the central Adirondacks; too cold, I guess. But I lived in rattlesnake country for a long time, out west, and they have a kind of fascination for me. I'll probably write to him and try to stay in touch.

8:30 pm October 12, 2002

Our end-of-the-season museum party was held today, at the Adirondack Hotel here in Long Lake. Almost everyone was there, and even Doris was well enough to come. We had a nice dinner with steamed clams and ribs. I won a hammered iron mallard duck hanger, which I think I'll hang in my kitchen. It was sad saying goodbye to everyone. I'll miss seeing my museum friends over the winter.

Now I'm home, feeling kind of let down and lonely, holding Miss Kelley in my lap and rubbing Huck's ears. I don't know what I'd do without them!

10:00 pm October 14, 2002

I'm sitting in what has become my favorite spot; just in front of the wood stove, hovering close to stay warm. The temperature has dropped into the twenties the last couple nights and, looking across the lake, you can see snow on the Seward Range. I am bemused by the presence of a new man in my life, Peter, eight years older than I. I first met him last year, when I was living with Harry. I ran into Peter in town recently, and we have struck up a friendship. I am lonely up here on this mountain, and his company is pleasant. Tonight we went to a charming little restaurant in Lake Placid, its decor an eclectic collage of everything imaginable. Afterward we wandered around a great old bookstore which occupies three stories and includes new and used books and art prints for sale. It was great fun.

9:00 am October 15, 2002

It snowed last night! Not much, but enough to cover the ground. The fire had burned out by the time I awoke, and even though I've rebuilt it, it's still chilly. So I'm wrapped up in my blanket, a cup of hot coffee warming my hands. I need to bring in the wood I split and stack it on the porch before it's buried in snow. Peter offered to come and help me, but I want to do it myself.

I pulled out my book of Robert Frost, a gift from Momma, and skimmed through it in search of his take on snow.

The way a crow shook down on me
the dust of snow from a hemlock tree
Has given my heart a change of mood
and saved some part of a day I had rued.

Frost is one of my favorites. His words resound with the rhythm of this place where I am living.

4:00 pm October 18, 2002

We have had more snow, mixed with rain, and when it froze last night this hillside turned to ice! I slipped going down the hill on my way to work at the diner. I mentioned it to Carl when I saw him this afternoon, and he said he would string a rope up along the steepest part so I could hold on.

Sitting here, I recall a comment I heard at one of the tables in the diner today which included the word nigger. Having grown up in the South (where I would have had my mouth washed out if I had used that word,) I am shocked by the racism I sometimes come across up here. "Colored" was the word we (and they) used for our dark-skinned neighbors in Virginia.

*****

One of the most beloved people in my life, Nellie, was colored. The story which comes to mind now is her story.

The Little Cottage in the Woods

Surrounded by Virginia pines and sweet gum trees, its paint peeled away long ago, there stood a little shingled, four-room cottage. The yard around it was dirt, with a few outcrops of wiregrass, dandelions, and daffodils which bent low when the wind blew. It was connected to the main road a half-mile away by a winding dirt lane, sometimes passable, often too pitted with potholes for a regular car to get through. Parked outside, most evenings, was an old blue Ford pickup truck. It had rested there, serene and comfortable as an old shoe, for many years.

Through the pines, when the light was right, could be seen the silhouettes of big houses newly erected on small plots of land, the native trees cut down and replaced with the flawless symmetry of nursery-grown saplings. These were expensive houses, belonging to newcomers to this woodland, who thought themselves very grand, and who didn't like the little cottage.

It hadn't always been like that. Just a few years back the little cottage was the only house out here. Not many people wanted to live in the boondocks of Short Pump, Virginia, and if they did, the Richmond people made fun of them. If the city brownstones and suburban tri-levels made fun of the little cottage, it didn't know it and would not have cared anyway.

The cottage had been happy then. It didn't care about the tall dormers and pillars or the multitude of empty bedrooms in the big homes. It didn't long for the expensive furniture; Chippendale reproductions and genuine antiques, which peeked through the curtained windows. Nor did it want the perfectly manicured yards, where no one dared step off the sidewalk. It loved the woods that surrounded it. It was, in fact, not the least bit envious of the big houses. It wished things could go back like they were before Short Pump became a prestigious place to live.

The little cottage was filled with love. In it lived an old man and an old woman. Their skin was the color of hot cocoa, dark and rich. When they moved into the cottage they were known as colored people; now in the time of the new big houses, they were called black. The woman, whose name was Nellie Bell, worked for a white family, looking after the young children and doing some cleaning. Back then, she was called a maid. Now, if she still worked, she'd be known as a housekeeper. Her husband Irving was called a plumber, then and now. He worked on the homes of other colored, or black, people.

The newcomers were too up-scale to use racial slurs, at least in public. If anyone had suggested that they wanted the couple to leave because of the color of their skin, they would have denied it with vigor. They were Northerners, after all. It was them that gave these people their freedom to begin with. They should have some respect. Their trashy little shack was keeping property values down, and the developers could build twenty fine residences on the piece of land occupied by that shack. The couple had been offered a good price; more than a fair price, enough for them to buy themselves a fine home. But the old couple wouldn't even talk to the realtor. There they sat, in that damned shack, interfering with the wishes of the whole community.

The developers sent in their lawyers. They took the old man and woman to court, using big legal terms the couple had never heard of. The realtors offered them a big check, assuring them that it was far more than their land was worth. When the couple didn't accept it, things began to happen. The creek that flowed by the oak grove on their land mysteriously dried up. There were veiled threats, phone calls from unidentified callers.

To no avail. The old man and the old woman were happy in their cottage. They did not understand why the white lawyers, developers, and homeowners complained. They had all the land surrounding them; wasn't that enough? The couple had lived there their whole lives, and they wanted to die there.

The old man did just that. One day his heart just gave out, and the old woman was left alone. She was content though. She missed the old man, but they had lived the life they wanted, and she had all her memories. Now she would stay in the little cottage until she joined him. With her husband gone, however, the developers renewed their efforts to get her out. Her children, all of whom were grown and living elsewhere, decided that she would be better off living in town, instead of at the end of a long rutted road surrounded by enemies. They tried to help her, filling the potholes when they got too deep, mending broken pipes, but they let her know that they did not approve.

In the end, it was neither her children, the developers, nor the neighbors who ended the battle. At least, not by themselves. It was the tax assessors that defeated her. It was "progress." You could even say it was her own land that brought about her downfall, and with it, its own final destruction. It became so valuable that neither the old woman nor her children could afford to pay the taxes. She was forced to sell. The delighted developers tore down the little house where the old man and old woman had lived and loved, bulldozed down the woods, and had their way.

I was one of the white children Nellie looked after. My parents taught school, so on weekdays Daddy drove Momma to her school and then drove down the dirt road (Nellie's Road, we called it) and picked her up. Nellie took care of my little sister, Nancy, during the day, and me when I got home from school. The basement (which Daddy had remodeled into a

*"recreation room") was her realm. She had her ironing board down there
and that's where our television (black-and-white back then) was. Nancy
and I stayed down there with her, watching "Amos and Andy," "The Andy
Griffith Show," and "Leave it to Beaver." Momma always made lunch
and left it in the icebox.*

*At Christmas time my father, brother, and I would drive down the road,
stop to visit with Nellie and Irving, and give them a box of homemade
cookies. Then we would hike into their woods with an ax and bring back
what we considered a fine short-needle pine tree (which Momma always
lamented because it was crooked and filled half the room.)*

*As time passed Nancy and I grew up and didn't need to be looked after,
but Nellie still came a couple days a week to do ironing and light
housework. Other afternoons, I would ride my horse down the dirt road
and visit Nellie and Irving. She would serve me milk and cookies at the
wooden table in front of the window. We would talk about little things;
my wirehaired terrier, Mister, and their big German shepherd, Jeff. We'd
talk about plants, about family. We became friends; not child and adult,
white and black, or employer and employed; just friends.*

*Later, after I'd moved away and the big houses were built and Irving
died, I'd drive down to see her on visits home. Sometimes now we talked
about race and discrimination. About how, when Nancy and I were young,
the colored kids in the neighborhood had gone to a different school.
About how things had changed. She told me how she had felt when, long
ago, her son had married a white woman. She hadn't liked it. She told me
that she had never thought Irving would go to a white person's wedding,
and how surprised and delighted she'd been when he came to mine. She
told me about the people in the big houses and how they were trying to
make her move. About how she didn't want to move and, later, in a tone
of resignation, about how she couldn't fight them anymore.*

*I remember the last time I saw her. She was in her late eighties, living
in a fine old home in Richmond, purchased with the money the realtors
had paid her. White pillars flanked the stairway and a foyer led into a
lovely parlor. There was a dining room with an antique chandelier and
wainscoting along the walls. Nellie and I sat in the kitchen, though, like
old times, at the scarred wooden table she had brought from her little
house in Short Pump. We had cookies with cans of soda and talked about
the way things used to be. She asked me how her "little girl," Nancy, was
doing. She wanted to know about my brother, Sandy, and my sisters Sally*

and Betsy, and their children. She told me about her grandchildren, attending a good school and living in a prestigious Southside suburb.

Sure, this was a nice house, she told me when I remarked on it, but it didn't feel like home. She wished she could go back to her little cottage; spend her last days there. I wished it too, but we both knew that our homes and the places we had both loved no longer existed. She gave me a big hug goodbye. "Law, Girl, you so tall. I think you's growed more every time I see you. But you always come see me, don't you? You never forget!"

Nellie died not long afterwards. I was in Arizona, and I didn't know about it till my next trip home. I spoke to her grandson's wife, a schoolteacher I'd met on my previous visits, and she told me about her last days of illness. They hadn't known how to reach me, she said.

I hope Nellie is with Irving now, and I hope they're living in whatever house they want, in a place where money and power don't call the shots; a place where no one judges you by the color of your skin or the monetary value of your possessions.

*****

8:45 pm October 16, 2002

Work was slow today, and I had time to visit with some of the customers. Barry comes in every day, driving over from Newcomb, another small town to the east, where he lives with his wife. The first time I saw Barry I did a double-take. He looks just like Maurice, the wealthy, egotistical crank in my favorite television show, "Northern Exposure." Appearance is as far as the resemblance goes. Barry is an agreeable kind of guy with a quiet sense of humor and not wealthy, as far as I know. Retired now, after 35 years of working at the Tahawus Mine, he answered my questions gladly.

The Tahawus Mine was near one of the first mines in the Adirondacks, he said. Originally called the McIntyre Iron Works, it had produced and smelted iron ore between 1832 and 1856. It had harnessed the power of the Hudson River and was the main support for the small village of Adirondac, a village which no longer exists. The mine went out of business because of its remoteness and inaccessibility and the difficulty of removing titanium impurities.

Later, in the 20th century, titanium became valuable and Tahawus Mine (which means Cloud-splitter in an Indian tongue) opened. The village of Tahawus was built around it, and Barry lived there. It had a post office, a school, two churches, a grocery store, and houses for the miners and their families. Barry operated the diamond drills, which bored into the rock for samples, and drove the heavy equipment at the mine.

In 1963 the houses in Tahawus were mounted on trucks and moved to an area of Newcomb known as "Winebrook." The mine ceased operation in 1989.

According to Barry, there's still plenty of iron and titanium there. I asked him if he thought it would ever re-open and he said no. But I don't guess anyone can tell the future. "You should go see it," he told me as he left.

6:30 pm October 18, 2002

The adolescent loons are still here. I can hear their distant wails from the lake when the wind is still. I expect the adults have already left, bound for the waters of the mid-Atlantic coast. I'm told that sometimes the young ones wait too late, till after the lakes have frozen, and they cannot take off. They then starve to death or freeze. I hope the ones I heard this evening leave soon.

9:30 pm October 19, 2002

I decided to take Barry's advice and go to Tahawus today. I got up early, gave Miss Kelley a handful of dry food, and headed out to the truck with Huck. We drove past the trailhead to Goodnow Mountain, which we had climbed the year before, through the hamlet of Newcomb, and over the bridge which crosses the Hudson River. We turned onto the Blue Ridge road and in a few miles came to what was left of the mine, closed now. I parked the truck at the entrance and Huck and I slipped around the closed gate, quietly, somewhat awed by the sense of mystery which enveloped the place.

We walked past Sanford Lake, which had been pumped almost dry back in the mining days. We passed the skeletons of cumbersome old machines, stopped dead in their tracks, and giant piles of ore (which Barry had called cobb rock) once buried deep in the earth, now exposed naked to my wondering eyes.

We returned to the truck and drove a little farther. The macadam on the road ended and we reached the edge of Adirondac, a once vital town, now inhabited by ghosts. I parked on the shoulder and walked slowly through the crumbling village, keeping Huck in tow. Deserted buildings lined both sides of the road, now falling apart and full of dust and dry leaves. Broken glass splinters still sat in the windows, the doors jerked sideways on their hinges.

Huck and I carefully stepped over a pile of fallen shingles and entered one of the buildings. This was where, in September of 1901, Vice-President Teddy Roosevelt, upon learning that President McKinley was dying, caught the stage that took him back down the mountain. One of the exhibits at the Adirondack Museum depicts the scene. It shows the stage coach hurrying through the night, carrying Teddy to North Creek Station, where he took the train to Buffalo and was sworn in as president of the United States. Looking out the back window, I saw the Hudson River, wending its way only a few yards away. Birds rustled the crackly brown leaves of a nearby black cherry tree, its branches still sporting a few dried pits. On the other side of the road, up the hill, stood what looked like a boarding house and maybe a bar.

I tried to imagine what it had been like a hundred years before, with children playing in the road and fishing on the banks of the river, women cooking for some church function, the men, just home from the mine, stopping in the bar for a drink. I shivered when I thought I heard the echoes of their voices, then realized that it was the complaining of crows perched on one of the roofs. On the way out I pulled the truck over at the blast furnace, located at the Upper Works. Here, according to the Adirondack Museum's mining exhibit, molten iron was poured into molds of "pig iron," which were later reheated to form higher quality "wrought" iron. Now all that is past, and the woods are silent again.

Sitting here with my journal, I have a strong sense of the passage of time, the transience of all things. I'm going to take Huck for his last walk, tamp down the fire, and go to bed.

8:00 pm October 23, 2002

I leave for Buffalo in the morning for another round of Head Start music sessions. I tried to get everything packed after work today, and then I drove over to Lois' house, on the Buttermilk Falls road. Lois has a great old farmhouse, built in 1894, with a view of the Raquette River; a home she lived in with her husband before his death. I got to know her at the museum, where she has worked for years. We had a cup of tea and looked at pictures of her family. Lois' grandfather was the school superintendent at Newcomb, the town eleven miles east of Long Lake. Lois said her grandmother taught there, and her mother wrote the words for the school song...There are so many stories in these mountains, it's hard to stay focused on my own.

Pat Garber

November 2002

7:00 pm November 2, 2002

Returning from Buffalo this afternoon, I found that Long Lake had been transformed while I was away. It's a winter wonderland, the trees draped in ermine stoles, the ground a carpet of shimmering diamonds! Bringing everything up the hill in the ice was a real challenge. I used an old sled I'd found in one of Carl's sheds, but it was not easy, trying not to slip and drop everything. Now the groceries are put away and I have a fire going in the woodstove. Miss Kelley is curled up on my lap and Huck's head is on my knee.

*****

Now my mind wanders back to a time filled with pain. A year or so after I returned to Virginia from San Francisco, my faith in the goodness of life, the infallibility of family, and the very existence of God fell apart. I was twenty years old when Sally, my oldest sister, adored and adulated by myself and my other siblings, became ill. Whether her illness was the result of too much social drinking with the "Navy wives," of an inability to accept the disintegration of her seemingly perfect marriage, or of a chemical imbalance unrelated to either, she whacked out. She became angry and dysfunctional, drinking herself into states of stupor and over-dosing on drugs prescribed her by doctors and psychiatrists. She spent the next few years ricocheting back and forth between waitress jobs, hospitals, and mental institutions; in the process losing her husband, her children, and all her material assets. She drove her family and her friends away and cast a cloud of grief upon my family. I had missed the signs of its coming when I lived with her.

Added to the grief over my sister was the loss of my brother-in-law, her husband, Turner, whom I had dearly loved, and of their children, who moved with Turner to Puerto Rico. It would be years before we would reconnect with my niece Debbie and my nephews, Chuck and Larry, and never with Turner.

The despair that I felt led me to turn to one of my long-time dreams; becoming a hobo. Woody Guthrie, with his freight-train-hopping lifestyle and his songs of compassion for the underdogs, was a hero to me. I wanted to emulate him, seeking not wealth but something more meaningful from life. I had horrified my eleventh grade teacher when, upon being asked to write a paper about the career I planned to pursue, I chose that of hobo. I didn't know how I was going to manage it, since I got homesick whenever I left home. But gradually I had developed a system, and it has worked ever since. When at the peak of either my courage or my despair, I put myself into a position requiring bravery, a position from which there is no easy way out. From there on, I let things go as they will.

Becoming a Hobo

"Oh dear god, what have I gotten myself into???"

I had just climbed out of a strange car in Dover, the capital of Delaware, assuring the driver that I knew exactly where I was and what I would do next. I knew neither, and as I gazed around the unknown neighborhood, a collection of gas stations, closed shops and ramshackle houses, I felt my stomach coil around itself in fear.

It was late, near midnight, and no one was around. It was also raining, though not as hard as when I had set out. I was exhausted and, seeing no other options, I approached a car parked on the side of the road. I tried the door but it was locked. Two more cars, and then, at the third one, the latch opened. I climbed into the back seat, pulled my sleeping bag over me, and tried to go to sleep. Tired as I was, however, my mind would not stop whirling, re-visiting the events which had led me to this moment.

I had been working at the Stratford Hills Veterinary Hospital in Southside Richmond. I liked my boss, Dr. Beller; I liked his volatile but kind-hearted receptionist, Virginia; and I liked my job. Along with the everyday work of cleaning kennels and holding cats and dogs, Dr. Beller taught me to develop x-rays, identify parasites, and administer sub-cutaneous and inter-muscular injections. He and I had an arrangement about unwanted pets which were brought to him. He would treat and neuter them if I would find them homes. We never put any treatable animal to sleep. I brought home cats with medicated ears, mutts with splinted legs, and a beagle with a broken pelvis which eventually found her way to my sister Betsy's home.

After I had been there a few months Dr. Beller brought in another veterinarian, Dr. Meres, to work with him. She did not, apparently, understand our arrangement. One day when she and I were working alone, a man brought in a big black tomcat who had been ripped up in a catfight. He was sick of paying vet bills, the man said. "Just put it to sleep!" I put the cat in a cage and when Dr. Meres asked me to bring it in I did so quite innocently, expecting her to treat the wound. I watched incredulously as she pulled out a bottle intended for euthanasia. "What

79

are you doing?" I asked in horror. She looked at me with an expression of annoyance. "I'm getting ready to put the cat down," she responded. I grabbed the cat back into my arms and there ensued a fierce argument, in which I flat out refused to let her near the cat. She was furious, but agreed to wait till Dr. Beller got back.

I waited in trepidation for Dr. Beller's return that afternoon, wondering if I would soon be looking for a new job. He called me into his office with a stern voice, giving me a long, hard look. "Are you going to get a home for that cat if I treat it?" he asked. I smiled in relief. "You bet!" I answered. "Well, bring it in then." Dr. Meres left the clinic not long afterwards, and I continued to enjoy my job.

After one of my sister Sally's bad weeks, however, I felt an unbearable need to get away, so I asked for some time off. I decided to go camping on Assateague, a wild and uninhabited island near Virginia's Eastern Shore, home of Misty and other Chincoteague ponies of Margaret Henry fame. I did not have a car, and as I had been longing to try out the life of a hobo, I decided it was a good time to start. I bade my parents goodbye and set out hitchhiking eastward from Richmond.

I made it without incident, journeying high above and far below the Chesapeake Bay on the 23-mile-long Chesapeake Bay Bridge-Tunnel and crossing the little causeway to the fishing village of Chincoteague. I walked through the village and across the bridge to Assateague, arriving just before dusk. Assateague is a national seashore, so there was a small ranger station near the entrance. I stopped in and told the ranger I would be camping in the backcountry there. He had me fill out a form-- name, address, etc., and I set out.

Assateague has always been one of my favorite places. It is home not only to wild ponies but to all kinds of water birds, including a large population of wintering tundra swans. It was spring now, so the swans had departed, heading for their breeding grounds in the far north; but other species were migrating through. I found a campsite on a high piece of marshland, pitched my tent, and ate a sandwich I had brought with me. Then I scooted into my sleeping bag and tried to get some sleep.

This was the first night I had ever spent alone. Now, miles from anyone, I regretted my decision to come and wished myself safely back home. I had no choice, however, but to lie there and listen to the strange sounds of island nightlife. Eventually I cried myself to sleep.

Meanwhile, back at the ranger station, the park ranger made a phone call. I had inherited from my father the sometimes beneficial, often *deleterious, trait of looking younger than my years. The ranger had not believed me when I told him I was nineteen, so he had called my parents to see if I was a runaway. They assured him that I was old enough to be camping on my own, and that I had their blessing. "Just keep an eye on her," they asked, "and let us know if anything goes wrong."*

Things looked better in the morning. I had, after all, survived, and the challenge of getting here had taken my mind off my sorrows at home. I explored the island, coming across a few rugged, longhaired ponies and the carcass of a dead one. I startled a flock of black ducks and watched a great blue heron spear a frog with its long beak.

The weather, however, was not looking good. The temperature dropped through the day and the clouds built up, forming a formidable gray canopy above me. Rain began to fall, and before long I was soaking wet. Camping no longer seemed like such a good idea. I climbed into my tent, pulled my damp sleeping bag around me, and decided I was outright miserable. After thinking about it for a bit, I decided to go visit my friend Sandy, newly married and living in St. Johnsville, New York. That would not be giving up, I consoled myself, since it would entail another adventure in itself.

I packed up my gear and hiked back out to the road. The ranger station was closed now, but by luck some late vacationer was leaving the park. I stuck out my thumb, still trying to get it down right, and soon I was on my way. A few long, slow but interesting rides later, following Route 13, I left Maryland and entered Delaware. My ride dropped me at the outskirts of its capital city, Dover.

So now, here I was, feeling like a true hobo and wondering what morning would bring. I finally fell into a restless sleep.

Rising at daybreak, I slipped away, thus avoiding the look of surprise and anger that my presence would no doubt have evoked from the car's owner. I wandered around for a while, finally locating a diner where I got a cup of coffee and a hot breakfast. I spent the rest of the day walking and hitching short rides north.

My last ride was a tractor-trailer going all the way to the outskirts of New York City. It was getting dark as I dropped my pack on the roadside and climbed down from the truck cab. I wasn't sure hitchhiking through New York City at night was such a good idea, but what the heck! I was actually enjoying the thrill of danger now, and it was proving to be a real cure for my depression.

Meanwhile, unbeknownst to me, the weather which had driven me out of Assateague intensified, developing into a full-blown nor'easter. The park ranger grew worried and set out to find me. Needless, to say, he was unsuccessful. He called my parents, wondering if I had returned home. When they told him they had not heard from me, a search was instigated.

I had not been standing on the highway into New York City for long when I was picked up by a young man with dark curly hair and an accent. Alfonsio was Italian, he told me, and lived nearby with his family. He invited me to spend the night with them, and I accepted with relief.

Alfonsio lived in a modest apartment in a lower Manhattan neighborhood, not far from the Brooklyn Bridge, with his parents and grandfather. First generation immigrants, his grandfather spoke no English, his parents a limited amount. They had already had dinner, but Alfonsio's mother insisted on fixing me a plate of spaghetti. (I wasn't about to complain, but I have to admit I was disappointed to find that Italian "spaghetti" was served with plain marinara sauce, not the rich meat sauce my mother made!)

Afterwards, Alfonsio and I went for a walk through the city. I had never been in New York before, and I was awed by its intensity, bright lights, and sheer size. We sat for a few minutes at the base of the Brooklyn Bridge, watching the cars and trucks pass above us, wondering where all the people were going. I slept that night on a cot in the small living area, sharing the room with the grandfather, who stayed on the sofa. The next morning, after coffee and toast, I thanked Alfonsio's family profusely. He gave me a ride to what he said was a good place to get a lift, and I was on my way, now having a wonderful time.

Back on Assateague Island the storm had abated. The ranger went back out to search for me again but found only the blackened sand where I had built my campfire. He called for help in the form of an NPS helicopter. At about the time I was arriving at Sandy's house in St. Johnsville, New York, a helicopter crew was hovering over Assateague and searching its surrounding waters for the body of a young-looking, longhaired, nineteen-year-old girl. My parents were, no doubt, suspended in an agony of apprehension.

I spent a couple days with Sandy, walking around her husband's hometown and empathizing with her tales of woe (married life, which she was finding, was not all it was cracked up to be.) Then I decided to hitch to Tom's River, New Jersey, and surprise my sister Betsy, who lived there with her husband. It was then that I learned about the storm in Virginia and the uproar I was causing. Betsy took one look at me, smiling on her doorstep, and gave me down the country. She escorted me to the telephone, where I called my parents and informed them that I was alive and well. The search was called off and I went home, resuming my job as a vet tech at Dr. Beller's.

Sally is better now. She has remarried and has a job waiting tables, and while she still drinks, she manages to function most of the time. We stay in touch, and I love her, but I still miss the sister I had worshipped and adored as a child.

*****

6:45 am November 5, 2002

It's snowing again, or perhaps I should say still. There is about a foot of snow on the ground. Carl said the bears are probably asleep now, so I can start feeding the birds without worrying about them pulling down the feeders. I had brought up the sunflower seed feeder that Mom and Daddy had used back home, and I'd bought a small suet ball at Northern Borne before they closed for the winter. I hung both in front of the window, so I can see them while sitting on the futon. A couple of black-capped chickadees are dining already.

My hours are cut way back at the diner, so I expect I'll have lots of time on my hands now. I took out my cross-country skis yesterday and tried skiing on the snowmobile trail. I had to leave Huck at home, since it's hunting season and I don't want him running free. The hills and curves are worse than I'd realized; I fell twice, though I didn't hurt myself. I'm going to need a lot of practice, I can see!

5:30 pm November 7, 2002

My feeders are alive with birds and red squirrels! I'm having a ball watching them. Besides chickadees, there are white-breasted nuthatches and blue jays. The red squirrels are the most fun. Also known as chickarees, they are much smaller than the gray squirrels I know from Virginia. They are lively and agile, hanging upside down and every which way to reach my feeders. Naturalist Clinton Hart Merriam describes them as "the most hilarious" of the squirrels and uses words like "jubilant," "arrogant," and "vexatious" as he writes about them. He credits them with having cleverness, industry, and an "insatiable love of

83

mischief and shameless disregard of all the ordinary customs and civilities of life." How could one not love them? Yet many folks up here hate them and the damage they do.

I took the snowshoes I bought at the museum's antique show last year off the wall today and tried them out. They are the old-fashioned kind, made of rawhide stretched over wood frames, about four feet long, known as Algonquins. The Raquette River, I've been told, derived its name from a pile of French snowshoes, or "raquettes" left behind during the American Revolution. I was pretty clumsy trying to walk in them and I managed to trip over Huck's leash and land in a big pile of snow. Trying to extract myself and Huck took a while; I expect that had someone been watching they'd have had a good laugh.

I've got a hot fire burning now, so it's warm inside, in spite of the 10 degree reading on the outside thermometer. My sister Sally says I must be nuts for trying to spend the winter here, but I've always wanted to try living in a log cabin in the North Woods. I guess I'm pretty lucky; not everyone gets the chance to pursue their dreams.

8;00 pm November 8, 2002

Sitting on the table beside me is a depiction of a mountain lake with a deer on the far bank and a hemlock tree in the foreground. It is carved on the cap of a shelf mushroom, which I found a few days ago while climbing up Mt. Sabattis. It was too soft to work with at first, so I set it on a shelf and tested it each day, until this morning I found it the perfect consistency for carving. I sketched a design on the creamy flesh with a pencil, then etched the lines with the tip of an empty ball-point pen. I finished it a few minutes ago, pressing texture into the mountains and tree with a blunt pencil. Studying it now, I am fairly satisfied with my work.

I first saw carved and painted shelf mushrooms at the Adirondack Museum where I work. Later, my 78 year-old- friend Doris showed me the ones she had painted, and Lois, also a friend from the museum, showed me one her son had carved years before.

Shelf mushrooms, or polypores, are large woody fungi that grow on dead trees, using their decaying matter for sustenance. This particular one is a birch polypore which, according to my mushroom guidebook, can be used as an anesthetic, a razor strop, or kindling for a fire. I have also collected a hemlock varnish shelf, false turkeytail, and several other kinds which I hope to paint. Most of them came from near my cabin, cut with my camping saw from the bark of their host trees.

My carved mushroom is actually just the fruit of the birch polypore. The main body, known as the mycelium, is a network of thread-like strands, or hyphae, which lie under the bark of the birch tree I cut it from. The hyphae take nourishment from the rotting wood of the dead tree to produce the fruit (the shelf mushroom I brought home) which contains the reproductive spores.

Mushrooms are, I am learning, mysterious and fascinating organisms which play an important role in our ecosystem. The mycelia of some species cover hundreds of underground acres and are busily engaged in decomposing all kinds of matter, recycling it into a usable form, without our even knowing they are there. Then one moist spring or fall day a fruit is produced, and we finally notice, exclaiming, "Look, a mushroom!"

I hope I can learn, come spring, which mushrooms around here are edible.

7:30 pm November 9, 2002

I found a new use for birch bark today. While gathering up some firewood from the pile near the cabin I picked up a few pieces of the bark, a bit thicker than that which I use for writing. I cut them into strips and then glued them into circles for napkin rings. They turned out great, so I am going to make some more for Christmas presents. I also cut out some stars and canoes and punched holes in them so they can be hung up. Birch bark Christmas ornaments! I may see if I can sell some of them.

5:00 pm November 10, 2002

I've been watching two hairy woodpeckers on the hemlock trees in front of the cabin. They are incredibly busy, tapping around the trees. I don't know what insects they're looking for but they must be finding something. One of them rips pieces of bark off with its bill and tosses them impatiently aside, then plunges its bill into the core of the tree. You can almost see the frustration on its face when it fails to find an insect. It moves quickly on to another spot.

I have started reading Reverend John Todd's book, "Long Lake." He was a minister who, back in 1841, came to bring God to "a little community of eight or nine families...shut out from the world" in what he called a "fairy land." He described the village. "They lived in their little log-houses and their boats were their horses, and the lake their only path." Would I have liked to live here then? I ask myself. I'm not sure.

4:45 pm November 12, 2002

I stopped on the way home from work and borrowed a book on mammals from my landlady, Margaret. She asked me to sit down and I did, just for a bit. Somehow we got on the subject of the mail. I knew that Margaret's daughter, Liz, works at the post office. Today I learned that her grandfather had been the postman here years before, delivering the mail on horseback. He would pick up the mail at Port Henry, on Lake Champlain, where it came in by boat, and deliver it to Long Lake on his horse, a journey of several days! Another story...

6:00 am November 15, 2002

I opened the door last night to see if it was still snowing. When I flipped on the outside light I saw a movement at the bird feeder. Two huge eyes stared at me from a chinchilla-like furry ball. It took me a moment to realize that I was looking at a flying squirrel. It stared back at me, its eyes dark and liquid and beautiful, then disappeared in a swirl of snow. I knew they lived here but this is the first time I've seen one. I looked it up in the mammal book Margaret loaned me. Both northern and southern flying squirrels live in the Adirondacks, it says, but northern squirrels are more likely to be found in coniferous forests, which this is, so that's what I'm betting on. It "flies" by stretching its legs, spreading its flight skin, and using its tail as a rudder. Cool.

Wildlife has always had a special place in my life. My mother says that the only way she could potty-train me, way back in my toddler days, was to sit me down with a book with pictures of animals.

7:30 am November 18, 2002

I pulled my back out yesterday while splitting wood so I guess I'll lay low today. Good thing I don't have to go to work. Maybe I'll try to finish the birch bark napkin rings and coasters I'm making for Christmas presents. Play my guitar. I'm trying to learn some new songs.

For now, I'm wrapped up in a heavy robe and, having brushed the snow out of my Adirondack chair, I've cuddled down with a blanket and a cup of hot coffee on my deck. The view is breath-taking, the trees draped with yesterday's snowfall.

I've been listening to a guy on NPR talk about Governor Pataki's proposed regulations to reduce acid rain in the Adirondacks. There are 500 lakes here considered to be "dead," supporting no life, because of acid rain. There are others whose fish are considered unsafe because of mercury released into the air by power plants and then into the water by the actions of acid rain. There are huge stretches of mountain where red spruce are dying, the calcium leached out of their needles as a result of acid rain, leaving them susceptible to injury from freezing temperatures. There are loons, otters, and other fish-eating species dying from mercury poisoning. All are the result of sulfuric dioxide and nitrogen oxide emissions released from coal-powered electric plants far west of here. Carried by winds to the Adirondacks, they are released in the form of acidic rain...what used to be, what ought to be, life-giving rain...

Every time we waste energy, we cause a tiny bit of some Adirondack lake to die. When we turn our hot water heaters up, take long showers, or leave lights on needlessly, we are helping to destroy some High Peaks red spruce forest or poisoning a loon chick. The tune and words to Malvina Reynolds' song, "What have they done to the rain?" echo through my mind. *"The grass is gone, the boy disappears, and rain keeps falling like helpless tears..."* Glancing up, I notice the kitchen light on. "Guilty as charged!" I berate myself...

4:30 pm November 19, 2002
Huck and I just returned from our daily trek, plowing through at least two feet of snow. Deer and snowshoe hare tracks zigzagged along the trail we followed, and Huck was crazy to follow them. But with hunting season in full swing, I 'm keeping him on the leash.

*****

Now I return to my past. I am twenty years old, home from my foray into hoboing but still mourning the dissipation of the sister I had loved and sinking quickly back into despair. I had wanted to ride my horse, Lady Caprice, out West, but Momma and Daddy were vehemently opposed to this idea. We compromised with a plan for me to visit England and Europe. I gave Dr. Beller my notice and bought an airplane ticket from New York City to London. Then, with tears in my eyes and a small bag of clothes slung across my shoulder, I set out for Kennedy Airport, hitchhiking again. Once I was on my way, my spirits soared.

Pat Garber

Two Dreams or
A Spiderling in the Big Apple

Like a newly hatched spiderling, spinning a lifeline of silk as she blindly tosses herself upon the wind, I ballooned into the world. Twenty years old, I was an idealist who believed that all one had to do was give life a chance, be true to oneself, and trust to Fate for good things to happen. I planned to prove that wealth, formal education, and all the trappings of class were un-needed for a truly successful life.

The wind that I rode (actually a tractor-trailer truck) deposited me on a highway leading toward the Big Apple, New York City. Adjusting my plaid canvas bag in the crook of my arm, I held up a sign and stuck out my thumb. I figured I could make New York City by dark. What I would do when I got there, I had no idea.

Not many cars had passed before one slowed down. Not being much of an automobile aficionado, I wasn't sure but I thought it might be a BMW. I cautiously examined the man in the driver's seat. While I believed in trusting to fate, I also believed in trusting one's own intuition, so I always checked out my rides before getting into their cars. I wasn't sure about this one. He was neat and well dressed, with short hair, a tie and the look of a businessman. While I didn't like to stereotype or show prejudice, experience had taught me to be wary of the type.

I chatted with him through the window for a few moments. He seemed nice enough, and I was pretty sure he was harmless, so I accepted a ride. James, as he introduced himself, and I talked on the way to the city. He was an attorney in Albany, he said, but had been away and was on his way home. It was Friday, so he was going to stop in New York City for a few days and visit his family.

In response to his questions, I told him that I was from Virginia, had dropped out of college and quit my job, and was now on my way to Europe. I had an airline ticket to London, I added, and was flying out of Kennedy Airport in three days. "No," I told him, "I had no idea what I would do when I got there." "Wasn't I afraid?" "Well, yes, but what other way was there to see the world?" "Did I know where I was going to stay in New York City?" "No, not yet." "Could I afford to get a hotel?" I laughed at that. "I have a hundred dollars to last for the next six months. No, I don't think I'm getting a hotel here! But don't worry," I said with a false bravado. "I'm sure something will work out!"

I was determined not to let on that I was scared to death of what the night would bring. I had a bad habit of making my plans in the morning, when my courage soars. About sundown, when fear set in, it was usually too late to back out of whatever situation I'd gotten myself into. As we drew close to the city I felt butterflies begin to wake up in my stomach. Soon I'd be on the street again, with darkness coming on and no place to go.

"Do you mind stopping at Saks," James asked me. "I have some shopping to do there." I was delighted. I'd never seen 5th Avenue, nor been in such a department store, bigger even than Miller & Rhoads in Richmond. I stared in fascination at the fashionably dressed shoppers and the elegant displays, though I didn't have much interest in the tailored clothes James was looking at. I looked a bit out of place in my cut-off blue jeans and worn tee-shirt, but if James noticed, it didn't seem to bother him.

When we got back in the car he turned to me and said, a little shyly, "I'm going to stay with my sister tonight. She has an apartment in Brooklyn. I'm sure you could sleep on her couch, if you'd like." If? "That would be great!" I assured him. His sister, Nancy, was attractive and artistic, with long dark hair coiled around her head and a long stylish skirt. Her apartment, located in an old brownstone, was nice, not ostentatious but tastefully furnished with interesting artwork and books. She and I hit it off immediately. After James and I had had time to wash up, they asked me if I'd like to go out "for a bite to eat" in a nearby cafe. "Our treat," they added. I accepted with gladness. Afterwards we went to a coffeehouse and listened to folk music. I explained to them my dream; to prove that a person could go into the world with nothing, like I was doing, and come out right. They listened thoughtfully and seemed to find it a worthy goal.

I woke the next morning to the smell of fresh coffee. Nancy poured me a cup as she explained that "James ran down to the deli for bagels and lox." It was my first taste of both, and I enjoyed them immensely. As we ate, they told me they were planning to go to their mother's house in Greenwich, Connecticut, and maybe take their boat out in Long Island Sound. Would I like to go with them? "I'd love to!" I assured them, and before long we were on our way. I stared in fascination as we drove through the city and across a huge bridge. I'd never spent time in New York City before, and seeing it with my new friends was exciting.

The smell of the sea was wonderful as we approached Long Island Sound, and the gulls called a shrill welcome. The neighborhood we drove through was impressive, with big expensive houses. We stopped at a gate where a gatekeeper smiled at Nancy and James and waved us in. They showed me around, and I stared in awe as they pointed out the homes of well-known politicians and tycoons. Finally we pulled up at their mother's house--a reconstructed 19th century barn, they told me-- and we went inside.

James and Nancy's mother was civil enough but not a bit like her children. She put on what I would call "airs" and talked constantly about her health. She was, nonetheless, very nice to me. She was getting ready to go to Europe, her husband already there on some business. James got the key to the boat, and then he, Nancy and I set out for the yacht club. We spent the afternoon puttering around Long Island Sound and had a lovely day.

I was scheduled to fly out of Kennedy Airport the next morning, I explained that evening, so I would need to get back to the city before then. I helped Nancy fix a salad while James grilled steaks on the deck. Afterwards he asked me to go for a walk. "Why don't you stay?" he asked me. "Forget about going to Europe? We could get to know each other better, and maybe... Who knows? You might decide to settle down here." I hesitated, staring at the man before me. He'd been very nice to me, a perfect gentleman. He would be, no doubt, a wonderful man to settle down with. But I was not thinking of settling. I had a world to see, a dream to make come true. I thanked him, but explained that I needed to do what I'd set out to do. He offered to take me to the airport in the morning, but I refused his offer. No use in messing up his visit home. Besides, I was getting too used to his looking after me and I was determined to be independent. His mother knew someone who was already going in, so I agreed to ride with them.

We got up in the wee hours of the morning. I said goodbye to Nancy, and James walked with me to the driveway. He handed me a paper with his address and phone number. "Call me when you get back to New York, okay?" he asked me. "Okay," I said, then added, "maybe." A quick goodbye, and I was gone.

I don't remember the people who gave me the ride into New York City, but I do remember that we passed a sign that said we were approaching Central Park. That was someplace I'd heard of but had never seen. I had several hours before I had to be at the air terminal, so..."I'll get out here, please!" I told them.

It was 4 AM--still dark--as I walked down the street that led into the park. I wasn't sure what I had expected, but I found it to be enormous and kind of frightening. There were only a few people around, and most looked as if they might be homeless. They stared at me as I passed, giving me an uneasy feeling. I heard a voice and, turning, saw a slender young black man standing nearby. "Excuse me?" I asked him, not having understood his words. He spoke again and I realized he had an unfamiliar accent. "Are you looking for something?" he asked again.

"No," I smiled at him, "I'm just taking a walk." "Can I walk with you?" he asked. He seemed like a nice young man, and I was feeling a little lonely and uneasy out here. I smiled at him. "Sure. Where do you want to go?" He showed me a lane that led down a hill to a meadow. "Are you hungry?" He asked. "I have a sandwich. You can have half."

We sat down and shared his sandwich and a couple cookies Nancy had given me. He told me his story, speaking with bitterness and staring at the ground as he spoke. He had come from Haiti, arriving in Miami a year ago, thinking himself in the "Promised Land." He'd had a dream of building himself a better life. He had tried to get a job, walking the streets every day, but he had finally given up. A friend of his, who lived in New York City, talked him into coming here. It was even worse. Everyone here treated him like he was less than dirt, and he still had no job. He wanted to go back to Haiti and was trying to get enough money together for a ticket. I wished that I could afford to help him out, but I explained that I too was going into the world with little money. All I could give him was a wish for better luck.

It was time for me to go. As I told him goodbye he said to me, "We're alike, you and me, huh?" I looked at him sadly and answered softly "Yeah, we're alike." The irony of his question hit me full force as I walked away. We had both arrived in New York City with nothing more than a dream. I had been treated like an honored guest. He had, in his own words, been treated like dirt.

I walked back out to the highway and held out the cardboard sign I had made. "Kennedy Airport," it said. Before long I was on a jet bound for London. I sent a postcard to James, telling him I had made it safely across the ocean, asking him to say hi to Nancy and his mom. I never called him, and somewhere along the way I lost track of his address. I took him and the kindness with which he and his family had treated me to be proof of my theory; but it was obvious that my theory needed revising. If you were a black male with a foreign accent, the dream didn't apply.

*****

3:30 pm November 20, 2002

My truck has been "plowed in," with snow piled up past the rear bumper, by the town plow, so I walked to work. It was pleasantly slow, with just enough business to make a little money. Talk centered around the weather and the ice on the lake, people guessing how thick it is and how soon the snowmobilers can get out on it. That's the big sport here in winter, and what supports the tourist business. Eve, Joey, and Jim are all big into it. I had gone snowmobiling a couple times last year with my friend Harry, and had even joined the Snowmobile Club. It's too noisy for me though. I'd rather be on skis or snowshoes.

Kathleen, who came in for breakfast this morning, suggested that we go snow-shoeing at the visitors' center near Newcomb. That's more my style.

Peter dropped by the diner for a cup of coffee and a short visit, something he rarely does since he's not crazy about some of the conservative "regulars" who come here. I invited him to come up to the cabin for lunch tomorrow. My boss Jim gave me a ride home after work and asked me how things were going now. "Great!" I told him.

I got a letter from my rattlesnake tamer friend. He's heading out west to drum up business and maybe get some more snakes. A most interesting way to make a living!

11:00 am November 23, 2002

I've been wondering what Miss Kelley stares at so intently, crouched in front of the floor-length window beside my front door. Today I found out. *Microtus pinetorum*, or in everyday talk, a woodland vole, has a home under the snow by the little balsam fir that grows a couple feet from the door. I saw it gathering remnants of the sunflower seeds that spill from the feeder, and then carrying them back into the hole, which serves as a doorway to his tunnel-home.

Voles look like mice. What most people call "field mice" are actually meadow voles. In fact, though, they are more closely related to lemmings and muskrats. They are herbaceous, feeding on seeds and other plant parts. They build long tunnels either below the ground, in warm weather, or below the snow in winter. Kelley caught a vole a few weeks ago in the woodpile on my back porch, but I rescued and released it. Another one died in her jaws, apparently of a heart attack.

I went snowshoeing with Kathleen yesterday at the Newcomb Nature Center, which has trails along Rich Lake and provides free, modern snowshoes, made out of aluminum. They were so nice—light and easy to walk in! I want to get some if I can. My "Algonquins" look great on the wall, but they are always tripping me up or coming loose when I try to walk in them.

We saw the tracks of red squirrels and what the naturalist said was probably a fisher, one of which lives near the lake. Fishers, says my mammal guide, are mustelids, similar to minks and martens but larger. They are not only good swimmers, but also climbers as well, which makes sense since the tracks we saw ended at the trunk of a hemlock. They dine mainly on snowshoe rabbits and porcupines.

I'm off now to the Warrensburg bus station to pick up my sister Betsy, who's coming to spend Thanksgiving with me.

7:30 am November 27, 2002

Betsy is still asleep in the upstairs bunk, so I may as well pull out my journal. One thing about being a 52-year-old woman, which I am not crazy about, is having hot flashes. They drove me crazy when I was so busy working at the diner and didn't have time to take a break. They drive me crazy here in the cabin too. I'll finally get the wood stove cranking so that the temperature is above 65 degrees, and all of a sudden I find myself stripping off sweaters and running outside into the cold. I told Betsy about this, and about how one night I pulled off my pajamas and went outside and sat down on a foot of snow in my Adirondack chair. We got to laughing and came up with the idea of taking a picture. I dug out my bathing suit and posed in the chair, surrounded by snow, pretending I was sunning on a southern beach, and Betsy snapped the camera button. Hope the picture turns out!

6:00 pm November 30, 2002

Peter and I gave Betsy a ride back to the bus station a little while ago. She and I had a nice visit, plowing around in the snow by day, drinking fuzzy navels in front of the fire by night, and talking about old times. The temperature dropped to −10 F, so staying warm was a challenge in itself. We cooked a turkey with dressing and sweet potatoes on Thanksgiving and invited Peter for dinner. He hiked up the hill in his snowshoes with a bottle of wine in his backpack and we shared a great meal.

Yesterday Carl strung a rope up the steepest part of the road leading to the cabin, where ice accumulates and makes it especially treacherous. Betsy and I laughed as we hauled our groceries and ourselves up, hand over hand on the rope, holding on as our feet tried to slip out from under us.

While she was here Betsy and I rehashed some of our childhood memories, often very different. If we both recall the same event in entirely different ways, which memory, we wondered, is true? Which is real, which imagined? And which is more important; what actually happened, or how we perceived it?

Alice McDermott explores that question in her novel "Charming Billy," concluding at the end, "as if...what was actual, as opposed to what was imagined, as opposed to what was believed, made, when you got right down to it, any difference at all." The 17th century English philosopher, Thomas Hobbs, said that memory and imagination are the same. According to poet W.H. Auden, "anything processed through memory is fiction anyway."

How much, I wonder, of the person I am today is created from my memories of who I was in the past? If those memories are imagined, does that mean that I am an imaginary person? If my memories are indeed fiction, am I simply a character in someone's dimestore novel? My mind spins at the possibilities. If I could imagine a different set of memories for myself, could I become a different person?

That is a moot point, I remind myself, for I have never been able to escape the implications of my own, very real memories. They torment me beyond reason.

December 2002

6:30 am December 1, 2002

Snow is falling again. The room is dark, the fire casting strange shadows on the wall. I stopped by Hoss's country store yesterday after work. Hoss's has a little bit of just about everything in it, including "yak traks," which are something like chains for your shoes. My sister Sally offered to give them to me for an early Christmas present after I told her how many times I had slipped on the ice while going down the hill. I bought a pair, and when I neared home I put them on. They worked great, and I clomped up the hill without slipping once.

8:30 pm December 2, 2002

I spent the better part of the day working on my mushrooms, trying to get enough carved for Christmas presents for my friends and family down south. It's really tricky figuring out when they are ready for carving. If you do it too soon, they turn to mush. If you wait too long, they are too hard to penetrate. I had to throw one away because I let it get too hard.

Work was not too bad today. I'm putting aside enough money, I hope, to get me through the winter; not too different, I guess, from what we used to do back home. We harvested apples, white and sweet potatoes, peanuts and butternut squash back in Virginia and stored them down in the basement for the upcoming winter.

*****

Thinking about our farm in Virginia brings to mind another farm I worked on in another time and another land. I see stone fences and cobbled lanes crisscrossing a bucolic English landscape. There is a stately old stone house, and nearby, in a garden, a girl picking flowers. She is twenty-one years old, wearing cut-off, patched blue jeans and a worn tee-shirt. Barefooted and braless, she has tucked a flower into the barrette that holds back her hair. The unbridled pleasure she feels is apparent. She still believes that all things are possible, and that happiness can be a permanent state of life.

I know, of course, that she came to England to escape a great sadness, the illness of her beloved oldest sister, Sally. A blight had settled on her family and sucked the joy out of her the way some claim that a cat will suck the life out of a newborn. How else would she have had the courage to cross the Atlantic, alone on a big airplane, with no destination and only a few dollars to her name? She, who was afraid to go down to the basement after dark by herself? Who cried every night for three months when she went away to college, homesick for Momma and Daddy? Nothing short of a desperation so intense that death itself held no threat could have given her the strength to set out on this trip. Yet here she is, with contentment on her face and in her heart. I long, for a moment, for the resiliency of youth, for that ability to absolutely believe in the future.

A Home in the English Cotswolds

"Potty, dear. I'm just dying for a cuppa. Would you care to join me?"

I paused, dust cloth in hand, and looked up at Mrs. Hunt. "I'd love to." I answered. "Shall I put the kettle on?"

"That would be lovely. I'll see if I can scare up a few biscuits."

I smiled to myself and shook my head. I seldom got through my morning's work without such a request. Not that I minded, of course. A cup of tea with my boss was always pleasant. But what a job! I certainly couldn't complain about being overworked!

A few minutes later we were seated at the kitchen table, chatting about the upcoming flower show at Stow-on-the-Wold. I enjoyed hearing about the local traditions and listening to her accent, including the way she pronounced my name. When I, with my Virginia intonations, first told her that my name was "Patty" (changed on a whim when I arrived in England from the "Pat" I had been going by recently) she asked me "Paddy?" "No, Patty" I explained, "with two tees." "Oh, Potty," she responded, and "Potty" it was, for the rest of my stay in Great Britain.

I had come upon my present employment about three months before, on a late spring day when the English countryside was as sparkling bright as the queen's jewels. I had been hitchhiking my way through the British Isles and had recently left Wales, where I had engaged in a brief but passionate affair of the heart with a fellow American traveler. Now, alone again, I was feeling blue. After being on the road for three weeks, sleeping under bushes, in deserted trucks, and on the floor of a college dorm, the notion of "home" seemed appealing.

When my ride delivered me to the little piece of England that was known as the "Cotswold Hills," I knew that I wanted, for at least a while, to make this my home. "You can let me out here," I exclaimed, on a little stretch of road between Moreton-in-Marsh and Stow-on-the-Wold. "Thanks ever so much."

"Good luck to you, my dear," called the London businessman as he pulled over on the left side of the road to let me out. I stood, with my

little black and red plaid bag thrown over my shoulder, breathing in the aromas of freshly cut hay and cherry blossoms. Gently rolling, emerald hills leaned against a sapphire sky where billowing cumulus clouds floated low on the horizon. Beneath them, looking like four-legged miniatures of the stately clouds, grazed a flock of Cotswold sheep. A pair of spry wooly lambs cavorted nearby, stopping for a moment to look me over before returning to their game. Farther up the hill, beyond a winding stone fence, were splotches of black and white which I knew were cows. The scene before me looked like a John Constable painting.

I sauntered slowly down the road, my heart singing with the thrushes and larks which rustled in the hedgerows. One of my ancestors, a man known as John Rives, had come from this part of England. A loyalist, he had sailed across the sea to Virginia in the seventeenth century to escape Oliver Cromwell's brief reign. I wondered if he had walked along this same road, his thoughts embroiled by the cruelties of England's Civil War, as mine often were over our War in Vietnam.

Before long I came to a small stone house, surrounded by farmlands. I walked up the drive and knocked on the door. "Hello!" I said to the woman that opened it. "I'm looking for a job. Would you happen to have any work?" "No, I'm afraid not," she said, but stood there thoughtfully before closing the door. "You're from America?" (My accent was always a dead give-away.) I think the Hunts, over at Manor Farm, may be looking for someone. Do you know where they live?"

She gave me directions, and in a just a few minutes I was turning down a lane that led me straight into the fifteenth century. A carriage house draped with English ivy stood beside an open gate. Following a crumbling stone wall I came to a large two-story house made of honey-colored Cotswold limestone. Two large chimneys emerged from its stone slab roof. Nearby was a barn, surrounded by a drywall stone fence where a number of cows milled restlessly. I heard a dog bark and then a voice.

Following the sound of the voice, I came upon a stocky, medium-sized man and a black-and-white sheep dog, both working hard to maneuver a small herd of cows into their milking stalls. I watched for a moment and then spoke, repeating my request for a job.

The man looked me over thoughtfully, considering my cut-off jeans, worn tee shirt, and bare feet. "American, you are, huh? Well, Mrs. Hunt might be needing some help in the house. Go knock on the door and ask her." Encouraged, I headed for the house, and before long I was making myself at home in a small but cozy upstairs bedroom. Then I joined Mrs.

Hunt in the dining room for a "cuppa." My new life in the English Cots-wolds had begun.

The Cotswold Hills lie in the heartland of England, a two-hour drive from London if you manage to hitch a ride straight through. The hills are composed primarily of limestone, the remnants of an ancient sea that once covered this area. Rising 1,000 feet above sea level, the limestone bends and folds into hills and plateaus, or "wolds" (the Old English word meaning "God's high open land.")

History lies like a colorful quilt upon every inch of the Cotswolds. Here, thousands of years ago, Neolithic Britons, predating the Celts, conducted activities that are wrapped in mystery today. The road I had arrived on, the Fosse Way, was laid by the Romans nearly two thousand years ago. Anglo-Saxon invaders from Germania stormed through these hills in the fifth century, overthrowing Roman rule and mingling with the Briton peoples. They were followed by the Vikings several hundred years later. The lovely little hamlets and Manor Farm itself were built by wealthy wool farmers and merchants who prospered here from the 12th to the 18th centuries. Oliver Cromwell housed prisoners in some of the churches during his revolt against the British monarchy. William Shakespeare, born only a few miles to the north in Stratford-upon Avon, left his footsteps along these lanes as well. The academic England I had visited in poems, plays, novels, and history classes had suddenly become real.

My daily routine at Manor Farm began at six a.m., when Mrs. Hunt would wake me up with a "Yoohoo...Potty" called up the stairs. I would slip on my cut offs and shirt, stop by the bathroom, and then slide into my chair at the kitchen table. Mrs. Hunt would be laying out a hot breakfast of newly gathered, poached eggs, toast made from a bakery-fresh cottage loaf, orange marmalade, and if Mr. Hunt had had time to pick any, wild mushrooms. And of course, a pot of hot tea.

We would wait for Mr. Hunt, who would come bustling in from the barn, having just completed the morning milking. After breakfast I would wash the dishes and then proceed to some chore, such as dusting, running the "Hoover" (as Mrs. Hunt called the vacuum cleaner), or polishing silver. Sometimes I would gather eggs in the hen house or pick vegetables from the garden. My favorite vegetables were the scarlet runner beans which, Mrs. Hunt explained, were the same vines that Jack climbed up when he visited the giant's house.

Then I would help prepare dinner, which we ate at noon. This meal would consist of vegetables from the garden, potatoes or Yorkshire pudding, and an entree such as fish, beef, mutton, ham, tongue or--I had trouble with this one--oxtail (cooked in a pot with the hair still attached to the end!) There was always a homemade dessert (my favorite was trifle, which we made with angel fingers, jam, and freshly whipped cream) and of course, hot tea. I would wash the dishes and then have the afternoon off to do what I liked.

During these peaceful afternoons I explored the farm, which had been the manor for the village of Broadwell. There was a stone brewery which dated to the fourteenth century and a lovely old church surrounded by ancient evergreen yews--St. Paul's. It still held services on Sunday mornings.

I roamed through the fields, visiting Mr. Hunt's three Percheron draft horses, petting the young Hereford (pronounced hair-e-ford here) cattle which the Hunts raised for beef, and scouting for red foxes. I loved watching the wonderful sheepdog "Bruce" as he patrolled his charges, the "Fresian" (known in this country as Holstein) milk cows. A young man named Jeff helped Mr. Hunt with the farm work, and he would give Bruce directions by whistling and pointing. Bruce was extremely obedient, but he had a mind of his own as well. One morning I woke up to find the yard full of bleating sheep which, it turned out, Bruce had rounded up and stolen from a neighbor who was driving them down the road to market. The neighbor showed up a few minutes later, and Mr. Hunt had to hold an indignant Bruce's collar so that the man could reclaim his flock. Bruce would allow me to pet him, but it was obvious that he considered his work far too important to interrupt it for long.

At about four o'clock Mrs. Hunt would lay tea, and if I was around I would join them. She would often have some delicious treat such as scones with Devonshire cream or pasties from the bakery. I would help clean up and then be off to read or explore until suppertime. Mr. Hunt usually had a glass of hard cider before supper, and Mrs. Hunt a sherry. They always invited me to join them. Sometimes I had what they called "root ale" which I soon learned was root beer back home. They also made a plum wine which I liked. I helped prepare supper, which was a simple meal; often eggs or mushrooms and toast. I would wash the dishes and my work day would be over. I was free on the weekends to do as I liked.

Mr. and Mrs. Hunt were an unlikely couple. She was eighty years old, small and spry and characterized by gentle English social graces. She loved to play Scrabble, arrange flowers, and share a "cuppa" tea with anyone who would join her. Her husband was at least twenty years younger and was loud-voiced and blunt, often using improper grammar and etiquette. He always introduced me as the girl who came from the Wild West, where there were cowboys and Indians, since he associated my home, Virginia, with the television show "The Virginian." I could never convince him otherwise, and I finally gave up trying. He also informed everyone about my other "oddities." "She's always drinking water!" and "She doesn't cut her food proper, with two hands, like we do!" Every night he would put a brick in the wood stove and, when it was hot, wrap it in a towel and lay it under the covers at the foot of my bed, so that it was toasty warm when I climbed in. I liked them both immensely.

While living with the Hunts I made several friends. Timothy and Mary lived just down the road, in the village of Donnington. Timothy was the bell-ringer for the church, an honored position which required great skill. The bells, housed inside the bell tower, each produced a different tone and varied in size from a few pounds to nearly a ton. They were attached by bell-ropes to wheels, which when turned, rang the bells. Ringing them (known as change-ringing or campanology) in the correct patterns for different occasions required physical strength as well as coordination and training. Tim invited me to join him on Sunday mornings. Climbing up the narrow winding stairs inside the fifteenth century bell tower was like reliving some English version of "The Hunchback of Notre Dame." You could smell the centuries in the damp stone. When Tim grasped the ropes and cajoled the great iron bells into melodies which resonated across the countryside, the journey into time was complete. He showed me how to turn the wheels and allowed me to ring a couple of the bells with him.

Tim's sister, Mary, was younger than us--seventeen--but she and I got along well. Much to my surprise, her parents allowed her to go with me to Stratford-on-Avon for a Shakespeare play--hitch-hiking to get there. We also took shorter jaunts around the villages.

One evening, when the moon hung above the horizon like a plump harvest pumpkin, Tim and Mary invited me to go with them for a walk. There was something mysterious about this outing, and we strolled along in silence. Coming across a hill, we stopped and gazed down upon a circle of stone slabs; a smaller, unpublicized version of Stonehenge. The stones cast long, misshapen shadows in the moonlight, and it was easy to imagine prehistoric priests performing pagan rituals. Here were my roots; whatever religion these stones symbolized was the religion of my ancestors, a religion that existed long before Christianity. We spoke in whispers. On Halloween, Tim told me, some of the local youth would come here to sit and watch, and some claimed to see indistinct forms moving among the stones. We saw no movement, but as we sat, silent, on that cold, barren hillside, the earth seemed to reek with the stale, mossy breath of ghosts.

Down the road a little ways, in Broadwell, lived Mr. Pond. He was a knight and a true gentleman. He took a liking to the young barefooted American girl and often stopped by with a small gift--a bar of Cadbury chocolate. He invited me to ride his horses, and afterwards I would join his wife and him for a cup of tea. One day they took me on a tour of the Royal Worcester Porcelain factory and bought me a lovely piece as a keepsake.

Mr. Pond and Mr. Hunt were fox hunters; in fact, Mr. Hunt was the hunt master for this part of England. I was there for one of the fox hunts, and it was an exciting event. It began on Manor Farm, where twelve men in scarlet coats and black hats gathered with their horses and hounds. Mr. Hunt did not have a hunter, so he rode one of Mr. Ponds. I don't know who owned the hounds. Mrs. Hunt and I walked down to see them off. Mr. Hunt blew the horn, and off they all dashed, sailing over stone fences and ditches, wherever the hounds led, raising their heads to bay out a mournful but ecstatic cry when they caught the scent of a red fox. I was rooting, of course, for the lovely little foxes which I saw on my daily walks, and I was glad to hear, when they returned, that although they had had a wonderful day, they had not gotten a fox.

One of the nicest things about my job at the Hunts was that I was free to come and go as I pleased. Every few weeks I would pack my little bag and give Mrs. Hunt a big hug. She would slip an envelope with a few quid (pounds) into my hand, and I would set out for some new adventure.

One bright morning in July I sat down beside the Fosse Way to wait for a southbound ride. I was headed for Cornwall, England's wild southwest coastline, described by D.H. Lawrence as "primeval...with great black jutting cliffs and rocks...a pale sea breaking in...like the beginning of the world, wonderful: and so free and strong."

More specifically, I was bound for Tintagel, known as the legendary site of Camelot. As a child I had reveled in the stories of Merlin the magician, Arthur, the great king, his wife Guinevere, and the ill-fated Lancelot. As an adolescent I had watched the movie "Camelot" and bought the sound track, memorizing the songs. On soft moonlit nights while watching my horses munch their hay, I would close my eyes and sing about the land where "the rain must never fall till after sundown; by nine p.m. the moonlight must appear," and I took to heart the admonition "Don't let it be forgot...that once there was a spot...for one brief shining moment that was known as Camelot."

Now I was bound for that "spot," a place where history and legend became one. The next morning I stood atop a slate cliff and perused the gray seascape, listening to the waves crash against the rocks below. I climbed down steep cliffside steps to the ruins of an ancient castle. Spending one of my precious quid on a book about the "real" King Arthur, I spent the afternoon reading and imagining. That evening I knocked on the door of some friends Mrs. Hunt had directed me to, and stayed the night there.

The next morning I decided to hitch a ride to Exeter where, a fellow traveler had told me, volunteers were needed for an archaeological "dig." By now I was nearly out of money, and the added attraction of the job was that it included two free meals per day. I found my way to the site and was told that one of the volunteers was leaving in the morning and I could take his place. I bought a loaf of brown bread with raisins and poked around the town of Exeter, exploring the ruins of the Roman wall which surround it and visiting its famous Gothic cathedral. Then I located a deserted truck and, finding the door unlocked, spent a chilly night therein.

I reported to work in the morning and I was shown to my "lodgings" (a tent which I was to share with another woman) and given a sleeping bag. Then one of the archaeologists took me around and gave me a short course in excavation. Once more I found myself journeying back in time. I was standing in a medieval castle, staring at a marvelous 12th century wall hanging. But this was not what we were looking for. Beneath it, someone had discovered an even more ancient marvel; a Roman mosaic. The castle had been erected on the ruins of a 1st century Roman palace, built not long after Roman soldiers, led by Julius Caesar, had invaded Exeter.

Soon I was sitting on a set of stone steps with a tiny paintbrush in my hand. I gently brushed away the dirt, moving through the layers of time and setting each object I found in a box. Two tiny bones and several pieces of turquoise tile were among the prizes I found. I was more than ready for lunch, a sandwich which I ate with other workers at a picnic table, when the time came.

I spent several days thus occupied, but then the damp, chilly weather for which England is famous descended upon us. When, for the second night in a row, cold rain poured down on my tent, leaked through the cracks, and soaked my sleeping bag, I decided to leave.

I wanted next to explore Devon. I had no money as I set out, so I spent the first two days dreaming hopelessly of the meat pies and Cornish pasties which stared out at me from bakery windows. By the third day, however, my hunger had abated, and I decided to see how long I could go without eating. Meanwhile, I wandered across the lonely granite moors of gorse and purple heather, keeping my eyes out for the rugged little Dartmoor ponies, sheep, and cows, which grazed the sparse grasses. I climbed up to the tors, hard granite outcrops left behind by erosion. Near the ocean's edge I collected fossil shells. On the seventh morning, as I sat on the passenger side of a big lorry (as the English call their tractor-trailers,) I felt myself slipping away into a fuzzy world. The driver noticed and asked in alarm if I was okay. Upon learning that I had not eaten in days, he insisted on stopping at the next restaurant, where he bought us both a big breakfast. Revived, I thanked him and decided that, my experiment in fasting over, it was time to go home to the Cotswolds.

Whenever possible, Mrs. Hunt invited me to join her on her social and civic outings. Usually I dressed in my normal fashion of jeans and bare feet, but occasionally, when required by the rules of propriety, she loaned me a pair of her shoes and a dress. One day Mr. Hunt drove us to Bourton-on-the-Water, built on the banks of the Windrush River, to meet a friend for Devonshire clotted cream and scones. On another occasion he took us to Moreton-in-Marsh to explore the old antique shops. Another time we went to dinner at the home of an earl. Unlike Mr. Pond, the earl and his wife put on great airs and hosted a quite pretentious gathering. Mr. Hunt never went to such affairs, making fun of them instead.

The flower show at Stow-on-the-Wold was a big event in Mrs. Hunt's life. She was one of the organizers and judges. She did not enter it herself, but she provided me with flowers, a pretty container, and advice in making an arrangement. Having participated in flower shows as a child at

Short Pump School, I had had some practice. Now it was great fun arranging the flowers and seeing my work of art displayed on one of the tables in Stow-on-the-Wold. I was not overly disappointed when I did not win.

The Harvest Festival, held in late summer, was another event of great local repute. A Celtic holiday, it celebrated the successful reaping of the corn, which I soon learned had nothing to do with the "maize" we grew in America. English "corn" is wheat, barley, oats and rye. Tim showed me how to weave the golden strands of wheat into "corn dollies," which we hung around the church and in the kitchens of our houses.

One idyllic afternoon, after dinner was over and the dishes washed, I followed my usual route through the fields to visit the Hunts' horses. They were grazing near the lane which bordered Manor Farm. As I stood combing my fingers through the gelding's mane, I heard a voice and, looking up, saw a boy standing at the fence.

"Hello!" he called to me. "Can I pet your horse?" I saw no reason against it, so I invited him in. He was about sixteen, I guessed, a lonely seeming lad. We talked for a few minutes. Then without warning he moved close and locked his arms around me. I was too shocked to move for a moment, but when I felt him pushing me roughly to the ground, his hand across my mouth, I began to struggle. He was not much bigger than I, but he was strong. Twisting my head, I broke away for a moment and screamed, hoping Mr. Hunt, working in the next field, would hear me. He pulled me toward him once more, but I screamed again and this time he must have become frightened for, glancing around him, he shoved me away and ran for the fence, then leapt over it and disappeared.

I turned, gasping with exhaustion and fear, and fled back to the house. Mr. Hunt had not, apparently, heard me scream, and I did not mention the incident. I kept an eye out for the boy for the rest of my stay in the Cotswolds, but I never saw him again.

While staying at the Hunts I pursued a new hobby I had discovered: brass-rubbing. Many medieval British dignitaries had been memorialized in brass effigies which were displayed in the old churches. With my pack over my shoulder and rice paper in hand, I visited these churches and created copies of the often life-sized figures. I got down on my hands and knees, placed the rice paper over the brasses, and then rubbed with a wax stick to capture the impression. The results were quite attractive and made nice wall hangings. I gave a matched set of a knight and his lady from the church in Cirencester to the Hunts, and they hung them in the hall. Others I packed away carefully to take with me when I returned to the United States.

Sometimes in the evenings the Hunts would talk about old times. Their favorite stories were about the War: the German invasion in the 1940s and the Battle of Britain. I tried to imagine the scenes they described: the roar of low flying planes, the scream of falling bombs, a much younger Mrs. Hunt seeking shelter from the rain of fire, the terror which hung like a cloud upon this bucolic countryside. The Hunts had grown crops and raised chickens and beef to feed the British fighters as they sought to defend their homeland. They showed me places where the bombs had destroyed the fruits of their labor.

None of us living in America know what it was like to have a war in our backyards. Yet even as I sat here, safe and secure, our country was waging a war in someone else's back yard. Far off, on the other side of the world, the bombs were still falling.

It was mid-August, and my twenty-first birthday was approaching. My parents sent me a check for $100 in a card, and Mrs. Hunt insisted on giving me a traditional English party. She made a plum pudding (which seemed to me to be more of a cake than a pudding) and invited Tim and Mary, their parents, the Ponds, and a few of the neighbors whom I had met. It was a nice affair.

I spent the next three months coming and going to and from the Hunts' farm. I visited Scotland and Ireland and caught a ride on a lorry that was bound across the Straits of Dover to Paris. Later I spent a quiet week with the Hunts and began thinking about returning to college. Mrs. Hunt asked me if I would like to stay with them and attend classes at nearby Oxford University, but by now I was growing quite homesick for my family in Virginia. I turned down her generous offer.

Saying goodbye to England and to Mr. and Mrs. Hunt was difficult. Our relationship as employers/employee had been tenuous at best. Over the months it had disintegrated and we had become family. I promised that I would try and return soon, but in my heart I doubted that I would see them again. They insisted on driving me to Heathrow Airport, near London. They waved goodbye as I boarded the airplane, and I watched through tears as they walked away.

I have no memory of the flight home or the rides I hitched south from Kennedy Airport in New York to Richmond. My only recollection is the story my Mother would later tell. She was teaching school one day, as usual, at Short Pump, when one of the teachers came hurrying into her room. "I'm not sure, Mrs. Garber, but I think I just saw your daughter Patsy walk by!" Momma rushed out and called to the lanky, barefooted young woman who was striding down the road with the same red and black pack slung over her shoulder.

A month later I enrolled for classes at Virginia Commonwealth University.

*****

5:00 pm December 3, 2002

I saw something today that I had never seen before, nor even heard of. You never know what to expect when you get up in the morning! I had just arrived at the diner, plowing down the snow-packed hill and across the sidewalk in my "yak-traks." I went to take my first order, from a young man sitting at a table along the wall. He was staring out the window, ignoring the menu. "Did you see the sun dog?" he asked me, pointing toward Mt. Sabattis, which stood stark and clear in the cold morning light. Rising above it, the sun shed its golden light upon the snow. On both sides, in two small arcs, glowed a rainbow of soft colors. A "snow bow" someone else in the restaurant called it. I stared, intrigued, until work called me back.

I looked it up at the library when I got off work, discovering its proper name, a "parahelia." In scientific terms, it is "a colored luminous spot caused by the refraction of light by six-sided crystals in the atmosphere, formed in the solar halo at points 22 degrees on either side of the sun and the same elevation as the sun." According to another definition, it is "a visual effect due to ice crystals in the upper atmosphere which align themselves creating unusual light refractions." Again, "colored disks resembling the sun caused by atmospheric distortions." I'm not quite sure what all that means, but I'm glad I got to see one!

9:00 am December 7, 2002

It's been snowing for days, and the outdoor thermometer reads minus twelve degrees. I've been watching the bird feeder all morning. It's much better entertainment than the television, which doesn't get the best reception, anyway. Most of my customers are chickadees. According to my bird book their favorite foods are insect eggs and larvae, but you'd never know it to see them go after the sunflower seeds. When I refill it they wait on the branch just inches from my hand, seemingly not in the least bit afraid.

The naturalist Aldo Leopold banded 97 chickadees in his quest to learn more about them. According to his calculations, 67 disappeared after their first winter, 19 lived two years, and only one survived to the age of five. He believed that most succumbed to dampness and wind in frigid temperatures, with a few becoming dinner for sparrow hawks, screech owls, and saw-whet owls. My guidebook says they lay six to eight eggs in spring, which helps offset their high mortality. They are certainly plentiful around this cabin.

Peter and I are planning to go skiing later on today.

3:00 pm December 9, 2002

It is snowing again, a fine, translucent, ongoing mist of confectioner's sugar sifting down from the slate-colored sky above. It is the twelfth day in a row that snow has fallen, save two. Sometimes the flakes flutter down like moths escaping from a flame. Sometimes they dance down from the sky in a herd, each a miniature winged Pegasus. Each flurry lays down a new of coat of frosting on the landscape; the snow on my deck is now two feet deep. Still the snow falls, "soft as froth and easy as ashes," to quote W.R. Rodgers; perfect crystals enveloping my cabin like an ermine coat.

It is said that no two snowflakes are alike, and Wilson A. Bentley, known as the "Snowflake Man" of Vermont, took photo-micrographs of hundreds of flakes in the late nineteenth century to prove it.

Betsy and I went to an exhibit at Buffalo's Museum of Science last month and saw them. Each individual flake is a hexagonal prism, having six-sides and six angles. Some are doubles.

There are seven types of snow crystals, we learned. Their size, shape, and weight are determined by such factors as the temperatures in the clouds where they form; the height of the clouds; and the water vapor content. There are snow banners, snow blinks, snow devils, and snow corn--terms I never knew existed before, but which I'm learning to know on a personal level now. The Inuits of Alaska, who know snow very well, have dozens of words to distinguish its various personalities.

Henry David Thoreau said of these delicate snow crystals: "I should hardly admire them more if real stars fell and lodged on my coat." Sometimes, when I walk outside at night, I imagine that my hilltop is the universe, and I am a black hole surrounded by falling stars...

Looking at my thermometer, I see that the temperature is dropping. Twenty-one degrees this morning; now at three pm, it is 11 degrees. The weather station says it will drop to minus 25 tonight. Carl, my landlord, calls up to remind me to leave the water dripping. Tonight, he says, will be the test. Will the cabin freeze up? Will I be able to live here all winter or not? The locals say this is February weather. It's not even winter yet! The snowmobilers are happy. They can't wait until the lake freezes solid. The same with the restaurants and hotels, since snowmobilers are their main winter customers and source of income.

11:30 am December 15, 2002

I woke up this morning in the dark, wondering why the cabin was so cold. A quick glance at the thermometer told me it was 19 degrees outside, which did not explain why the indoor temperature had dropped to 48. I took another look and realized I had misread it. My sleep-clouded eyes had missed the minus sign. It was minus 19 degrees. I added more logs to the fire. It is burning greedily now, consuming the wood and spewing warm air across the room.

*****

Now I'm looking back in time, thinking once more about that trip I made to the British Isles. I spent a few weeks of it in Ireland. So much happened there, however, that as I look back, it feels more like months or even years. Time is relative, I think, and sometimes deceptive.

I've always tried to do things my way, make my own rules. It doesn't always work, of course, but if you don't try, it won't happen. The young woman I see now, "Potty," has thoroughly overcome her fears and is thriving in the role of vagabond. Now she is bound for the bonnie land of *Eire*. I am amazed at her courage and audacity.

In the Shoes of an Irish Scuttlemaid

Bits of hay scratched my bare legs as I lay back in the old wooden wagon, trying to get comfortable. The plodding hoofs of the dun gelding stirred up a mist of dust, mingling with the smell of the hay in a not unpleasant aroma which reminded me of the barn at my parents' home in Virginia. My eyes grew heavy as I relaxed into the softness. It had been a long day.

I had set out from Cork early that morning after a visit to Blarney Castle, where I'd climbed the tower and kissed the famous stone, a useless effort on my part. "Blarney" (the gift of gab) never has been among my gifts. Having no special destination in mind, I chose a lane that headed west, crossing an area of Southern Ireland that had no towns marked on the map. The countryside was lovely; a mix of pastoral farms and deserted moors, and I was enraptured as I strolled along. Eventually, however, I realized that the dearth of vehicles, from which I planned to hitch a ride, could be a problem. One automobile passed, but it was headed in the wrong direction. I was beginning to think I might have to spend the night under some shrub, shivering in the damp chill, when I heard behind me the thump of horses' hooves and the creaking of wagon axles. The driver was stolid, even taciturn, as he gestured for me to climb in the back. He was devoid, it seemed, of any curiosity which could have been satisfied had he invited me to share the front seat. Sitting in the back, I had time to reflect on the past week, my first in this island country known in its own Gaelic language as Eire, more familiar today as Ireland.

I had taken the boat from Scotland to Larne, located near Belfast in Northern Ireland. It was 1971, a time when the anger and violence in that country was at a peak. The six Protestant counties in the north, known as Ulster, had split from the rest of Ireland in 1921, the Partition Act making them part of Great Britain. The other 26 counties became the Irish Free State. The Catholic groups Sin Fein and the Irish Republican Army, however, opposed the partition, and were engaged in an ongoing war of terror to reunite Ireland.

I'd spent the night at the home of a Protestant family, friends of the Hunts in England. They were Anglo-Irish gentry, descendants of Englishmen to whom the Crown had given land confiscated from the original Gaelic inhabitants. Known as the Orange-Irish, they were hated and resented by most of Ireland's Catholic poor. I found them to be quite snobbish, and I was repelled by the pathetic preserved fox heads and tails which adorned the walls of the house, constant reminders of their obsession with fox hunting. Neither they nor I was comfortable with my visit, so I left the next morning, hitchhiking south.

One of the first rides I got was in a huge covered wagon pulled by draft horses and driven by tinkers, often mistakenly referred to as Gypsies. These wandering families were originally tinsmiths, it is believed, but evolved into nomadic horse traders, barterers, and scavengers. I took turns sitting on the big bed, which filled half the wagon, with three unruly children, or perching on the seat next to the driver, alternately husband or wife. They described their unusual way of life. The different families belonged to tribes, each of which had a leader. They followed the fairs that took place all over Ireland, and they invited me to join them. I was thrilled at first; what an exciting way to live! Soon I found, however, that the quarters were cramped, the plodding pace excruciatingly slow, and the conversation, after the initial exchanges, uninspiring. I changed my mind and got off the wagon near a town south of Dublin. I soon found myself regretting my next move.

On the boat to Ireland I had met a fellow American hitchhiker, a young man who described to me how, when he was broke, he often asked for a bed at some local gaol. "It's easy!" he had said. It was late, nearly 11:00 pm, when I arrived in the town of Limerick, and my funds were low, so I decided to try my luck. The paddy on duty at the police station seemed shocked at my request, so I quickly said "Never mind, I'll find somewhere else." But no, he stopped me. "Let me see your passport!" "Oh, I didn't bring it with me," I told him. "I was afraid I'd lose it, so I left it in England!" "How much money do you have?" I pulled out my paltry handful of cash. "A few quid, at least!" I announced, trying to sound cheerful.

"Vagrancy!" was the charge. "You're not going anywhere!" He was actually quite a nice bloke, but he decided that I was a runaway American teenager, and no amount of persuasion could convince him otherwise. "I'm 21 years old." I told him. "My parents know where I am. They even approve!" He didn't believe me, and now he insisted that I would spend the night in gaol whether I liked it or not. But when he tried to find a cell for me, they were all full of men. He didn't know what to do.

A few phone calls later, and he had found a solution. Soon we were walking up the steps to a huge, forbidding abbey, with turrets and steeples and ominous looking rooms. I was put into the care of a Catholic nun, with the admonition, "Keep a close eye on her. I'll be back to get her in the morning." She took my bag and, using a flashlight, escorted me through a large, dark room lined with cots containing blanket-enshrouded bodies till we reached an empty one. By this time I was exhausted, so I crumpled into it gratefully.

I was almost instantly asleep, when I realized there was a light shining down on my face. I opened my eyes into the beam of a flashlight and listened with something akin to shock as a deep, scratchy voice asked me, "Are you Catholic?" "No!" I responded, indignant at being waked up. "What religion are you?" "None!" "None?" I amended my answer. "Indian! "I believe in the American Indian religion!" Peering over a notebook with her light, she wrote down my answer, then vanished into the darkness.

The room came to life in the eerie shadows of pre-dawn. Shapes emerged from the cots. Bent silhouettes tottered and ambled to a far door and disappeared through it. I threw off my blanket and followed them, then stared in amazement. Before me was a room full of old, very old, men and women. Clothed in the rags and brown, wrinkled skins of the destitute, they were lining up in front of a black cauldron. Each had a bowl, which he or she held out to a nun, dressed in black, sitting beside the cauldron. Into each bowl she ladled a spoonful of porridge. Few words were spoken as they took their bowls to various tables and sat down. I watched for a few moments in fascination.

But I was hungry, so I decided to join them. I took a bowl, lined up and was given my portion of porridge. I went to sit down at one of the tables, but was admonished by an angry voice; "That's my seat!" I moved to another table but was again repelled: "That's Mrs. O'Don-nally's place."

Well, I wasn't THAT hungry! I felt quite insulted and unwanted, so I decided it was time to make my exit. I slipped back into the room where I had slept and quickly searched the desk at one end. I found my bag in a drawer, then tiptoed down a long corridor till I came to a heavy door. It was locked. I continued on, wandering through dark hallways until I located a door which opened when I pushed it. I found myself outdoors just as the sun crept over the horizon. Keeping an eye out for my paddy friend, I set a good pace, hiked to the edge of town, and put out my thumb.

Now it was the next day, and I was pleased to be sitting in the back of this wagon. After an hour or so we trotted into the hamlet of Glengariff, a poor but charming village with stone fences and modest houses. The driver pointed out a rambling building, where he said I could find food and lodging.

Deciding to part with some of my small fund of cash, I approached the inn. I asked hopefully if there was some work I could do; a job in exchange for room and board, but was told no. I was shown to a low-ceilinged upstairs room where I deposited my bag. Then I followed the stairs back down to a dining room with four tables. Three were occupied, so I sat down at the remaining one and ordered a bowl of hot potato and beef soup. Afterward I stopped by the pub, located in the next room. It was dark and gloomy, and the five men who occupied the stools sat with somber faces, staring into their glasses trying, it seemed, to discern some hidden message in the contents of their Guinness. The bartender handed me a glass of cider, but if he was surprised at my American accent or my presence in the pub, he kept it to himself. This was not the rollicking, jolly Irish pub I had expected. Feeling out of place, I quickly drank my cider and went upstairs.

It seemed like I had slept for only a short while when I heard a tap at my door, then a creak as it opened. The innkeeper's wife was leaning over me, peering down into my face. "Are you awake?" she asked. "I have a job for you if you want it."

The scuttlemaid, it seemed, visiting her family a few hamlets away, had sent a message that she was sick and would not be in to work that week. I would take her place and wear, in a manner of speaking, her shoes for a while. I moved into her room, took over her chores, even put on some of her clothes and her long, slightly dingy white apron. Just like that, I had a new identity.

There was no time to waste. Dawn was breaking, and I had to set the tables for breakfast. I quickly ate a bowl of porridge and tried to follow the instructions that were hurled at me. "Slice potatoes, serve the bacon and eggs, wash the dishes!" "Faster, not like that!" I seemed to do everything wrong...If I had thought this would be easy or fun, I was in for a surprise. After breakfast was behind us I was ordered to "hoover" the carpets and then to make the beds in the guestrooms. "Hurry up! You're too slow!"

Working with me was an adolescent boy as sweet and charming as my employers were petulant and demanding. Peter knew his job and worked quickly and efficiently, giving me pointers along the way. No longer a paying guest, I found that my lunch would be pig's feet and cold cabbage. Peter and I ate together. He showed me how to drain some of the grease off of the feet, and then pick them clean with my teeth.

After serving and cleaning up after lunch each day, I had a couple hours off. During this time my employers took a completely different attitude, treating me as a respected guest. They were fascinated by my life in America and asked me all kinds of questions. As soon as it became time to work again, however, they became stern and unreasonable taskmasters. It was so for the whole week that I was there.

Peter was also fascinated with the young lady from America, and tried to spend all his spare time with me. He had, I found, far less time than I did. During my week at the inn I learned the story of Peter.

Peter was one of eleven children born to very poor parents who lived in a nearby hamlet. They had made an arrangement with the inn owners which I doubt was strictly within the workings of Irish law, but which was probably common in this part of Ireland. To my naive and indignant eyes he was a slave, sold to the inn for a sum of money that he never saw. Twelve years old, he had been pulled out of school the year before to go to work. Clearly intelligent, he had a book in his hand whenever possible. His greatest wish was to finish school and go to university. But, he explained, in defense of his parents, his wages were needed to help feed his younger brothers and sisters.

Peter was up and already at work when I got up each morning, and his last job, scrubbing the floor of the pub, was not done till after 1 am. He kept his cheerful manner and sweet expression through threats and cursings, keeping out of the way of his often angry employers.

When we both had time off, we went for walks through the village and countryside. On Sunday the road was closed to traffic and the farmers ran their cows and sheep through the streets to market. We chattered and laughed as we trotted through town, trying to avoid the cow pies. He showed me all the special secret places he knew. One afternoon we went with the owners' daughters to cut peat; on another we wandered through the moors picking flowers. I told him about America, and he told me about his dreams.

When supper dishes were done I would go to the Pub, where the owner of the inn was tending bar. I would wash the used glasses and then sit down with a pint of cider, my day's work done. On the third night I met a young man named John, a tall slender fellow with a slash of black hair hanging in his eyes. He invited me to go to a party with him, and soon I found myself in the midst of a younger and far livelier crowd. As they consumed glass after glass of stout they grew more and more garrulous. Soon we were all standing, arms around each other's waists, singing Irish ballads and anthems. The talk switched to the coming Friday night, and before long I realized that I was in the midst of members and sympathizers of the Irish Republican Army. This was the part of Ireland where the rebellion had been born, and sentiment was still strong. John explained that a shipment of guns was coming in, and he and several others would go to the coast and pick them up in one of their wagons. Their Irish patriotism was contagious, and I found myself in full sympathy with their plans, which in England would be considered treason.

Back at the inn the next day, I learned that Peter felt as passionate in his Irish loyalty as the young men. It was his dream to get an education and fight in the courts for Irish freedom. With naive idealism, I came up with a plan to help him. I would take him back to Virginia, where my parents could adopt him. He could go to school there and have all the advantages I had known. Then, if he chose, he could return to his homeland. I had no doubt that my parents would agree, so the difficult part would be at this end. He nodded shyly when I asked him, so I made arrangements to visit the priest in his village.

Head held high with what I considered a noble goal, I approached the little Catholic diocese. I explained my plan to the priest, thinking he would find it a marvelous opportunity for Peter. Instead, he interrupted me with a question. "Are your parents Catholic?" No? Then it was out of the question. I needed to leave things as they were. Peter was living a good Catholic life and I shouldn't interfere. No, he would not direct me to Peter's parents' home. There was no sense in disturbing them with this outlandish idea. I was heartbroken when I left, and I dreaded telling Peter. He nodded slowly. His good-natured acceptance of his fate broke my heart.

At the end of the week the regular maid returned and I received a small payment for my labor. I exchanged hugs and best wishes with my employers, promising to stay in touch. Peter, who was scrubbing floors, was not allowed to stop for a real goodbye. I ran my hand lightly over his dark head and whispered a wish for his welfare. I don't recall his words of farewell, but I remember the look in his eyes and the brave, hopeless smile he gave me as I left.

After returning to England, I wrote to the Irish family a few times and got a letter or two back. I was surprised to learn, when I got back to Virginia, that they had written my parents, concerned when they did not hear from me as soon as expected. They never mentioned Peter, and I never found out what became of him.

*****

11:00 am December 13, 2002

Huck was restless this morning, continually glancing toward the window. When I looked out, I saw two white-tailed deer cleaning up the sunflower seeds spilled from the feeder. They were beautiful. I foolishly thought I might get a picture, but when I opened the door they vanished, just a flash of tail waving like a flag of truce as they leapt across a snow-covered log.

A lot of people feed them up here, buying big bags of cracked corn and setting it out for them. I'm tempted, but I don't want them to come to count on me, since I'll be gone part of next month. Besides, there is a law against it. Wildlife officers are afraid it will cause deer to congregate in small areas, thus aiding the spread of chronic wasting disease, a fatal neurological brain disease which deer and elk have contracted out west. I think they're over-reacting, since it hasn't been found in the eastern part of the country. I'm not going to buy any corn, but I won't be offended if they want to clean up the spilled sunflower seed.

6:00 am December 16, 2002

I am developing a very personal relationship with my wood stove. It is the first thing I think of when I wake up, and the last that I attend to at night. Fire and snow have become the elements of my existence, every thought and action taking them into consideration.

Morning is now painting the scene beyond my window visible, and I can see the sky, grim as an old gray dog. Flakes of snow drift down like bits of dandruff kicked out by a scratching hind leg, landing softly on the shoulders of yesterday's snowdrifts and vanishing into them.

9:30 am December 17, 2002

I got stir-crazy yesterday afternoon, so I decided to snowshoe over the hill and through town to the Adirondack Hotel. I ordered a draft beer and a sausage and mushroom pizza to go, and while I waited for the pizza I began talking to a man sitting next to me. I had seen him around but had never actually met him. He is a trapper, he told me, at least in the winter. He uses the leg-iron traps I hate, but I know that trapping is a traditional way of making a living in these mountains.

Then he told me what he does when the snow starts to melt, and I was really intrigued. He clears land for people, using not a backhoe or tractor, but draft horses. He really loves his horses, and we talked a bit about them; about how a person can have a spiritual relationship with them that one doesn't have with other animals, or with people either. I was sorry to learn, somewhere in the discussion, that he was married, for I found him not just intriguing but quite attractive.

When my pizza arrived I broke it down so it would fit into my backpack and headed home, using a flashlight for the last part of the trek up the hill. Huck and I ate half, sharing a few pieces of sausage with Kelley.

10:30 am December 24, 2002

It's Christmas Eve. I sat in front of the open wood stove this morning, playing remembered carols on my accordion and searching the flames for hidden spirits. A dragon, a piece of twisted wood from whose mouth flames shot out, licked hungrily about for something to consume. I watched it, mesmerized, as my fingers sought out the keys for "It Came Upon the Midnight Clear" and my arms moved the bellows in rhythm. Tears slid, unbidden, down my cheeks. I didn't bother to wonder why.

Later on I'll take my cross country skis and meet Peter for a ski trip in Whitney Park, near Little Tupper Lake. No pre-Christmas hustle and bustle this year. Now, staring into the flames, I think about the heat coming from the logs I split last month, cut down in their prime the year before. Now sharing that energy with Huck, Miss Kelley, and me.

7:30 pm December 25, 2002

The Christmas holidays are almost over. This is the first I've spent away from family or close friends. It has been strange, in a way, but not so bad. I've been to a few parties: a cookie exchange at Wendy's house in Indian Lake with my museum friends; a dinner party at the Blarney Stone for the Diner employees. I had breakfast with Cathie and Avis today, and later went with Cathie to a Christmas party at her cousin Cindy's house. I didn't stay long, however. I wanted to be home with Huck and Miss Kelley. The hostess wrapped me up a turkey dinner and I brought it back and shared it with them.

When I got home I talked to Betsy, Nancy, and Sally on the phone, and had a brief conversation with Mom. She had trouble hearing me but I think she knew who I was.

5:30 pm December 30, 2002

A whole flock of birds descended on the snow beneath my feeder today. They looked something like the house finches I know from down south, but were smaller and had distinctive red caps. I was befuddled and called Peter, who's a real birder, to ask him if he knew what they were. "Redpolls!" he told me immediately. I looked them up in my bird guide. They are a far northern species, related to the finches. "Irruptive" is the word used to describe their occasional forays into the United States.

When they do show up here, it is usually in great numbers, like the flock here. They're still rummaging around busily, both on the ground and at the feeder.

*****

Traveling back to my past again, I recall a brief time--two weeks--that I spent in Paris. After leaving Ireland I returned to the Hunts' farm, where I spent a few pleasant weeks working and visiting with my new friends. Before long, however, I decided it was time to make my way to Europe. I planned to start in France and then continue on to other countries, but that was not to be. Foolish is a word I would use to describe the young woman I see before me now, but also resilient and maybe even brave.

An Excursion in Paris

"Let me in! Please!" It was sheer desperation that brought me to those glass doors. I banged my fists against the wide panes, raising my voice in a plea for attention. If I had had a rock I would have smashed the glass. Tall buildings surrounded me, a jungle of macadam and concrete. I was not afraid of woods, of open fields or deserts; but being lost in the middle of a huge city which seemed to have no end, where no one understood a word I said, inspired a fear beyond reason. I raised my voice higher, shrieking through my tears: "PLEASE! Somebody let me in!!" There was no one in sight. The building was obviously closed. But walking around the side, I had seen a group of men sitting around a table, apparently at a meeting. I wasn't about to give up until one of them came to the door.

Finally I saw a human figure approach. The man, obviously irritated, stood on the other side of the door and gesticulated, glaring, for me to leave. "Go away! We're busy!" His words were music to my ears, the first English I'd heard all day. He could have been crooning a love song, so delighted I was to hear him. I raised my voice louder and pounded harder. He finally shook his head and turned the latch, opening the door wide enough to stick his head out. "Please," I begged," forgetting all sense of dignity, "I want to go home! Please send me home!"

He let me in, finally, and I told him, through sobs, my story. I had left my home in the English Cotswolds the morning before, hitching a ride through London, along England's southeastern coastline, past the chalky cliffs of Dover. I had gotten a ride with an English lorry driver, sitting in

118

the cab of his truck as we crossed the English Channel to Calais. I was going to Paris, I told him. "Don't you want to ride with me to Switzerland?" he asked me. "It is much nicer than Paris." Nope. I planned to go there later. Paris was my first destination.

I didn't worry when he warned me about how big Paris was, how hard to get around, how frightening it could be. I'd been making my way around the British Isles for five months, after all, and had done just fine. Where did I want to get out? "Oh just drop me off anywhere," I told him, blithely. "I'll find my way."

He looked doubtful as he pulled off on the side of the four-lane highway that circled the city. I brushed away my doubts as I realized how far away the city looked--at least a half mile. "No problem!" I said. "I need some exercise." I watched him drive away, then squared my shoulders and, with my pack on my shoulder, headed for the lights of "Gay Paree."

There was nothing gay, however, about the outskirts of the Paris where I found myself. I climbed down ditches filled with broken glass, stumbled across a railroad track, and finally ended up in a desolate landscape of factories and huge storage sheds. Everything looked gray, an impression that was not helped by the drizzle of rain that fell from the ashen sky.

I was not discouraged. If I just kept walking, I was bound to reach a better part of town soon. I trudged along until I finally saw signs of life; dingy apartments where grim-faced people went about their dreary lives. This must be part of Paris' ghetto. I approached a middle-aged woman. "Parlez-vous Anglais?" From the way she looked at me you'd think she didn't even parle Francais! She shook her head impatiently and walked away. I tried again several times, trying to ask directions in my two-year-high-school French accent. They looked at me as if I was speaking Swahili.

Finally I saw a bus. It pulled over for a couple passengers and I ran up to it. I repeated my questions to the bus driver and he answered me impatiently in a language that did not remotely sound like the French I remembered from 11th grade. He was obviously in a hurry and wanted me to either get off or pay up. I had no idea how much it was, and besides, I didn't have any French money. I held up a handful of English coins and he shook his head, gesturing for me to leave. I wasn't about to get off that bus, however, so he took a coin, muttering what sounded like a rude expletive, and motioned me to a seat.

Now I had it made, I was sure. I would just ride the bus till I reached someplace where someone spoke English. I rode it all the way to its final destination, without reaching anything that looked promising. I tried asking the people on the bus, but no one even tried to figure out what I was saying. "Hostel!" I tried, thinking that because youth hostels were found all over the world they would all have the same name. "Ou est un hostel?" No luck. I remembered, too late, the reputation the French have for disliking Americans. I had a feeling that I was not doing anything to improve their opinions.

The last person got off the bus and the driver indicated that I should do the same. I did. "Oh well, I told myself," trying not to be too discouraged. "I'll just take the next bus and try again. Eventually one of these buses is bound to go somewhere I want to be." I don't know how many buses I rode that day, or how many ways I tried to ask directions. Paris must be a huge city indeed, for after all those miles I still hadn't seen anything that looked like the Eiffel Tower, the Palace of Versailles, or even a motel.

Finally I got an idea. If I could just find a school, they might have an English teacher! "Ecole! L'ecole?" I asked now, and finally someone directed me to a big stone building with wide steps. I entered the dark hallway timidly. School was over for the day, but I found someone, perhaps a janitor. He took me to someone else, not an English teacher, but someone with whom I could at least marginally communicate.

By now I had thought of another word which I could try. "Embassy! Embassee American!" He looked it up in a book and pointed me back toward the bus stop, this time telling me what bus to look for. It took several more transfers, but finally I was there. When I ran up the stairs of the imposing building and found the doors locked, my courage and pride dissipated in a flood of hysterical tears. I had had enough of Paris. I didn't care about seeing anything else! I wanted my Momma!

The man at the embassy allowed me to talk, and when I was calmer he gave me a handkerchief and suggested that if I got to the tourist section of Paris I would be all right. I blew my nose and explained that I had been planning to stay at a youth hostel. One was not far away, he told me. One more bus ride and I was there, surrounded by other people my age, of all nationalities, many of whom spoke delightfully accented English. My fear dissolved as I was assigned a bed at the hostel and told to make myself at home. The shyness I usually felt among strangers was over-shadowed by my by relief to be there, and I soon made friends.

For the next two weeks I played the American tourist, exploring the Louvre, the Museum of French Impressionism, and all the well-known attractions. My newly found friends and I lived on long airy baguettes, bought in the open-air markets, fresh cheeses, and cheap wine. I practiced my French and found it much improved, (though I suspect that it was mostly because the French people here, dependent on the tourist dollar, were more tolerant of bad French.) I met a nice young man, two years older than I, from Switzerland. We made plans to travel together through Europe, first visiting his home in the Alps, and then continuing on to Spain and other destinations.

There was one slight problem, which as it turned out, became an immense problem. The French did not like bare feet, and I had no shoes. After being expelled from the Palace of Versailles and threatened by a gendarme for walking down the street without shoes, I decided to swallow my principles and submit to the rules of society. I took my precious stash of French money and went shopping for a pair of shoes. As I looked through the display of footwear I decided that, since I would probably never have another chance to buy shoes in Paris, I should buy stylish shoes that looked like they came from Paris. I could get tennis shoes or sandals anywhere. Instead, I found a pair of patent leather high-heeled Granny shoes, the "in" thing at that time, and I put them on in the store.

I wore them for the rest of my visit in Paris. It was fun at first, but before long my feet began to hurt. They grew worse, and by the time I realized that I should stop wearing the shoes, it was too late. I could no longer walk, even when I took them off. I couldn't hobble my way through Europe like this, so I reluctantly said goodbye to my Swiss friend, purchased a train ticket, and limped my way back to England. A trip to an English podiatrist confirmed that, by confining my feet in shoes like that after going unshod for five months, I had severely damaged the tendons, perhaps permanently. I would not be wearing my new shoes, or any other tight shoes, for a very long time.

Such are the penalties for betraying one's principles and submitting to feminine vanity!

*****

Pat Garber

January 2003

5:30 am January 1, 2003

I woke up early this morning. It is New Year's Day, and I told Jim I would work, since I didn't plan to stay out late and get shit-faced last night, like most everybody else. I have only a few resolutions: drink more water and less booze, do more snow-shoeing and skiing. I want to go ice fishing and try ice climbing if I can. Most important, I want to finish this self-scrutiny that I have begun. But for now, I need to get dressed and get down the hill to the diner in time for the breakfast crowd.

Later...

There were three young whitetail deer at the feeder when I got home. They trotted off when they saw me, waving their tails high above them and looking miffed. Now, with Huck and me in the house for the evening, they are back, searching the snow crust for sunflower seeds tossed out by the birds and squirrels. Elk and moose used to be regulars here in the Adirondacks, as well as deer, but they were hunted out sometime in the last century. The deer almost disappeared too, but they are back in force. The moose are making a comeback too, but not the elk. A reintroduction program failed, and because of a disease they are susceptible to, carried by the deer, they may not be here anytime soon.

5:15 pm January 4, 2003

I walked to work today, as I often do, and when I got there I realized I'd forgotten to bring my tennis shoes. I was wearing my lined rubber fishing boots (purchased at a commercial fishing shop in Manteo, North Carolina,) which are warm and waterproof, but hardly suitable for wait-ressing! The customers got a kick out of it anyway, and no one complained.

I actually like going to work now. All the bad feelings seem to have vanished, and I feel quite close to the people I work with. I'm also be-coming fond of a lot of our regulars.

What I don't like is the feeling of condescension I get from some of the customers. I wanted to think that I didn't care about that stuff, but I guess I was deceiving myself. When I noticed that one of the women in my station was reading a book about creative writing, I mentioned that I was a writer. She just looked at me strangely. On another day I heard two customers talking about archaeology. I told them that I was an anthropologist and had worked at several archaeological sites myself. They looked quite uncomfortable, as if they were sure I was making it up and didn't know how to respond. Being an educated waitress seems to be against the rules, and most people don't like the rules to be broken.

I don't want to look down on anyone, and I like to think that I don't; but I absolutely hate thinking that others look down on me. On Ocracoke, the North Carolina island where I live when not up north, no one looks down on anyone; or at least, that's what I like to think. If they do, they need to move on.

8:40 am January 9, 2003

I awoke this morning to the sound of my cat's hunting call, a tiny noise she makes deep in her throat when instinct takes over her more refined house-cat manners. She was crouched on the shelf above the loveseat, eyeing a handsome gray squirrel who had discovered my bird feeder. The squirrel was putting on quite an acrobatic show in his attempt to reach the sunflower seeds, and Miss Kelley was entranced. I watched for a moment, admiring his thick, glossy coat and his impudence. Gray squirrels are far less common here than in Virginia, where I grew up. This one appeared to be larger and more robust than the ones I had known farther south. I pulled on my boots and, wrapping my bathrobe around me, took a handful of seeds out for him to eat.

*****

I had trouble sleeping last night. I kept waking up, thinking about a dream I'd had about my former husband, Pete, and the roller-coaster ride that was our life together. I guess it's time to go back there, back to 1972, the beginning. Pete and I had met not too long after I returned to Virginia from the British Isles. He was trouble, I was warned, but I paid no heed to the warnings. The next eight years of my life were entwined with his, for better or worse.

Now, looking carefully, I see the interior of an old, hand-painted black van. It is decked out in paneling with curtains, a small table, and a bed with pull-out drawers underneath. A tall, handsome man with a dashing mustache and golden locks spilling over his shoulders is sitting behind the steering wheel, a Marlboro cigarette resting on his lower lip, a can of Pabst Blue Ribbon beer in one hand. Three other young men, also long-haired, are lounging about, one rolling a joint. There is no young woman to be seen, but I know she is there. She is curled up in a fetal position, long hair tied back with a bandana, in one of those drawers.

Pat Garber

Caught in a Spell

"Let me out!" I yelled, trying to push open the drawer where I was hidden, knees curled up and head bent down. "It's boring in here and I'm getting claustrophobia!" A hand, held against the front, stopped me. "Be quiet! You can't come out yet. Just stay there!" I muttered to myself in frustration but gave in, allowing him to push the drawer tight again. What the heck was I doing in here anyway?

But I knew. I was in love, swept off my feet by the man behind the hand. There was no doubt in my mind, nor in anyone else's that knew me. Pete might not have been my family's first choice for me, but they couldn't dispute my feelings. I had met him a few months before while attending college at Virginia Commonwealth University and working part time at the "Round Table," a combination bar and restaurant located not far from where I lived with my parents in Short Pump, Virginia. Tall and lean, with an aristocratic nose, compelling gray eyes, long blonde hair and a mustache, Pete looked like a cross between Jesus Christ and a Caribbean pirate. That kind of described his personality as well. He had the devil-may-care, risk-taking bravado of a buccaneer and a way with words which made him a born storyteller. He could be tender and caring and considerate, and could play a mean guitar and sing to beat the band. His charisma enlisted him an entourage of disciples, which included men and women, children and older people. He could also, as I was to learn, be cruel, dishonest and coldly uncaring.

Pete came regularly to the Round Table, where I worked, until he was kicked out by my boss for refusing to wear shoes. He swept me off my feet in swift order, and it was not till later that I learned he was married (though not living together, he said.) He would wait for me till I got off work at 1:00 am, then whisk me off in his convertible Triumph sports car, jump-starting it from a run since the starter didn't work.

He told me romantic stories of his grandmother, a princess from White Russia, who fled to America in the Bolshevik Revolution. He showed me the white-columned mansion where his father had been raised, and where he had met Pete's mother, a governess hired to care for his children by a previous marriage. (His first wife, so the story went, had run away to Europe with a movie actor.)

We took a whirlwind trip to Mardi Gras in New Orleans, where we were literally carried into town, the tiny Triumph (with us in it) borne on the shoulders of Bourbon Street revelers.

Caught up in my infatuation, I ignored the warning signs: the debts Pete had incurred, the money he cajoled out of his reluctant mother, the bad check notices, the constant consumption of cans of beer, which he drank while he drove, while he worked, all day, every day.

Together we planned an exciting trip. I finished my semester of college and he quit his job delivering mobile homes. We bought an old Dodge van, minus engine and most other working parts. Pete spray-painted it black and installed an engine. We built cabinets and a bed, I made curtains and slipcovers, and we turned it into a mini-home. Now, spring of 1973, it was ready for the road.

At first it was great. We rolled across the countryside, listening to the sounds of Ten Years After, the Beatles, and Led Zeppelin. Pete drinking Blue Ribbon beer and smoking Marlboro cigarettes the whole time. We had brought along a little, semi-feral black cat named Smut from Short Pump, and she was proving to be an excellent traveler. Heading north, we visited, at my request, Walden Pond and the homes of Ralph Waldo Emerson and Louisa May Alcott. We spent our nights in forbidden parking places, trying to evade the ubiquitous police who would shine their flashlights through the window while we struggled to pull on our clothes.

We spent a few days on Cape Cod and then picked up a hitchhiker who told us about a big concert in Watkins Glen, New York. Sure, we'd give him a ride. We saw other hitchhikers along the way, many holding signs that read "Watkins Glen." We picked up a few more and soon had a van full of longhaired, pot-smoking concert-goers. When we got near, however, we heard on the radio that the concert was sold out. "Don't worry," one of our passengers told us. "I have a friend who's making counterfeit tickets. I'll get you some." We stopped in town to get the tickets and to leave Smut at the ticket-maker's house. There was, however, only one ticket left. No problem. Pete had a solution. "You climb in the drawer," he told me. "They won't know you're there, and you can get out once we're inside the gates."

"Why me?" I protested. (There were three other passengers as well.) "You're the smallest!" he answered with his irrefutable male logic. So we took the clothes out and I scrunched down and slithered into the drawer Pete and I had built a few months before. Then we headed for the concert.

So here I was, in this absurd position, uncomfortable and feeling like a fool. It was mid-summer and we didn't have air conditioning. Let me tell you, it was hot inside that drawer, not to mention dark!

"Are we there yet?" I kept calling out. I felt the van slow down, then stop. We were not, however, there. It seemed that all of New York State was going to the concert on that two lane road. We were caught up in the biggest traffic jam you ever saw (well, technically I didn't see it.) We inched forward a little, then stopped. Again and again. It seemed like hours. The odor of marijuana smoke drifted through the van. The van ran out of gas. Our hitchhikers went from vehicle to vehicle, trying to buy enough to get us started again. Finally they returned with a can full, enough for us to continue.

By then I was fed up with lying in that drawer, but Pete kept shoving it back every time I pushed it open. "Be still! Don't you want to see the concert?" Word trickled down from the front that the concert grounds were full and no one else was being allowed in, tickets or not. We sat there for a while longer. Then word came that the fences had been torn down and people were going in anyway. Then, that the authorities had given up trying to keep us out. They were allowing everyone in, no tickets required.

Hallelujah! I pushed my way out of the drawer and struggled to my feet, stretching my cramped limbs. We left the van where it was and headed, in a great exodus of sweaty, semi-drugged bodies, for Watkins Glen.

Watkins Glen is a beautiful little valley carved out of limestone by a rushing creek which tumbles over rocks and small cliffs, forming cataracts and waterfalls. Its fame, however, is based on the fact that a stockcar racetrack is located there, drawing great crowds of hollering, beer-drinking, gambling fans who traipse through the valley without noticing its wildflowers and breath-taking beauty.

Now it was over-run by six hundred thousand hippies, all smitten with the sounds of the Allman Brothers, the Band, and the Grateful Dead, along with the thrill of free love, drugs and a heady sense of rebellion. The clear liquid pools, usually home to brook trout, seethed with nude bodies engaged in all manner of sexual contortions. The soft melodies of dragonfly wings and warbler songs were lost in the pulsing beat of drums and bass guitars. The grass was trampled by bare feet and sandals, and every tree and shrub hid a human body, sprawled in drug or alcohol-induced sleep. Pete and I were absorbed into the great miasma, part of and yet separate from the 599,998 other concert-goers.

Birchbark Chronicles

Three days later we made our way back to the van, which still stood parked in the middle of the road. We picked up Smut and headed west, to Buffalo, where my sister Betsy lived with her family.

I guess we looked pretty ragged by then, for her neighbors called her when we showed up (she was not home at the time) and told her there were some suspicious looking hippies hanging around her house. Did she want them to call the police? After a short visit we drove across the border to Canada, stopping to gaze in awe at the spectacular Niagara Falls.

We traveled across Canada, from Ontario into Manitoba, then down through the Dakotas and Nebraska. One night, somewhere in Nebraska, Pete drove through a grove of trees and parked the van in a cornfield. When morning came we found that we were stuck, our wheels mired in the red clay mud. Pete rummaged through a nearby barn and came out with the key ("they always keep them in the toolbox," he smiled) to a big green machine he called a corn picker. He complacently started it up and headed for the van, bumping across the ditches. "You drive this," he told me, having hooked a chain between the two, and I'll drive the van.

"NO!" I protested. "I don't know how!" (I had been protesting about the whole idea of "borrowing" the corn picker, anyway.) But he won, as usual, and I climbed up onto the metal seat. After a few heart-stopping attempts in which I was sure the picker itself was going to lurch through our windshield and crush Pete, we got the van out, it and us covered with mud. Pete returned the corn picker to its resting place and the key to the toolbox. Then we skeedaddled. I'll bet that farmer scratched his head and wondered about the tracks we left behind.

On one of our stops I met a man who had recently captured a family of baby striped skunks and had them de-scented. They were the cutest things I'd ever seen and I was sure I had to have one. Pete reluctantly agreed and I parted with the last of my cash. Violet, as I named him, joined our family.

We were out of money by the time we reached Colorado, both ready to stop for a while. The little town of Manitou Springs, nestled at the foot of the Rocky Mountains, in the shadow of Pikes Peak and overlooking the Garden of the Gods, seemed an ideal place to live. Pete got a job at a mobile home hauling business and we found a little apartment on the highway that wound through town. It had a great view of the mountains, was within walking distance of funky little shops and restaurants, close enough to the wilderness that I could hike into canyons and up mountain-

129

sides. Our new home was named after the Indian word for god (Manitou) and a sulphur spring which lay within walking distance of our new home. Bottles of Koolade were turned magically to carbonated sodas when I added water from this spring.

Things couldn't be more perfect, or so I thought. Pete didn't want me to work so I spent my time fixing up our apartment. I decorated it with interesting rocks and twisted pieces of wood I found in the canyons. Pete brought home lamps and trinkets from the repossessed trailers he moved. I attended a nearby ceramics class and made dishes and Christmas presents. I fell in love with a little cast bronze burro, loaded with gear for the gold mining which had once been the mainstay of this community, and was thrilled when Pete went to the gift shop where it resided and bought it for my birthday. I painted pictures on wood scraps and put up a poster that said "Home is where the Heart is" and I believed it with all my heart. I was, at first, euphorically happy.

Smut, the little wild cat we had brought with us from Short Pump, sat in the picture window and waited each evening for Pete to come home. So did I. We waited longer and longer each night. Summer turned into fall and then winter. Pete started working weekends. Still we waited. I spent hours playing with Violet and Smut.

I wandered the streets of Manitou Springs and the canyons outside the town, growing lonelier with each day. I cried each morning before Pete left, begging him to take me to work with him, or to go somewhere together when he got home. He said he didn't have time and we couldn't afford to go out. I had no car, and when I asked if I could drive him to work and then use the van myself, he refused.

Wanting some money of my own, I got a job at a little restaurant I could walk to, but he grew so angry that I told the manager I couldn't keep it. Pete came home later and later, smelling of beer and explaining that the guys all went out after work. It was part of the job. It was too cold to stay outside for long now, so I sat in the apartment, huddled up with a book when I had one, miserable. I felt like I was locked in a drawer again.

Finally Pete grew tired of working in the snow and cold and quit his job. Unhappy as I had become, I hated to leave Colorado, for I had fallen in love with the mountains, the canyons, the feeling of the "old west" which still pervaded. I gave Violet, whom Pete disliked intensely (and vice-versa) to a friend who wanted him, and we headed back to

Virginia. Maybe now things would get better. They didn't. Not, at least, for a long time, and even then, not for good.

All these years later, I still wonder why I allowed Pete to control me the way he did. I have to assume some of the blame myself, for I was not some young innocent who had never been on her own. I was the same young woman who had hitchhiked across the British Isles, alone; who had found herself a job in a remote Irish pub; who had looked after herself in a number of difficult situations. The hours I allowed myself to be locked in that van drawer were few and rather comical. The months that I allowed Pete to lock me away, first in the Colorado apartment and later in a dingy little office in Richmond, Virginia, were long and frightening; frightening because I allowed him to do so.

I was like a moth fluttering around a candle flame; entranced when Pete shone the light of his attentions on me and willing, like the moth described in Annie Dillard's essay, to let it destroy me. It was love, but love combined with some malignant force that we were both subjected to; a kind of spell that changed us both. It took years to break that spell, years more before we were free.

Even now, I sometimes find myself longing for the mesmerizing, all-consuming flame of that doomed love affair.

*****

6:45 pm January 12, 2003

The gray squirrel is becoming a regular at the feeder. Yesterday he was hanging upside down and eating seeds as nonchalantly as if that were his normal position. I tried to figure out how his back feet were holding on; there didn't seem to be anything to grip. He (or she) is really beautiful; if I believed in wearing fur coats I might want to abscond with his!

There was a bit of a break in the weather today so I drove east toward Newcomb with Huck and turned down the road to Santanoni. Santanoni was a Great Camp, designed by architect Robert Robertson and built for the Pruyn family in 1893. When, in 1971, the owner's grandson disappeared in the woods, the state's largest manhunt was conducted. It was unsuccessful and, after the hunt was called off, the family left for good. The camp, including 12,900 acres and 45 buildings, became part of the Adirondack Park.

I stopped at the Gate Lodge and parked; then took out my skis and called Huck. The camp lies on Newcomb Lake at the end of a 4.7-mile-long road, closed to motorized traffic but accessible by foot or skis. It passes by once-productive farm buildings, over the River, and through beautiful forests. It took most of the day to ski in, share a picnic lunch with Huck, and explore the lovely though eerie buildings. Huck followed the trail of a deer which led across the open porch of the main house; once teeming with human life, now being slowly reclaimed by Mother Nature. On the way out I met John Mallory, also on skis. John and his wife Jackie are musicians, outdoor enthusiasts, and of a more liberal inclination than most people here. I'd like to get to know them better.

1:00 pm January 15, 2003

I didn't have to work today, so after enjoying my coffee, I drove to Tupper Lake and got groceries and a big bag of sunflower seeds. I stopped by the diner, where UPS had delivered my new aluminum snow shoes, so when I got home I tried them out. They worked great! They're much like the ones I'd tried on the nature trail at Newcomb.

8:00 am January 18, 2003

It is 24 degrees below zero! There were four deer outside the cabin this morning when I got up. They looked so cold and unhappy, I wished I could bring them inside! People are saying that a lot of them will starve this winter because of the cold. I am tempted to set out a bucket of sunflower seeds for them, but I remind myself that, in the long run, they do better without human interference. I have stopped letting Huck run free because, even though he chases them in fun, the energy wasted in fleeing from him could be, for them, the difference between life and death. He does not understand, I know.

All the bucks have shed their antlers, so I don't know which deer are male or female. There are two small ones, born last spring, I'm guessing. For the last few days a large deer with an injured leg has been coming around. I wonder what happened to it. Occasionally I see one with a collar around its neck. I mentioned it to Carl and he said it was no doubt part of a research project out of Huntington Ecological Center, a couple miles this side of Newcomb.

The deer I see on a daily basis are one of my absolute favorite things about living here. Their beauty is magical, their dark liquid eyes intriguing. I do not disapprove of hunting if the meat is properly used.

I've eaten my share of venison and enjoyed it. But I do not see how anyone could bring himself to actually draw a bead, take aim, and pull the trigger to kill one.

4:30 pm January 20, 2003

The days slip by like coyotes, moving in and out of the shadows. Work was slower than ever today, with almost no one coming in. Those who did shook the snow off their jackets and shook their heads at the cold. A new couple sat down at my counter. After I served them coffee we got to talking, and they said they were leaving soon for a Caribbean cruise. I told them about my own version of a cruise I took when in my early twenties, hoping they would have better luck.

*****

It was in the Virgin Islands, on the little isle of St. John. I had left Pete and the desolate office in Southside Richmond once more in desperation, thinking that this time I might break away from the spell he seemed to hold me under.

Adventure on the High Seas;
a Brief Sojourn in the Virgin Islands

"Hey Pat!"

I turned quickly, surprised to hear my name. I didn't know many people here. I recognized a girl I had met a few days before, her dark hair pulled back in a braid, and smiled as I searched my memory for her name. "Wendy!" I responded. "How are you?" "Great! she answered. "Remember that sailboat I told you I wanted to buy? Well I bought it yesterday. How would you like to go sailing?" "Cool!" I'd like it fine, I told her, and we agreed to meet the next morning down at the beach.

She trotted off and I turned back to the book I was reading, stretched out in a hammock under a coconut palm. Having lost my train of thought, however, I settled for a little reminiscing. I had arrived in the Virgin Islands two weeks earlier, flying in a big airplane from Richmond, Virginia, to St. Thomas, and spending a brief visit at Charlotte Amalie, the capital city.

Then I rode a tiny ferry to Cruz Bay, here on St. John, from which I hitched a ride across the island to Coral Bay. Half of the island and a large underwater preserve are protected from development by their designation as a national park. Laurence Rockefeller once owned the land and donated it to the U.S. government, which established the park in 1957. The beautiful beaches, ruins, and Amerindian petroglyphs entice a few tourists, but the island is relatively quiet and peaceful.

Coral Bay, the little hamlet where I was staying, was the island's first settlement. The Danes, who had seized the islands from the natives, had raised sugar cane here. There were over 100 sugar plantations in the early 1700s, worked by a large number of slaves brought over from Africa. In 1733, after hard times fell upon the plantations and the slaves were allowed to starve, they revolted. The revolt was successful at first, but soldiers were sent from the other islands and all of the 150 slaves who had participated were killed.

Little evidence remained of those tumultuous times. Coral Bay was a sleepy little village, now part of the United States, along with the rest of the island. I was staying in a room at the little bar/restaurant where I now relaxed. I worked in the kitchen at suppertime in exchange for some of my rent. Dead broke, I was trying to live off the fruits which grew in profusion, as well as a loaf of bread here and there. I had met a most handsome young man, Jeff, originally from Jamaica, and while he had no money either, he knew where to go to find fruit or an occasional fish. I'd brought my guitar with me to St. John, and he loved to borrow it and sing. "Jamaica Farewell" was my favorite of the songs he knew, and he was teaching it to me.

Jeff said he was falling in love with me (which I suspect he said to a lot of the young women who showed up there.) I certainly found him attractive and engaging. But I was in love with someone else, and while it seemed to be a doomed affair, I could not bring myself to forget him. I had come here, to the Virgin Islands, to try and figure things out.

Pete and I had spent five months living together, first in our van and later in a Colorado apartment. Things had not ended well, but I was still hopeful, wanting to move somewhere we could make a new start. We had returned to our homes in Virginia for what I thought was a short visit, but Pete had decided to stay and buy a business. My parents had asked that we not live together, unmarried, in Richmond, where people might talk, and I had agreed. So I moved back in with my parents. Pete (who was still legally married to someone else) and I had not discussed marriage.

Pete's new business, which he called United Mobile Transport, was moving mobile homes for people. He said I could work for him,

134

answering the phone and booking jobs. Pete was good at driving the truck and setting up the trailers, but doing paperwork and handling money were his downfall. The office he had rented was a dingy little building on a big highway in Richmond's Southside, where I knew no one. I did not have a car, so when Pete dropped me off in the morning I was stuck there until he picked me up and took me back to my parents' house.

Pete bought a big truck and hired his best friend, Frankie, to work for him. Frankie liked to drink beer too, and when they'd finished working they'd stop off at the nearest bar. Maybe they drank up the profits, or maybe there weren't any. There was never enough money for Pete to pay me. "Just be patient!" he'd say. "Don't you trust me?" He'd pay me when business picked up.

Sometimes he didn't show up till 11:00 at night. Sometimes he didn't show up at all, and I spent the night without supper, curling up on the couch with a blanket, trying to sleep. My parents watched helplessly as I grew more and more unhappy. Finally, I knew I had to leave. Momma and Daddy offered to buy me a ticket to wherever I wanted to go. So here I was, in the Virgin Islands, getting a great sun tan and mulling over my broken heart.

I met Wendy the next morning, as we had planned. She brought another friend with her, Jane, a slightly pudgy, cute young woman I hadn't met before. We set out on our adventure with enthusiasm. It was an old wooden sailboat, Wendy explained as we walked to the harbor where it was docked. She'd gotten a good buy since its owner wanted to leave the island. We jumped aboard and pushed off from the dock as Wendy loosened the lanyards and raised the sail. It was a beautiful day, and the sail filled as if by magic, driven by a steady wind. We watched the shoreline diminish, and in our exuberance we flung off our bathing suits, sailing nude beneath the Caribbean sun, fancying ourselves young goddesses.

It was a shock when Jane called out, "There's a boat!" Sure enough, bearing down on us was a cabin cruiser. We dropped everything, hearing the leering cheers of men's voices as we reached for our bathing suits. As we hurried to pull them on our boat swung around, or "came about" in sailing jargon. "Watch out!" Wendy cried, and I looked up just in time to see the boom swing into me. It knocked me across the deck. "Are you okay?" I rubbed my arm where it had hit, shaken but not seriously injured. "Yeah, that was stupid of me," I replied. The other boat was well past us now, and we realized that the swells striking our boat were formidable. Looking back, we noticed how far from shore we were. "Maybe we'd better head back," I said. "It's getting rough."

We resituated ourselves, a little more sober now, and Wendy pulled the tiller toward her as I tightened the lines of the sail. The boom swung around the other way, and Jane dodged just in time. We had a head wind, and Wendy's boat did not want to sail into it. We tried to tack, sailing at an angle, but none of us was an experienced sailor. We struggled until we were exhausted and frightened, making no headway. We looked around, hoping the cabin cruiser would return, but it was gone. We searched the horizon, hoping for another boat, but none was in sight. I felt a twinge of fear.

"Maybe we should drop anchor," I said, "and swim for it. Come back for the boat later." Wendy agreed. Jane said nothing. Wendy went forward and dropped the anchor over the side, while we prayed that the line would be long enough to reach the bottom.

"Yes!" I saw the line go slack in her hands, which meant it had hit solid ground. We let it out some more, till we were sure it had caught. The boat rocked restlessly, and we stared at the distant outline of St. John's shore. It was then that Jane spoke in a small voice.

"I'm not a very good swimmer. I don't know if I can make it."

Wendy and I looked at each other grimly. "You have to make it," we told her. "We don't have any choice."

Leaving our gear on the boat, we slipped over the side and began swimming. We were about a third of the way back, staying close together, when I heard Jane gasp. She had swallowed water and was starting to go under.

I had taught swimming with my father in our backyard pool for six summers. I did not get my lifesaving certificate till years later, but my father had taught me what to do. Trying to control my fear, I instructed her to relax and lie on her back. I would take care of her, I said. I started to panic when she grabbed my arm. I knew the danger. She could pull me under and we would both drown. Sliding away from her grip, I seized her chin, flipped her onto her back, and slipped a hand under her back. "Relax," I told her. "Just relax." It worked, but before long I found myself breathing hard and losing my strength. I swallowed a mouthful of water. Wendy took over. We took turns, helping Jane and making slow progress toward shore. I thought we would never get there, but finally I felt sand beneath my feet. In a few minutes we staggered onto the beach and collapsed, all of us exhausted, gasping and shaking. We had made it.

Wendy went back that evening with Jeff, our Bahamian friend, who asked a friend to take them out in his boat. They found the little wooden sailboat, still anchored, and Jeff sailed it back. All's well that ends well, they say. Lady Luck may not have been sailing with us that day, but she seemed to have been keeping an eye on us. How many close calls does it take, I wonder, before she gets disgusted and turns away.

I stayed in the Virgin Islands for another week or two, snorkeling, exploring the ruins of an 18th century Danish sugar cane plantation, gazing at ancient petroglyphs, and visiting the British-owned island of Tortola.

One night I called Pete's office. I did not expect an answer, but his friend Frankie picked up the phone.

"Hi," I said in an uncertain voice. "Is Pete there?" "He's here," said Frankie. "He's been here every night since you left, hoping you'd call. He hasn't gone anywhere."

Our conversation was short, Pete's voice low and hoarse. "Are you coming back?" I told him I didn't know. "I miss you." I hesitated before I answered, and my voice was a whisper. "I miss you too."

I stayed a few days longer, but I knew after that phone call that I would be returning to Pete. I was sure that now things would be different. When I got back Pete told me that he had filed for divorce, and if I wanted to, we could be married the next month. We began planning a small wedding, hoping for the best as we embarked on our voyage into married life.

*****

9:15 pm January 21, 2003

Today I packed dog biscuits, a tuna sandwich, and a few oatmeal cookies into a small backpack and called Huck to join me in the truck. We drove out the North Point Road past Buttermilk Falls to a barely visible trailhead, hidden in the snow. I'd heard about a pond back here, now frozen over, which I'd never been to. I was ready for an adventure. I pulled on my new aluminum snowshoes and we set out along the trail, just discernible in the deep drifts. It was great fun--the pond silent, beautiful, and mysterious under its blanket of white. It was farther than I'd expected, however, and by the time we got there and turned around to head back, I realized that it would be getting dark soon.
"Hurry up, Huck," I said nervously. "We have to get back!" Hurrying in

snow shoes is not easy, however, and I was getting scared. I was berating myself for not bringing a flashlight, and beginning to panic at the thought of being stranded for the night, when I heard a voice.

"Hoorah!" I thought to myself, "There's someone out here in the woods!" I heard more voices. "Wow! They're having a party!" Realization hit suddenly, and I felt a flash of terror. The voices belonged not to humans, but to coyotes. There was a pack of coyotes, possibly quite hungry, not far away. Huck seemed as worried as I, and we sped homeward, moving faster than I would have thought possible on snowshoes. We made it back to the truck just as darkness began to obscure the trail.

Boy, am I glad to be here now, cradling a glass of wine in front of the warm fire.

9:30 am January 23, 2003

My skiing is improving a bit, though I still have trouble when the trail winds down a hill. Yesterday I skied on the lake, stopping by Eve's house on the opposite bank and then at the Adirondack Hotel to warm up with a cup of hot chocolate. Snowmobilers who had passed me earlier stopped in as well, teasing me for what they consider a slow, "too much work" sport. There is an on-going feud, sometimes friendly and sometimes not so friendly, between cross-country skiers and snowmobilers. I picked up a carton of eggs at Stewarts and tied it to my backpack, then headed up Mt. Sabattis. I made it home without breaking any eggs.

I noticed two red-breasted nuthatches at my feeder today. They're smaller than their white-breasted cousins and more colorful. My bird guide says they smear the entrance to their nest-holes with pitch, perhaps to keep away intruders.

I don't have to work today, so I think I'll snowshoe the Sagamore Road with Huck. I'll write for a bit first.

*****

The piece I now pull from my memory took place about a year after my marriage to Pete. Our wedding had been a small and lovely affair in the back yard of my parents' farm in Short Pump, with the horses and dogs in attendance. I, the bride, wearing a cream-colored granny dress with daisies in my hair, was given away by my father and attended by my younger sister Nancy and my best friend Sandy.

Pete and I rented a small house in Goochland, Pete's home town, but shortly thereafter we moved to a lovely village on the James River known as Claremont. I look now at one particular day in 1975 which has baffled me for years.

The Day the River Blew Away

I was a country girl back then, not too well educated, and some folks might say I was crazy. But I saw what I saw, and I know what I know, even if it's a secret shared only by a river and me.

The James, down Claremont way, is a big tidal river, nearly a mile wide if it's a foot. It begins far away where a thousand springs and seepages in the Blue Ridge Mountains flow together, and then takes shape where the Cowpasture and Jackson Rivers converge. From there it flows east for 340 miles, passing near the Peaks of Otter; through the rapids of Richmond, and past Hopewell, growing ever deeper and wider and straighter. Down here, in what's called the Tidewater, it's wide and deep enough for ships to sail. As it continues on its eastward journey, its fresh waters mix with the sea's saltiness, and it becomes brackish, hosting blue crabs and oysters. The James is over two miles wide where, at Hampton Roads, it finally empties into the Chesapeake Bay and loses itself in that great estuary.

The James, named after an English king, is kind of like royalty herself; you could call her the queen of rivers in Virginia, and since Virginia once upon a time included everything from Canada to Florida, west to the Pacific, you could call her the queen of this country. (She's definitely a lady, in spite of her name.)

Every inch of the James River is a-swirl with history, and the part around Claremont, where this story takes place, is no exception. Go west and you come to a whole string of antebellum plantations, and, a little farther on, the seven hills of Richmond, where Union soldiers built the Dutch Gap Canal, hoping to use the river to capture the city.

To the east is Jamestown, where the English claimed to have built the first permanent colony in America (despite the fact that the Powhatan Indians had lived here for thousands of years--that's not permanent?) and where Pocahontas is said to have saved the life of Captain John Smith. Nearby Hog Island, now a wildlife refuge, is where three hundred English colonists once lived and kept their pigs. It's said that Blackbeard and other pirates used to sail these parts and, according to one legend, buried a whole pile of treasure on one of the islands out here in the James.

In 1974 I, along with my husband Pete, moved into an old farmhouse on the shore of the James, just a hop, skip, and a jump from the village of Claremont. With us were Bojay, a loveable black lab cross, our gray kitty Foxey (daughter of my old momma cat Tiger, still living with my folks in Short Pump), and a floppy-eared doberman pup named Princess. Our beloved semi-feral cat Smut, who had traveled the country with us, had disappeared when a repairman had come to our house in Goochland to fix the refrigerator and had left the door open.

Our home sat alongside a sandy, shell-strewn river shore at the bottom of high bluffs, an area known as Claremont Beach. Huge, ancient cypress trees grew in our yard, poking their odd-shaped roots (often called knees) up any old place, as if Mother Nature had designed a sculpture garden just for us. Our house and a big old wooden restaurant/dance hall, closed at the time, were the only buildings on the beach. Pete and I were trying to buy the house, but it shared a septic system with the restaurant, which proved to be an insurmountable legal obstacle.

A winding lane, edged with redbuds, dogwoods, and loblolly pines leads up the bluffs. Draped along the branches of the trees are huge rope-like vines of wild grapes and honeysuckle. At the top, the sleepy little village of Claremont sprawls in a haphazard manner along marshes and around cliffs which overlook the south bank of the James, at the spot where the Upper Chippokes Creek meets the river.

This was once upon a time the principal village of a group of native people who called themselves the Quiyoughcohannocks. That's what the stone marker at the end of town says. It also says that on May 5, 1607, English settlers visited here (Captains John Smith and George Percy) which no doubt explains why a stone marker is all that's left today of the Quiyoughcohannocks.

According to John Smith, who documented his visit, he was met by the tribe's werowance (chief) and men playing flutes made of reeds. Their bodies were painted crimson and they wore chains of beads. They sat on a mat spread on the ground and smoked a pipe amidst the "goodliest corn fields" Smith had seen. There are still plenty of "goodly" cornfields around Claremont today; green with promise in the spring, pregnant in summer with their plump crop, and eerie in winter with the rattling of dry husks.

In 1621 the English colonist George Harrison (no relation to the Beatle) was given a land grant at Claremont. A year later, not far away, on March 22, Chief Opecanough attempted to defend his people against occupation in what's called the "Great Massacre" of English settlers. The attempt was ultimately unsuccessful, and ten years later another Englishman, Arthur Allen, later a Speaker in the House of Burgesses, obtained 12,000 acres at Claremont. Forty-some years after that Nathaniel Bacon led his famous rebellion against the English government, also unsuccessful, nearby.

In 1750, William Allen, a descendent of Arthur Allen, who was once the wealthiest man in Virginia, built Claremont Manor. The village developed around it and was incorporated in 1886.

Sometime before we moved to Claremont, Pete had, much to my dismay, bought himself a mobile home hauling business. (That's how we'd ended up here, him having moved a trailer for the woman who owned the farmhouse.) He left every morning to go to Southside Richmond, where his office and two trucks were located. I waited tables a few nights a week at a pizza place in Richmond, but I spent most of my time here, wandering along the river. The James River was a constant living presence in our lives. Even when the shades were drawn, the sky black as pitch, you'd know she was there, just outside the door, moving great volumes of water silently, inexorably to the sea. Carrying stories and secrets right by your window.

We fed off her bounty, sitting on the bank and throwing a line in, squirming worm attached, and pulling up big catfish. Catching the cats was an easy matter, but cleaning them was something else entirely. You couldn't just scale them with a knife; they had to be skinned, like a deer. They'd been living on the muddy river bottom, so I'd soak them in water to remove the taste of mud. It helped but, if truth be told, they always tasted a bit like maybe you'd dropped them and not quite managed to wipe off all the dirt. We knew about the mud but what we didn't know about was the undetected chemical, Kepone, being pumped illegally into the James by Allied Chemical upstream in Hopewell. A year or two later the officials in Richmond put the screws to Allied and banned eating fish from this part of the James, announcing that they could cause you to come down with cancer. But it was too late by then; we'd already ingested a good share of them.

In spring we'd take nets and head up the creeks to dip for herring. There wasn't much in life that was more fun than herring season. We would hike to one of the creeks which fed into the river, carrying buckets and nets, trying to avoid poison ivy and prickly blackberry vines and keeping an eye out for water moccasins. We'd find a place to sit at the creekside (no old logs, of course; you didn't want to come home with a belly full of chiggers!) Most likely there would be robins trilling around you and the scent of redbuds in the air, and of course the babbling of the brook as it hurried to meet up with the James. Fighting their way up the creek, heading for some secret spawning place recorded in their genetic memory, were thousands of herring, or alefish. Herring are anadromous, like salmon and shad, which means they live most of their lives in the ocean, going to freshwater to breed and spawn. Dipping our nets into the creek, we'd scoop them up by the dozens and deposit them into our buckets. Finally, with enough for a year's supply, we'd carry them home.

I'd learned how to prepare herring from my momma. First you washed quart or gallon jars, soaking them in boiling hot water. You packed them tight with the fish and poured salt water over them, after which you let them sit for months. Many of the herring we caught were ripe with eggs, or roe. These we carefully scraped off to cook for breakfast. Later, after the herring were cured, you'd soak them overnight to get the salt out, roll them in cornmeal, and fry them crisp. Nothing better!

Surry County, which was where Claremont was located, was peanut country. Peanuts got to Virginia by a round-about route--having been carried by Spanish and Portuguese explorers from South America, where they were a favorite food of the Incas, to Spain and then to Africa, where they became known as goobers. From Africa they were brought by captured slaves to Tidewater Virginia, where they've been thriving ever since. The best peanut soup in the universe was served at the Surry House, not far from where we lived, and we always took out-of-town guests there to try it.

Not long after moving to Claremont, Pete and I got ourselves a boat, a sixteen-foot wooden runabout with a 35 hp motor. It was old, but it stayed afloat just fine, and the engine worked at least half the time. We traversed every inch of that river, one or the other of us usually on water skis. Our skis weren't new or fancy, but they worked, and we learned to jump wakes with the best of them. We traveled east, past Smithfield, where the best smoked hams you ever tasted (never mind the carcinogens) are cured. We passed the site of old Fort Bee, where my great-grandfather, Sergeant-Major Jenkins, watched the Merrimack battle the Mo-

nitor during what he called the War for Southern Independence. We slowed our engine and drifted through the shadowy hulls of the "Ghost Fleet," where naval vessels are put to rest; an eerie group of silent gray ships anchored in a watery graveyard, their lines creaking like wailing voices when the winds blow. We headed west, to an island where we spent a day digging for Blackbeard's treasure with a couple friends we'd gotten to know. The only thing we took home with us was poison ivy, but it was fun imagining the possibilities.

One day Pete had shut off the engine and we were just drifting, having a bite to eat, along with a couple beers, when we heard a whistle. Looking up, we saw a tugboat bearing down on us, pushing a loaded barge in front of it. Pete jumped up to start the motor, but when he pulled the starter nothing happened. He tried again with no luck. And again. Meanwhile, the tugboat was tooting its head off and coming at us hellfire for damnation. I checked the fuel tank and Pete tried everything he knew to do, but she barely sputtered. We could hear the tugboat hitting its brakes but stopping a loaded barge is no easy thing, and I was thinking we'd best hop off the boat and swim for it when Pete noticed that I'd set our cooler on top of the fuel line, knocking it loose. He sent the cooler flying and re-attached the line, jerked the starter, and by jiminy, she started. We skedaddled out of there, right happy to be gone, and waved an apology to the tugboat captain, which, judging by the language he used as he went by, he didn't accept.

As soon as I could, I brought my horse Caprice from Short Pump. I found a place to keep her in a big pasture near Claremont Manor, about a mile from our house. Caprice was an American Saddlebred, a big beautiful sorrel mare with white socks and a half stripe on her face. My parents had given her to me when I was sixteen, as an early high school graduation present. She'd been a two-year-old then, gentle but untrained. I'd never put a saddle on her, and I'd trained her to follow knee commands, so I didn't have to use a bridle.

Riding Caprice was the next best thing to being a wild animal. On her back I mingled, barely noticed, with red foxes and cottontails, whitetail deer and muskrats. We followed hidden trails and riverbanks, sloshing through marshes and galloping through meadows of wild flowers. One spring day, as we waded through a shallow spot at the edge of the river, I looked down and discovered that we were surrounded by snakes. Hundreds slithered, like tiny coiling ribbons, around Caprice's feet. A sensation of horror seized me. I am not phobic about snakes, but the sight of all those sinuous dark bodies awoke in me a primordial fear. I wondered, in the brief moments it took for us to leap away, if they could be moccasins or copperheads. Once safely back on land, I climbed off Caprice and peered into the water, watching in morbid fascination for a long time.

Pete was lead singer in a rock & roll band in those days, and most of the time when he wasn't driving his truck he was practicing or playing with the other guys in the band. I went along sometimes, but mostly I stayed home. The band, calling themselves "Salt Air," got its name from this part of the James. Sometimes they came out and practiced at our house, and then we'd all pile into our boat and head out into the river.

The James River was an all-encompassing presence in our lives. So when I looked out the window one late winter morning and she wasn't there, I had quite a shock. Shaking my head and rubbing my eyes, I stumbled to the door and, opening it, peered out. It was true. The river was gone. Where, the day before, her waters flowed deep and strong, reflecting the moods of the sky above, there was only mud and sand. Calling the dogs to join me, I walked over to the edge of the vanished river. Far off, toward the middle, I could see a ribbon of water, deep and narrow, still flowing. All else looked like a bizarre waterlogged moon-scape, with an occasional pool of water where a few fish flopped. The elegant river lady, suddenly defrocked, lay naked and exposed to sky and air, unable to shield her nakedness. It felt brazen and rude to stare, but I couldn't take my eyes away.

Bojay and Princess had already trotted out, following their noses to enumerable doggy treasures that lay before them, a veritable banquet of canine cuisine. I was more hesitant. There was no one around to question, to explain. I wondered if there was quicksand lurking in that vast expanse. I also wondered what would happen if the water, so mysteriously vanished, were to return. I pictured a huge tidal wave; a tsunami of epic proportions, sweeping down the riverbed and washing everything in its path out to sea.

So I stepped gingerly, wiggling my toes in the cool mud. Soon, however, I became engrossed in the scene before me. I loved to beachcomb, and was always picking up bits and pieces I found along the shore, flotsam and jetsam washed up and left behind by the impatient river. Now, spread before me, lay all the trinkets and treasures she had dropped as she hurried to the sea. There were bottles and rusted cans, shells and bones, fishing lures and pieces of twisted wood and metal. Farther off, I spied a larger shape rising out of the mud.

The dogs galloped ahead of me, determined to beat me to my destination, and they were already sniffing around the water-logged hulk when I approached. It was a boat, I realized, or what was left of one. I stepped gingerly across her hull, staring at the battered remains. Blue paint still clung to some of the boards, and she seemed to be pretty much intact. What was her story? How long had she lain on the bottom of the river, a home for fishes? How had she gone down? What secrets did she hold?

I let my imagination take flight. I thought of drug boats, modern pirates searching for a place to bury their treasure, discovered and destroyed by other pirates. I pictured a great storm with waves crashing over the gunwales and a gallant escape with a desperate swim to shore. I stepped cautiously into her cabin, half expecting to see the bleached bones of some former captain or mate; but all I saw were a few bleached and broken boards. Still in place were a brass captain's wheel and a porthole, their metallic sheen tinted green by the action of salt water. I stared through the porthole at the eerie landscape outside. Suddenly, I wanted to get away. I shook off the creepy feeling that had come over me and called the dogs. We headed back home.

I puttered around the house that day, but I couldn't keep my mind on anything. The absence of the river was as palpable as the loss of a loved one. We didn't have a phone, and there were no nearby neighbors to talk to.

By the time Pete got home, later that afternoon, the water was rising again. I told him about the wrecked boat, and we high-tailed it back out into the muddy expanse. Pete brought a saw along and we removed the brass porthole and captain's wheel. We took them home and I spent hours cleaning them.

The next morning when we looked out the window, the James River was back, pretending she'd never been gone. There was no sign of the boat, her presence hidden once more in the riverine depths. The river looked the same as usual, giving no sign of her recent disappearance, giving no clue as to where she had gone or why.

Years later, I tried to learn the explanation. I had, in the intervening time, visited the narrow, swift-flowing mountain stream which was the James at her birth. I had paddled her whitewaters, bumping across the rapids east of Richmond in a canoe with my brother. I had sailed up the

James in a 27-foot Cape Dory sloop, from the Chesapeake Bay to the mouth of the Chickahominy, just east of Claremont. I had run into no one, however, who remembered the day the river blew away.

I talked to family and friends who knew the James. "Do you remember the time...?" No one did. "Have you ever heard of this happening...?" A few people had heard of it happening in other rivers, other countries, other times, but never in the James. I thought back to an old folk tale I'd read about five Chinese brothers who drank up the sea and then spit it out again. Had someone mysteriously drunk up the river for a day?

I called nearby colleges and universities; they suggested I call the U.S. Geological Survey. The folks there referred me to the Virginia Marine Resources Commission, but the scientist I talked to had no idea. He suggested that I call the Virginia Institute of Marine Science in Williamsburg. There I talked to Steve Kuehl, who had never heard of the event, but had some ideas. Gradually I pieced together possibilities; perhaps an astronomical low (or neap) tide, combined with a long-term, persistent off-shore breeze, pushing the waters seaward.

I tracked down a professor he mentioned, retired now, who was supposed to be an expert on the James. Dr. Nichols had studied the James his whole life. But when I mentioned the day in question, he had no clue. "It's impossible!" he said. "Sometimes," he added, with a touch of humor, "I have dreams like that..."

"Well," I told him, "I have a captain's wheel and porthole from a boat my husband and I found that day, and they don't look like they came off a dreamboat!"

He thought about it. There are some really low tides in February and March, particularly March...did it happen then, by any chance? Round about then, I answered. And strong north-westerly winds blow that month, sometimes for days...they could move a lot of water. If there were a lot of siltation, a lot of shoals..." Let me get my charts," he said. "Won't take a minute."

He studied the charts, and then announced, with a hint of excitement in his voice, that there were foot-deep shoals off Claremont Beach. They stretched for 200 yards and then gradually deepened over another 100 yards to a depth of about 25 feet. "And," he added, "I see there are a lot of wrecks out there! The mud could have piled up behind them, accounting for some heavy siltation, making the river unusually shallow there. If the wind blew strong enough, if the tide was low enough, it's just possible..."

I had my explanation, or at least as much as I figured I'd ever get. A lot of unique conditions, all working together, had produced an unheard of moment in time. I had been there at that moment. I thanked Dr. Nichols profusely and said goodbye.

Not long afterward, Hurricane Isabel took out Claremont Beach, at least all the man-made structures there. I walked along the familiar shore, sat on the foundation of the old restaurant, and stared at the empty yard where Pete's and my house had once stood. Our house, the restaurant, all the cottages built in the intervening years, had been swallowed by the James in a moment of Mother Nature's wrath. They were now scattered in bits and pieces somewhere on that river bottom; flotsam mingling, perhaps, with the remains of the boat I had discovered on that long-ago day. In a nearby lagoon, amidst the floating garbage, I saw a pair of swans, tilting their heads in graceful arches and ignoring the devastation that surrounded them...

I picture the house as I had known it, its green paint peeling away in the sultry Virginia heat. I see the young woman, galloping her horse along the banks of the grand old river, splattering through its mud and scattering silver droplets of its precious water. I imagine the boat, submerged again and slowly decaying, wrapped in river seaweed and mussels, fish swimming through the absent porthole, her captain's wheel now adorning my wall. House, horse, and young woman are gone now, but the mighty James flows on, passing on her stories and keeping her secrets, forever.

*****

6:00 pm January 26, 2003

I got a chance to talk to Bunny at the diner today. He was waiting for his wife Evie, who was late. Bunny is one of the Adirondack guide-boat builders for which this region is famous. I learned a lot about guideboats at the museum. There is one whole building devoted to boats and boating, including a real person building one in the exhibit.

Before white trappers and settlers arrived here, the native people got around in dugout canoes, paddling on the rivers and lake. When white folks first moved here there were no railroads and few roads, so they also used the waterways for transportation. They designed a special boat which was easy to row and light enough to hoist up on shoulders to cross the "carries" between lakes. Many Adirondackers served as guides and used these boats to take visitors out hunting and fishing. (Still do, in fact.) Hence, the name guideboats.

Bunny Austin is a fifth generation guide boat builder. His wife Evie canes the seats for his boats. He invited me over to see one and the shed where he works, once it warms up. He also told me a little about his life. He'd grown up poor, in the part of Long Lake known as Kickerville, and had done all kinds of jobs. But about the time the Korean War started he joined the marines, and ended up a pilot flying secret missions during the Cuban Crisis. He'd later gone to Bible College and become an ordained minister, and that's not to mention riding into Long Lake on the fire engine as Santa Claus!

7:30 pm January 31, 2003

I've been packing for my trip south. I asked Jim if I could take a month off to go home, and he said yes. I plan to leave day after tomorrow.

Peter and I drove to Buttermilk Falls this morning with Huck and his dog Chelsea and, in our snow shoes, clambered over the embankment created by the snow plows. The falls looked like the setting for Tchaikovsky's "Snow Queen;" an elaborate stage of frozen sculptures through which flowed the heart of the Raquette River. All but the channel was stopped in motion, tiers of ice in graceful formations wrapped around snow-covered boulders. Deer tracks formed trails in the three-foot-deep snow, and Huck pulled at his leash, wanting to follow.

February 2003

10:30 am February 1, 2003

I woke up early this morning and am sitting in front of the woodstove, thinking about my upcoming trip to Virginia and North Carolina. Going back to Richmond will be hard; seeing Momma the way she is, missing Daddy, passing the home where someone else now lives. Still, it will be great to see my sisters and brother and their children, my old high school friend Sandy, and yes, Momma too. I hope I don't get caught in any snow storms on the way south!

I sip my coffee, gazing into the firebox, and let my mind drift.

*****

Looking back in time, I see a sun-bronzed woman in her mid-twenties, living now in Apache Junction, Arizona, east of Phoenix. Still youthful-looking, her sojourn into marriage has added years to her psyche, and her innocence is all but gone. Her husband Pete has sold his trailer hauling business in Virginia and now, 1975, they have come west.

The Other Side of the Law

The rich colors of the Sonoran Desert flashed by, a calliope of reds and browns, as Pete whipped our Honda 350 around the curves of a small Arizona roadway. The rush of hot air against my face, the snarl of the bike's motor, the precarious angle at which we tilted as we zoomed around curves and through intersections provided a glorious rush of adrenaline. Then, from behind me, I heard the shriek of a siren. A glance back revealed the fast approaching, flashing red and blue lights of a state trooper. I leaned against Pete, his long blonde hair sweeping my cheek, and screamed into his ear. "Cops!"

Pete gunned the engine and a moment later we slid with squealing tires onto a little dirt road. The police car was gaining on us. I bent low to reduce friction, streamlining myself to the shape of the bike. Then, "Hang on!" Pete called to me. Soon we were flying across the ditch that ran beside the road and thumping across the rugged terrain of the desert. I heard the police car screech to a halt, its siren still raging. A quick look showed him out of the car, fist clenched, watching us bounce across rocks and ditches. I held tight, trying to dodge the spines of cholla cacti which reached out for us. I felt the bike slide as Pete barely pulled it out of a fall when we shot into a rocky arroyo. Finally, out of sight of the road,

Pete released the accelerator and we came to a shaky halt. "That was a close one," Pete grinned. "Good thing we don't have a license tag; he was sure close enough to read it!"

I was shaking now, and I clung limply to his waist as we leisurely explored the hillocks and canyons where we found ourselves. The forbidding Superstition Mountains, home of outlaws and the renegade Indian chief Geronimo, loomed above us. We felt right at home. "Old Smokey may be looking for us," Pete said, "so we'll wait till after dark to go home. Then we can slip in with our lights off."

This was one of several times we had evaded the police on our illegal, unlicensed motorcycle out here in the Arizona desert. We didn't have an unlicensed motorcycle exactly by choice. We hadn't had much money, and this bike had been a really good deal--the only one we could afford. But the title was missing, and without it, we could not get tags. And without tags, we had no choice but to try and outrun the cops.

I didn't really approve of the wild, illegal rides I took with Pete, but the bike was fun and the heady exhilaration was hard to resist. Pete ignored my mild protestations, and I knew that if I objected too strongly, he would go without me. So I just held on and reveled in the thrill of the chase and the stark beauty of the Superstition Mountains. When Pete killed the engine and pulled a beer and a blanket from a side pack of the bike, I allowed him to lure me into an evening of love-making under the violent colors of the desert sunset. Then we bounced our way back across the desert and slipped through the darkness into the safety of our house.

We had rented a small terra cotta cottage here a few months before, in the little hamlet of Apache Junction. Pete had a job transporting trailers for Continental Mobile Homes in nearby Mesa, which lay just outside the monstrous, sprawling city of Phoenix. I helped Pete sometimes and waitressed a few nights a week at the Village Inn Pizza Parlor. Most of my time, however, I spent wandering in the desert, enthralled by the flora and fauna that flourished in this rough, arid environment.

We spent a year living in the Sonoran desert. Saving our earnings, we bought a jet boat and explored nearby Canyon Lake, a breath-taking, though environmentally devastating, lake created by damming the Gila River for hydroelectric power. Taking our dogs, Princess and Bojay, with us, we water-skied in its aqua waters by day and camped along its rocky shores under canyon walls at night. We rented horses and searched for the lost gold mine which, according to legend, could be found by following the shadow of Weaver's Needle. We never found the gold, but the riches offered by the mountainous desert were worth far more than gold.

The Sonoran desert in spring was a garden of jewels. There were scarlet blossoms of ocotillos, which conserved water by shedding their leaves in drought; sunshine-yellow blooms of barrel cacti, which hoarded their water in their round bellies; fuchsia-tinted flowers of cholla cacti, whose spines seemed to jump out to seize onto any passersby; delicate hues of pincushion cacti, barely visible in the desert sand. Watching the giant, stately saguaros don their caps of pearly white blossoms, seeing the once-in-a-lifetime profusion of canary-colored flowers on soon-to-die, agaves, or century plants--these were the riches bestowed by the desert.

Fleet-footed roadrunners, spry jackrabbits, huge, hairy tarantulas, and night-dwelling kangaroo rats all lived here. Spiny horned toads (actually lizards,) harmless kingsnakes, and deadly rattlers, even a Gila monster--these were its hidden treasures. Once, scrambling across a pile of talus, I came face to face with a wily bobcat, who stared at me through mysterious golden eyes before disappearing into the brush.

Pete and I never did get caught by the police, but our motorcycle riding came to an abrupt end one autumn morning when Pete, alone on the bike, took a flying leap across a rocky crag and landed in a pile at the bottom. I was watching from a nearby hill, and I ran down to him with my heart in my throat. A trip to the emergency room revealed that he had broken his collarbone and damaged his shoulder. We sold what was left of the bike and, not too long afterward, packed our van and headed for California.

Our bike-riding adventures were not the only times Pete and I found ourselves on the other side of the law. Our relationship had been born flouting authority, and it never changed tracks. Pete and I always seemed to be evading the police, or "pigs," as he called them.

The months we'd spent traveling and living in our van, it seemed like every other night we'd wake to lights flashing in our eyes. We'd grab blankets and pull on clothes with trembling fingers as knuckles tapped on our windows, flashlights exposing our every move. They'd sniff the air and search through Pete's ashtray, looking for signs of marijuana or other drugs, but beer was the only drug we had. They would tell us we were parked illegally, so move on.

"All right, all right! It's not like we're doing any harm, for gosh sakes!" we'd tell the ubiquitous cops. Sometimes they'd tell us where the nearest campground was, (as if we could afford it!) "Okay, we're leaving," we'd

tell them. Then we'd drive on down the road and find another illegal but free place to spend the rest of the night, cursing a society where, if you didn't have money or sign on the dotted line to be like everyone else, your very existence was against the law.

There was the time that Pete's rock and roll band "Salt Air," playing at a big outdoor party near Richmond, got raided by a whole slew of policemen. Pete had the microphone, and he began warning the party-goers; "The pigs are here! Swallow your dope everybody. The pigs are here!" One of the officers jumped up on stage and snatched the microphone away from him, telling him to go home. Pete backed off, but as soon as the cop moved away he grabbed the microphone again and repeated the warnings. As two policemen rushed back up to the stage Pete told me to take his guitar and make a run for it. He grabbed his amp and the two of us hauled ass, in his terminology, running into the woods and coming around from the back to get to our van. Then we took off.

Pete bought me a big, beautifully tooled leather pocket-book for Christmas one year. I was thrilled by his generosity, till I realized that he had an ulterior motive. He could stash three cans of beer in it and sneak them into places they were not allowed!

Upon arrival at a big outdoor Lynyrd Skynyrd concert one day in Arizona, I found out why he had encouraged me to wear long pants and a jacket. He stuffed beer cans down every nook and cranny he could find, then strolled in beside me in cutoffs and a tee-shirt, innocent as a babe. I was the one who got searched and thrown out of the concert! Most of the time I grinned good-naturedly and loved him all the more for his wild ways.

Accepting the financial irregularities in his, and now my, life was more difficult. I never adjusted to the fear and shame of having bill collectors knocking on the door, bad check notices filling the mailbox. Pete did not seem to let such things bother him. When our electricity was cut off in Claremont he went out to the box and cut it back on. When it was turned off again he turned it on again. I was the one who was there when the meter man, now furious, returned the third time. He put a lock on the box and reamed me out thoroughly, threatening to bring the police next time.

I didn't grin when I had to pick Pete up at the local jail for drinking and driving, or when the neighbors told me our house was under police surveillance for drug-dealing.

Something of an anarchist myself, I can't claim that Pete taught me all my law-breaking ways. My parents were good law-abiding citizens, my father honest to a fault, but I was always eager for new experiences. I had tried shoplifting a pair of sunglasses while in high school just to see what it felt like. It felt awful, and I couldn't sleep until I returned them (it was much harder sneaking them back into the store than it had been getting them out!)

I'd been thrown out of uncountable restaurants for refusing to wear shoes, lost job opportunities for refusing to conform to dress codes. I'd been picked up by the state police for hitchhiking in Tennessee and hauled into the jailhouse. (After scaring me to death and threatening to lock me up for a week, the policeman bought me a bus ticket home to Richmond.)

My earlier ventures, however, had been the purposeful, idealistic acts of a young middle class woman rebelling against what she considered the inequities and false values of a materialistic society. She might walk in the shoes of the down-and-out, wear the sandals of law-breakers, but she knew there were other shoes in her closet.

Over the years I spent with Pete the thrill and excitement dissolved. The piquancy of belonging to the class of underdogs gave way to the reality of being poor and despised. The person I became during the years I was with Pete was no longer middle class or acting on idealistic principles. She was no longer playing a sympathetic role. The shoes she now wore were the only pair she had, and sometimes they were pretty down-at-the-heels.

I learned how bank tellers look at you when they tell you that your account is overdrawn. I learned what it feels like to beg for a waitress job. To stand in line for government surplus cheese and flour. To pay for your groceries with food stamps.

I learned how, once you're down, it's next to impossible to get up. How our society, whether by accident or intent, rigs all the ropes so that the poor stay poor; so that breaking the law seems like the only way to survive. I learned how it feels when you believe that however bad it gets, you deserve it anyway. I learned the meaning of helpless anger, of hopelessness. I learned the meaning of shame.

I watched Pete try to get up over and over. "Bad luck," he kept saying. I heard it from others, our friends, and I started to believe it. But it was luck brought about by our own shortfalls, and by a system that gives no mercy to renegades. It was luck brought about by believing that you didn't really have a chance anyway, so you may as well grab for whatever solace you could get, be it beer or drugs or a stolen chainsaw blade. And if you did manage to achieve success, you didn't have any practice in knowing how to use it, so you blew it. Pete and I did a lot of "blowing it" back then...

Thinking about it now, I do not regret those days. They were, as Charles Dickens once said, "the best of times and the worst of times." They taught me things I never learned in graduate school. They taught me that living by your conscience is not necessarily the same thing as living by the law. That some of the most decent people are, by American standards, losers; and some of the most successful, jerks. They taught me to be slow to judge and quick to try and understand, and to remember the words Jesus purportedly spoke, "Let he who is free of sin cast the first stone."

*****

10:30 am February 4, 2003

Snow again. It falls almost daily, and the temperature seems to be doing the same. It was minus 14 this morning. I get up several times each night to add another log. The fire in my woodstove has become the focal point of my life. When it goes out, the room feels as empty as if a lover had walked out the door.

Yet I live in fear of that same fire, particularly when I am gone. Chimney fire! It's a specter that haunts all who depend on wood heat. I had a chimney fire at my house in Washington one winter. It was terrifying, producing what sounded like a locomotive thundering through my living room. I was lucky; that fire stayed in the chimney and did no harm other than some smoke damage. I bought a fire suppressant-- "ChimFix"--made specifically for putting out chimney fires, the last time I was in Tupper Lake. It sits on a shelf not far from my woodstove. I hope I don't have to use it.

It was Prometheus who brought us fire, having stolen it from the gods (at least that's what Greek mythology says.) Zeus was furious! Fire gave man the ability to do things formerly reserved for the residents of Mt. Olympus. Things were never the same again.

Anthropologists are more inclined to give lightning the credit for men learning to use fire. It was probably many eons after discovering the value of fire that they learned how to produce it themselves. In the meantime, being the keeper of the fire was a job of Olympic proportions.

When I was eleven, I helped my father put out a fire that started back home in our woods in Short Pump. I remember the fear, quickly overcome by the rush of adrenaline and the sense of purpose that had us beating out the flames with our jackets. By the time the fire trucks arrived, Daddy and I were exhausted, covered in soot, and coughing from breathing in the smoke. But we had put the worst of it out. The firemen sprayed down the blackened ground with water to be sure, and then tried to determine its cause. We never knew for sure, but our neighbor had seen hunters there that day. We guessed that they had thrown a cigarette into the leaves, then walked carelessly away. Frightening!

For now, though, fire is my best friend.

6 pm February 7, 2003
On the way home I saw a coyote standing on the side of the road. I slowed down and watched him. He stared back at me, his yellow eyes unfathomable, before turning and slipping silently into the woods. Most people here hate coyotes. They creep into their yards, they say, working in packs to snatch their cats or small dogs.

They weren't here when these mountains were first settled. They've moved in, like ghosts, to replace the gray wolves that once roamed these mountains. These eastern coyotes are much larger than the ones out west. Some people say they're really small wolves, though the park rangers deny it. In the museum's "Woods and Waters" exhibit there is a stuffed wolf, his eyes protruding in what appears to be an expression of outrage.

Wolves or coyotes, I like them. They have more right to be here, I figure, than I do, although I hope they stay away from my cabin. I'll try to keep Miss Kelley inside. I would not want them around if she decided to slip out the door.

There are foxes here as well, both red and gray. I sometimes see one down near where the old Sagamore Hotel stood, and I often see tracks near my cabin. It is of foxes that I am thinking as I work on this next piece.

*****

Pete and I had moved again, leaving Arizona so Pete could take a job hauling mobile homes in southern California. We rented a modest little house in Riverside, outside of Los Angeles, and I rode with Pete, as his assistant, as he delivered trailers to San Diego, San Juan Capistrano, and Palm Springs. We camped at Big Bear, in the Joshua Tree National Park, on the shore of the Salton Sea. Once our van broke down on a torrid 110 degree summer day in Death Valley and we had to be rescued.

We were happy for a while, but as usual things started going downhill. After a year we decided that it would be best for me to go back to my parents' home in Virginia, and then we would see what happened...

Living with Foxes; Living on the Edge

It was 1977, the year of my sister Nancy's wedding. She and Jim were married in Colorado Springs, and my husband Pete and I drove there from California, having just moved out of our house in Riverside. We arrived just as the final rehearsal began, and I was rushed by my family out of the van and into the chapel. I was, after all, the matron of honor and played an essential role in the proceedings.

They were upset that I was so late, which I could not understand. I'd made it, hadn't I? In the van, a white 1971 Ford Econoline, were Bo, a black lab mix; two doberman pinschers, Princess and Maybe; five of Maybe's puppies; and two cats, Sam and Foxey. It is hard to travel fast with such a load, and besides, the van had been acting up, I told them. I did not explain that Pete had been playing music and drinking with his friends when he should have been working on the van, and as a result we were a day late leaving.

It was a little tricky convincing the Sheraton Hotel to allow all those animals in the room, but we did. The wedding went off without a hitch.

Afterwards Pete and I headed east. Pete was taking me, the dogs, and the cats back to Virginia, after which he planned to return to California. We did not call it a separation. I do not recall what we told my family. I do not recall what we told each other.

An hour outside of Colorado Springs the van stopped moving. It simply slid to a halt. Pete, the dogs, the puppies, the cats and I were stranded in the midst of a flat, empty landscape which stretched to the horizon. Pete started walking, with Bo tagging along; I stayed with the other animals. Cars passed, but I ignored them, lying on the bed in the van and staring at the ceiling with a numbing sense of despair.

Eventually a pickup truck pulled up behind me, and Pete got out with a weathered, red-capped rancher. He took a toolbox out of the truck bed, and they set to work under the hood. Pete came back in a little while, his face covered with grease and a grim expression. "What is your sister's phone number?" The transmission, it seemed, was gone; shot; ruined. The "acting up" that it had been doing on the trip to Colorado Springs had now acted "out" of ever working again.

The rancher took a liking to Bo, and vice-versa. Pete told the rancher to keep him, and I was too numb to argue. Under the circumstances, letting him have him seemed like the logical thing to do.

My new brother-in-law Jim interrupted his honeymoon and came to pick us up. We returned to Colorado Springs, where we all moved into his apartment (he and my sister were staying at a motel.) Pete called his mother for money, and three days and a new transmission later, we set out for Richmond again. Pete left me there and returned with his dog, Maybe, to his job in California. I took back my old job as a waitress at Gim Din, a Chinese restaurant where my sister Sally worked. I spent the next two months serving up dishes of wonton soup, shrimp fried rice, and moo goo gai pan.

Then, in June, I got a ride back to California with my best friend, Sandy, and another friend of hers, both wanting to see the west. Princess and Sam stayed with my parents. The puppies had, meanwhile, been sold or given away, and my beloved little grey kitty, Foxey had disappeared.

We had a pleasant trip and I was soon reunited with Pete. He was living in his van in San Bernardino, a border between the sprawling city of Los Angeles and the Mohave Desert., which is how and where I came to share a home with a family of red foxes.

The plan had been for Pete to return to his job in L.A. and save some money, while I did the same in Virginia. Then, when I returned, we would set out again in search of a new life. Except that when I got there, Pete hadn't saved any money. We had to stay there so Pete could continue his job working on mobile homes.

The van was parked in a barren area of eroded desert, rock, and arroyos; a place claimed by no one, where we could trespass at will. It appeared to have been a dumping ground for abandoned washing machines and pickup trucks at one time, their decomposing skeletons now half-buried in dried tumbleweed. Twisted cholla and sprawling prickly pear cacti pushed up through the arid soil, and an occasional stunted palmetto suggested that once there had been water here. Small Joshua trees crouched beside rock out-crops, their hairy arms twisted in unlikely positions, as if ordered to freeze in the midst of a wild dance.

Derelict spires rose from scorched, still-sharp skeletal leaves left behind by century plants after their once-in-a-lifetime orgasmic blooming.

It was a sort of hinterland, somehow left behind and forgotten by Southern California's boomtown economy. Pete had the use of a company truck to drive, and sometimes, when his boss had work for me, I went along and did odd jobs. Most of the time, however, I stayed behind in the van, reading, sketching, and wandering, a stranger in a strange land.

One day I noticed the red fox. She was standing atop a huge rock, on a hill not far from the van. She was watching me, standing perfectly still, her coat a burnished red, a flash of white on the tip of her tail. Then she was gone. I saw her again the next day, and then a day later her mate was there, on a nearby outcrop. We became accustomed to each other. I watched them enter the crevice in the rock, carrying a gopher or garter snake, sometimes still alive, and come out empty-mouthed. Then one day I saw the kits, two at first, then a third. They were playing at the entrance to their den. As soon as I moved, they disappeared.

Over the next few weeks, however, they became accustomed to Pete and me. The vixen would lie on the rock, eyes half open, as the kits frolicked below, chasing grasshoppers and snapping at each other in real or pretend disputes. It became apparent that they were establishing their dominance, and soon it was easy to pick out the alpha kit. I would sit nearby and watch their aerial contortions and pouncing games. Later, the adult foxes would disappear, leaving the kits out in view. I pretended that I was their babysitter, entrusted by the parents with the protection of their young. Perhaps it was true.

I wandered along the barren gully, littered with broken beer bottles and used-up shotgun shells, seeking respite to my boredom and despair. I discovered where a burrowing owl had its home, a nest-hole in the ground, and I sat for hours, watching it as it ventured out to hunt. I located the entrances to gopher holes and waited patiently for them to stick their heads out. I picked out the erratic tracks left behind by sidewinders, the small desert rattlesnakes who never moved in a straight forward line.

I mulled over the enigma of my marriage. I loved Pete with a passion that was obsessive, but my life with him seemed to be headed down a ravine as full of discarded dreams as this gully. Looking ahead, I saw no gleam of light at the end. Only the foxes seemed to thrive in this wasteland.

Pat Garber

We took a trip to the Baja Peninsula of Mexico, camping along desert beaches and cooking gulf lobsters on campfires. We hid two young, swarthy-skinned men, fleeing from the Mexican border patrol, in the back of our van, later trying to emulate a proper accent as we answered "No problema" to their effusive cries of "Gracias." We watched a dog spin in circles, its drunken owner doubled over in laughter, calling "tequila!" in a gleeful Spanish accent when he saw us watching.

One morning when we returned to our van after camping near the water's edge, we found that it had been broken into. We spent a frustrating day at a police station where no one, we were told, spoke English. We gave up eventually on even reporting, much less retrieving, our stolen goods.

Having endured an intimidating drug search by Mexican Federales, we recalled stories we had heard about drug plants in this country; about Americans locked up for months for drugs they had never possessed.

Later, we spent three nights with an old Mexican couple in a sod shack, and the senora showed me how to cook tortillas on a wood stove. We swam in the surf nearby with Pacific harbor seals, as intrigued by us as we were by them.

It was an exciting trip; an idyllic break of the kind that kept me coming back to Pete, feeding my starved love just enough to keep it alive.

Then we returned to San Bernardino. We saw the foxes a few more times. The kits were growing, and from a distance it was hard to distinguish them from their parents. They roamed farther from their den, seeking out berries and other food. They stalked desert mice, seizing them with cat-like, semi-retractile claws and dagger-like teeth. They were preparing for their own solitary lives in the desert.

Finally, realizing that we were getting nowhere, Pete and I returned to Virginia. We rented a small house in Oilville, just west of Richmond. That lasted three months. Then I moved out; another mini-separation. He went to Myrtle Beach, SC, where he was going to make lots of money putting siding on condominiums. Something went wrong and he came back penniless.

We rented a tiny apartment, crawling with cockroaches, near the Chinese restaurant where I once again worked. For entertainment Pete (when he was there) lay on the couch and threw darts at the roaches as they skittered along the walls. He was going to get a job, but it didn't pan out. Two months later I left again, broken-hearted. Princess and I fled in a little orange Honda Civic, heading for an ambiguous destination...West.

160

*****

But I have lost track of myself. It was foxes I was talking about. Now I am once again living with red foxes, at the edge of this Adirondack wilderness. I see their tracks in the snow every morning when I head down the hill to work, crossing the path just a few feet from the cabin. Huck sniffs their scent in excitement when he passes by. A book I recently bought about them says that they thrive in the vicinity of humans. Because of their adaptability they have the widest distribution of any carnivore in the world.

I raise my eyes now and gaze at the fox on the opposite wall; a young red vixen I painted years ago with watercolors, sable bristles, and soft strokes. Self-portrait, perhaps I should call it. For I am a fox now, traversing the edges of different worlds; watching, taking pictures and notes in my mind, almost but not altogether a part of a hundred habitats, seeking answers in my self-imposed solitude. I like the sound of it, the way it slides across my tongue; "I am a red fox, living on the edge."

It is getting late now, and I have a long trip tomorrow. I am going to Richmond and then to Ocracoke. Time for bed.

6:00 pm February 27, 2003

I got home from Virginia last night after a long, difficult drive. The weather forecast predicted good weather, but apparently the weather gods weren't listening. Somewhere north of Binghamton, snow began to fall and soon I found myself in a white-out. I crawled along, scared to death, till I saw a motel sign and an exit off I-81. I didn't think twice about what it would cost--I got a room and collapsed in relief, then spent the rest of the evening watching cable tv with Huck and Miss Kelley curled up next to me. It was still spitting snow in the morning, but not too bad, and it stopped soon after I reached I-90 and passed Syracuse.

I went skiing today, reveling in the sharp twang of the sub-zero-degree air on my face as I glided up and down the hills. Now I'm sitting before the wood stove, trying to reconnect with the cabin and trying to process some of the things that happened while I was in Richmond and Ocracoke. I think back to two conversations I had while I was in Ocra-coke. One was on an evening when I had dinner at the home of two good friends. When I asked how their daughter was doing, they answered, "She's decided to make Pat Garber her role model, and frankly, we're scared to death." I didn't know what to say. "Don't get us wrong," they added. "We admire you greatly, but we're worried about her trying to live like you do."

The second conversation was with a person I'd never met before, an older woman who knocked on my door one afternoon as I was roasting yaupon tea in my oven. She'd been looking everywhere for a copy of my first book, *Ocracoke Wild,* to buy for her sister, and was distressed to learn that it was out of print and could be found in none of the shops. She'd bought a copy of my second book, *Ocracoke Odyssey,* she said, but desperately wanted *Wild.* She apologized for bothering me and asked if there was any way I could get it for her. I told her that she was not bothering me, and that I still had a few copies and would sell her one. Before she left, she told me that, in looking back over her life, she wished that she had lived hers like I was living mine.

What, I wonder, do those two similar yet disparate statements mean? What responsibility do they lay upon me and how can I possibly live up to it? I remember other conversations. Another friend, before she moved away from Ocracoke, told me about her daughter in Washington who was trying to pursue an idealistic dream without considering money or benefits. "I keep telling her it can't be done," she said, "but then I think about you. You do it all the time!"

I recall the phone conversation I had with a secretary who had organized one of my *Ocracoke Wild* book talks. She told me that after reading the book and hearing me speak she had decided to quit her job and change the way she lived her life. I didn't know what to say.

What is there in my life that is good, that people would want to emulate? I see so much that I regret, that I would have done differently. The hounds of guilt nip constantly at my heels, and I feel like a hypocrite when others look at me with respect. I envy those people who are content with what they have, not always yearning for something more. I envy those people who have a husband and a family, not just a string of crazy dreams and stories. I need to find a way to weave these stories into some kind of foundation upon which I can build the rest of my life, a life that I can believe in and truly be proud of.

6:45 pm February 28, 2003

There was an article in the newspaper today about Canadian wolves crossing the St. Lawrence Seaway and entering the United States. I read it while working at the diner, and it got everyone at the counter talking about wolves coming back to the Adirondacks. Some people think they will follow the moose back. A lot of people swear that they are here now. Some think that they were never completely extirpated; others that the Adirondack Park Agency re-introduced them without letting anyone know. My friend Peter says that the canids that live in the Adirondacks are really hybrids anyway; half eastern red wolf and half western coyote. I love the idea of wolves re-colonizing the Adirondacks. This newspaper story reinforces that possibility.

Pat Garber

March 2003

10:15 am March 2, 2003

My job at the diner has not resumed yet, and without a work schedule to put a date on the days they meld together. I am a hermit again, snowshoeing down the hill to buy milk and eggs, then returning to my solitude.

The snow is deep, the temperatures well below zero every night. I've been playing my guitar all morning, sitting in front of the woodstove with a blanket wrapped around me. Practicing old songs I haven't sung in a long time--"Dust in the Wind," "Stairway to Heaven," "Diamonds and Rust." Wondering what they mean, what emotions and stories inspired their creation. Another song pops into my head, drawing me back in time. I find myself once more walking away (driving, actually) from my marriage to Pete, listening to the throbbing lyrics of Bob Seeger's "Stranger in Town."

*****

I look at the woman I see now, 27 years old, embarking on a new life. Devastated when she left, she now feels like a different person, a person she doesn't quite recognize but wants to get to know better...

On the Oregon Trail

"Polly want a cracker?"

I peered across the counter at the bearded man before me. "It's not a Polly," I informed him dryly. "And he doesn't eat crackers. He likes fresh fruit." The object of our discussion, a two-year-old double-crested yellow parrot, chose that moment to squawk out a rather ragged "Get Lost!" causing the man to jump back. I grinned. "Hi John. Good to see you!" Glancing at my watch, I informed him that I had another hour to work.

This was my day job (I also worked three nights a week as a cocktail waitress at a nightclub called Bogey's.) I'd started work here, at the Dog Chalet, two months before, waiting on customers and taking care of the odd assortment of animals we had. Jake here was one of my favorites, with an amusing vocabulary and an ornery tendency to bite when least expected.

We also had a boa constrictor, several tarantulas, cockatiels, para-keets, finches, guinea pigs, gerbils, and rats. One of the rats, a large black one of venerable age, was sitting in my lap at the moment. I held

*him up, his long tail a' dangling, and introduced him. "Sam, meet John."
Then, opening my hand, I let him scurry up my arm and nuzzle into the
folds of my long straight hair, from which haven he turned and studied
John, his nose twitching.*

*John was a tall, rugged-looking man with a full beard and a head of
wavy brown hair. I'd met him a few months before, when I first arrived in
Oregon. He was a forest ranger, living in the town of Corvallis. He'd
driven across the Cascade Mountains today to visit me here in Bend, the
rugged little mountain town, nestled in the shadow of the Three Sisters,
which I now called home. He thought he'd take a walk, he said, and meet
me back here at five. It was a slow day, so after he left, I sat back on my
stool, stroking Sam and remembering the day John and I had met.*

*I had, in great anguish, left my husband Pete three weeks before,
driving due west from the grungy, cockroach-ridden apartment we were
renting in Richmond, Virginia. I was traveling with Princess, my doberman pinscher, in a little orange Honda just purchased with a loan from
my father. I'd gone to Riverside, California, for a visit with my sister
Nancy and her husband Jim; then headed north. I was planning to meet
my parents, on vacation and traveling by train, in Bend, Oregon.
Somewhere along the way I hoped to find a place to live. Nancy and Jim
had given me an early birthday present, a tape player for my car, which
Jim installed. I had splurged and bought Bob Seeger's tape, "A Stranger
in Town," and I had listened to him sing about broken hearts and "Who
needs tomorrow?" all the way to Oregon (which may, in a certain way,
have accounted for my getting to know John so quickly.)*

*Having left Riverside, I had stopped in a small northern California
town for the night. I couldn't find a campground, but I saw what looked
like a nice little house with no one living in it. There was a cot on the
back porch, so I laid my sleeping bag on it, called Princess up to sleep
next to me, and cried myself to sleep. Which would have been fine, except
that I learned the next morning that it had been full of fleas (no longer;
now Princess was full of fleas instead!)*

*I listened to her scratch as we drove north, and when we arrived in
Corvallis, where I planned to spend the night, I looked for a drugstore
where I could get flea powder. I didn't see a drug store, but I did see a
cozy looking tavern. A cold beer sounded great, and I needed to make a
phone call, which I was sure I could do there. I got a beer, found a seat in
a booth, and tried to make my call. The phone was busy. In the booth
behind me were three men. They spoke to me when they saw me repeat-*

edly walk to the phone, and asked me if I would like to join them. I was lonely, so I agreed. They were forest rangers, I soon learned, just getting off work, all quite attractive. We talked for a while, and in the conversation I admitted that I had no idea where I was going to sleep that night.

I soon had three invitations. All three men, it seemed, were single and had spare bedrooms or at least couches. Quite a dilemma! How was I going to decide? I thought about Princess waiting for me in the car, still scratching, no doubt. "Well..." I asked, "Do any of you happen to have any flea powder?" John won. He had recently lost his dog, but still had a container of flea powder!

I followed him to his house, a nice but simple bachelor's pad. He ordered a pizza and, while I dusted Princess and took a hot bath, he picked it up. Pizza, a bottle of wine, and the memory of Bob Seeger's song, "Here we are, both of us lonely, searching for love..." Well, I didn't need the extra bedroom.

He fixed breakfast the next morning, neither of us saying much. He had to go to work, and I still had miles to drive. Neither of us mentioned tomorrow; neither of us asked for phone number, address, or even a last name. I drove away with an empty feeling, not expecting to ever see John again. On across the Cascades, their snow-capped peaks glistening in the thin air, through towering red cedars and hemlocks, to the land of red-barked ponderosa pines and ancient volcanoes. When I crossed the Deschutes River and pulled up in Bend, I knew immediately that my journey was over. This was where I would stay! I met my parents and we spent an enjoyable few days. Nancy and Jim drove up from California, and we went to Crater Lake and Mt. Rainier. After they left, I set about finding a job and a place to live.

It didn't take long to connect with Kathy, a young, cute, and vivacious dog-groomer who needed a roommate at her new apartment. The Grizzly Bear Pizza Parlor needed help, and that meant not just a job, but free pizza! I was all set. But I was still lonely, missing Pete. I blocked him out of my mind, but allowed my thoughts to return to John. Maybe I should give him a call...

I had no idea, however, how to get hold of him. All I knew about him, really, was his first name and that he was a forest ranger. I wondered how many Johns worked for the U.S. Forest Service in Corvallis. I decided to find out...

The first John was the wrong one, which was a little embarrassing. "Hi. Is this the John I spent the night with a few weeks ago?" "Um...Nooo...I don't think so..." It took me a couple days to get enough courage to try the next one. I wasn't at all sure he'd be happy to hear from me, if I did find him. But he was. He was thrilled, in fact, and wanted to come visit me on his next days off.

We began dating, him driving to Bend whenever he could find time. He told me about his life as a ranger, fighting fires and policing the woods. Originally from Minnesota, he had come to Oregon to study forestry at the university in Portland, and had stayed. He brought me smoked salmon, which he had caught in the Willamette River and smoked himself. We went to the Bend Woolen Mill, once a working mill, now a sometimes rowdy bar. He told me that I was his fantasy woman, a concept which I found hard to believe. I could not imagine being any man's fantasy, but it was an exciting idea.

Meanwhile, I was falling in love with Bend, central Oregon, and my new life. Sharing an apartment with Kathy, I learned, meant sharing her life: her friends, her activities, her never-ending string of crises. Which, since I had no life of my own, was just fine.

Kathy was a rich kid, an only child, who had decided to drop out of college, move away from her parents' home in western Oregon and make it on her own in Bend. She took a dog-grooming course, found the apartment we were to share, and jumped in with both feet. She was not used to the sparse living which her decision required, however, and she was not used to jumping through the hoops needed to set up her own dog grooming business. She seemed to be constantly at the edge of financial ruin. Her relationship with her boyfriend was always at the point of traumatic collapse or romantic making up. Her constant dilemmas, each accompanied by histrionics and tears, drew my attention away from myself and gave me something to concentrate on. Kathy's generosity and ability to laugh at herself made her faults forgivable, and she was always able to cheer me up, even in my most morose moods.

Bend in 1977 was like a frontier town. It still had a touch of old west wildness to it, and the fragrance of ponderosa pine stirred my soul. Perched in the foothills of the Cascade Mountains, it was surrounded by reminders of its volcanic origins. Bear Creek Butte loomed to the east and Mt. Bachelor, a volcanic peak which now served as a ski resort, towered nearby. Jagged hills and craters of old lava begged for explor-

ing. Just out of town were several waterfalls which, when winter came, froze into exquisite ice sculptures.

I hiked and camped with Kathy and her friends, taking Princess everywhere I went. One day, having back-packed to remote Culter's Lake with three friends, I watched Princess tear up to me with an anguished expression and a nose-full of porcupine quills. Kathy's boyfriend had a plier-like attachment on his pocketknife, so he pulled them out, one by one, as I held her, whining, in my arms. Another time she met up with a skunk, which left his mark on her for a number of days, despite the tomato juice and vinegar baths I gave her.

I did not make much at the Grizzly Bear, so I had to watch my pennies closely. I fell in love, however, with a large watercolor print, a limited edition signed by B Forbes and titled "Westward." It depicted a plains Indian against a background of, at the top, a bison, and at the bottom, a train. The Indian is a complete man at the top, but his form almost disappears where back-dropped against the train at the bottom. The print symbolized much of what I believed about human ideas of progress. Not having enough money to buy it outright, I put it on layaway, putting a little of my tips towards its purchase each week. My sense of pride when I was finally able to take it home was immense.

My job at the Grizzly Bear came to an abrupt end when Fred, a new assistant manager who thought he was hot stuff, gave me a ridiculous order, which I refused to obey. He told me that if I didn't, I was fired. I took off my apron, shoved it into his hand, and walked out. A few days later when I went back to get my paycheck, the manager, who had been out of town, told me that Fred did not have the authority to fire me and was, in fact, being terminated himself. I was welcome to come back, he said. I had by then however, already found the job at the pet store, and I wanted to keep it.

I loved working at the pet shop, though I knew it was a seasonal job and would end after Christmas. I learned everything I could about the animals, and I met interesting people. Carol, another employee, was an animal lover and outdoor woman. Carol became my good friend, and we spent a great deal of time together.

In Bend, I discovered that I liked women, and they liked me. I had, in recent years, made only a few friends, finding little in common with the women I waitressed with or Pete's friends' girlfriends. I assumed that I had some abnormality; a social faux pas that precluded normal friendships and having a good time with other members of my sex. In

Bend I learned that there were other young women with the same interests and values, who actually enjoyed my company. It came as a shock. I stopped trying to be someone different than who I was. The experience was exhilarating.

I saved my money and when the first snows arrived, in November, I bought a pair of cross country skis. What a world of wonder that opened up! I could ski right out the door of my apartment into a winter wonderland. From then on I skied every day I could, meeting new people and exploring new places.

I missed Pete terribly, though I tried hard not to think about him. I had not spoken to him since walking out the door all those months before. To my knowledge, he had no idea of what I was doing or where; and I wanted it that way, with no chance of false hopes or broken dreams. John, who loved Bend, was trying to get transferred to the Forest Service here. He came as often as he could, and we had some good times together. But now, as I sat in the pet shop stroking Sam and contemplating our relationship, I realized that it was going nowhere. I saw him a few more times and then told him a final goodbye.

I dated a few other guys, but nothing serious. I was not, I realized, ready to fall for another man. Hard as I tried to suppress my feelings for Pete, they were still there. There was nothing, however, to limit my love affair with Bend and central Oregon. I wandered through old lava beds, the black glass so sharp it would cut through the soles of my shoes. I picked up pieces of obsidian and volcanic lava, tucking them into the pockets of my jeans. I visited an observatory on a nearby hill one night and stared through a telescopic lens at a black hole: the remains of a star, billions of miles away, that no longer existed. I camped on a high desert landscape where still-existing stars spanned the sky like falling snow.

One night, as I lay in bed after an evening working at the nightclub, Kathy out of town, I heard the doorbell ring. I turned on the light and peered at the clock beside my bed. It was 1:30 a.m. Who on earth??? Pulling on a bathrobe, I padded to the door and opened it. On the doorstep, backpack sitting on the stoop beside him, stood Pete.

I never asked him how he'd found me. It didn't matter. I never asked myself if it was wise to take him back. Wisdom had never played a part in our relationship. We stayed in Bend for another month or so. I introduced him to my friends, and we had some good times, tubing on the snow-packed mountainsides, talking over mugs of beer. We spent Christmas in *a log cabin on Paulina Lake, in the mountains, snowmobiling to the cabin with Princess running alongside.*

But this was my life, not his, and I think we both knew we would be leaving. He couldn't find a job in Bend, and my meager salary could not support the two of us. He was offered a job working as a mobile home serviceman in Chehalis, near the Washington coast, and we decided to go. Pete had left his van with a friend somewhere to the south, so he hitchhiked back down and drove it back. Then we headed out.

I left Bend, taking with me only my dog Princess, my cross-country skis, the "Westward" water color, and my newly discovered sense of self-worth.

Years later, I returned to Bend, hoping to find what I had left behind. The interim years had changed the little town. It had grown by leaps and bounds. The pet shop was gone, my friends untraceable. The frontier aura, the feel of the Wild West had been replaced by what seemed to me an artificial facade of yuppie prosperity and tourism. The apartment where I had lived, on the edge of town, remained, but it was barely recognizable, crowded in the midst of new structures. The Bend Woolen Mill was still there, but I recognized no one when I stepped inside. The landscape was still beautiful, but I drove away with a sense of sadness and nostalgia, an unknown stranger in the town which had helped me to know myself. I still have the "Westward" print I had worked so hard to buy, and I still treasure it.

*****

7 pm March 3, 2003

The trails through the woods here are deep now, carved out of the snow by deer, followed by the many creatures who inhabit this mountain. Today I decided to follow one. Hoping to see some such creatures, I left Huck at home with Miss Kelley.

Putting on my snow shoes, I started down the snowmobile trail to where I knew a deer trail crossed, and detoured onto it. The snow rose two to three feet on each side of the narrow, winding path. I walked carefully, placing my snowshoes one in front of the other. When it forked, I took the left fork. It forked again and I followed the right one. I continued on, studying the tracks I saw along the way, wondering who had made them--fisher? fox? maybe a bobcat? Where were they going, and why? Looking for signs--bark stripped off tree trunks, scat containing hair or plant matter. Deer pellets were everywhere, but then, I already knew deer used this trail. They followed it to my cabin each morning, when the first rays of sunlight were filtering through the treetops, to feed on the sunflower seeds I had set out by the woodpile.

Finally, as the sky darkened, I stopped and turned around. I started back, but as I tried to retrace my tracks I found myself lost. The marks made by my snowshoes, which I had thought I could follow, were indistinguishable amidst the other tracks. This path, which I thought would lead me back to the snowmobile trail, just led to another crooked deer trail, more wilderness blanketed in snow. I doubled back, but could not find the original trail.

Soon I found myself more confused than ever, and I started to panic. I wondered how long I could wander before coming upon some sign of human presence, how long before total darkness would encompass me. I wondered how long it might be, were I to really disappear, before someone would come to my cabin to check on me. How long Huck and Miss Kelley could survive alone there. As I stumbled on, I felt a strange calmness descend upon me, as if such a fate was meant to be.

I knew, of course, that I was not truly lost. The highway lay at the bottom of this mountain, and while it might be a long and gnarly trip, if I bushwhacked my way down toward the sound of those distant, annoying lumber truck jay-brakes, I would eventually reach civilization. I allowed myself the exhilarating terror, however, of imagining that I was truly lost in the wilderness. Then I stumbled by accident onto the snowmobile trail and headed home.

Now I have pulled out Reverend John Todd's book, "Long Lake," written in 1845, and I read what he wrote then. *"The sensation of being lost in this vast forest is horrific beyond description...It is probably as near derangement as can be, if there is any difference..."*

I could understand what he meant.

11 pm March 5, 2003

There was only one red-breasted nuthatch this morning. I looked out the window repeatedly, hoping to see its partner. Always, they were together, though I did not know if they were mates. I am saddened as I wonder what has become of the missing one. Songbirds have, I have read, an annual mortality rate of 80%. It boggles my mind whenever I think of it. Four out of every five birds I see will most likely be dead this time next year. This is reality, truth as we know it in the 21st century. There is a huge array of threats out there...cats...picture windows and towers...loss of habitat.

Loss of habitat, that is the biggest threat, particularly as the rain forests in Central and South America get mowed down daily. But birds are not the only ones who lose their homes in the name of dollar signs and progress. My home in Short Pump is gone now, destroyed by the deception and greed of the Catholic Church, or at least some of its businessmen, who promised my parents that, if they sold it to them, our house would be preserved. Hah! They turned around and sold it to developers, who tore everything down. It is the same thing that's driving the red-cockaded woodpecker, the bobwhite quail, and the Bachman's warbler to extinction. Too many people and that ugly, uniquely human characteristic, greed...

It's pointless to sit here mourning for one little nuthatch, I know...

The coyotes are about tonight. I can hear their howls resounding from the hilltops. It sounds like they are everywhere, but I know that is probably an illusion. Huck heard them first. I felt him lift his head, then step quietly off the couch. He is nervous and barks with a low woof every few moments. Miss Kelley, too, is nervous, pacing about the cabin. What, I wonder, causes them to lift their heads and produce such melancholy, eerie moanings. My wildlife book says they are communicating their locations, letting each other know where they are. But why tonight? Why now?

7:30 pm March 6, 2003

Another cold morning, minus six out, with a light dusting of snow drifting down from the sky. The natives say it's the coldest winter they've seen in years. The deer have eaten all the sapling trees and stripped the bark off the taller trees as high as they can reach. Many are starving. All the creatures of the woodland are hungry. My birdfeeder is a busy place. It reminds me of the diner when it's tourist season. Chickadees and goldfinches flutter in the trees, waiting their turn to get at the sunflower seeds and suet ball.

I've started back at the diner, but we were so slow today that I didn't make much money. I did bring back a big container of chili, though, so at least I have supper. Now I'll get back to my writing.

*****

The woman I see, reunited with her husband Pete after a six-month separation, is now living in western Washington. Despite the turmoil of their past years, despite what lies ahead in the future, they have now embarked on a wonderful journey into an idyllic life; an experience that I would not have missed for anything.

Looking back, I relive that sense of absolute joy, and the words of Edna St. Vincent Millay's two-stanza poem come to mind;

"My candle burns at both ends, it will not last the night.
But oh my friends and ah my foes, it gives a lovely light."

Lovely was the light that shone on the good times I spent with Pete in western Washington, but how dark the night when it burned out.

A Dream Farm in Gate, Washington
or Painting with Sand

The Navajo people have a healing ceremony in which they create a beautiful work of art, making intricate designs with colored sands, and then destroy it. The shaman purposefully sweeps all the sand away, flinging it across the earth, so that the healing can take place. It is the transience of the painting that makes it so beautiful.

The five-year span I spent on a small farm in Gate, Washington was, it seems to me, like a sand painting; a thing meant to achieve ultimate beauty and then, too perfect for this world, to be whisked away. It was my Camelot, doomed by desire for perfection; my Eden, betrayed by the serpent of greed. My spirit had grown sick. I was in need of healing.

I found it one spring day in 1978 while perusing the real estate ads in a western Washington newspaper. My search seemed like a gesture in futility, for my husband Pete and I had no money and no credit. I was so miserably unhappy in the tiny apartment we were renting in Centralia, however, that any glimmer of hope was better than nothing.

"Fixer-upper," it said. "Old farm house on river, five acres with barn, outbuildings; owner financing; $28,000." It wouldn't hurt to call. We had no telephone, so I walked to the nearest phone booth. The realtor I talked to was not encouraging. "It's in terrible shape," he said. "It's been on the market for a long time because no one is interested. We have some other properties that are much nicer." I was interested, however, and I talked to Pete that night when he got home from work. I showed him the ad. We

called the realtor back and made arrangements to see it the next day. I fell in love at first sight.

The house was indeed in bad shape, but my eyes moved quickly past it. The farm's front two acres faced a small dirt road with tall western cedars on both sides. There was a large garden plot to the left of the house; a garage and pump house to the right. To the rear was a yard with, on one side, a large barn, on the other a chicken house. Then the land dropped off, sloping down about twenty feet to three acres of pastureland. Beyond that was the Black River, its banks lined with blackberry vines, black willows, and alders, its waters alive during springtime with migrating salmon. In the distance, to the east, loomed the snow-capped volcanic cone of Mt. Rainier. Closer by, just a few miles away, rose the Black Hills, their slopes covered with great forests of Douglas fir, hemlock, and western cedar. The splendor of the landscape over-shadowed the squalor of the run-down house.

The place looked deserted, although the realtor assured us that there was a man living there, an Indian. No flowers grew in the yard, no vegetables in the garden. The lawn was composed of wiregrass and weeds, and all the buildings needed repair and paint. Piles of junk littered the property. The house, a century-old, two-story clapboard, painted yellow, was the worst. The local bank, we were told, had refused to finance it. We followed the realtor inside, studying its gloomy interior. It had been remodeled at some point with cheap paneling and cheaper green carpet, now stained and worn. There were a few pieces of dilapidated furniture, nothing worth keeping. The wiring was shot, we were told, the plumbing minimal, and there was no heat.

Pete and I cared not an iota for the setbacks. Pete was a mobile home repairman. He had a fair amount of carpentry skills and access to building materials. I had an artistic bent, my father's propensity for fixing things, and an unlimited amount of enthusiasm. We were sure we could turn the old farm into our dream home. We asked the realtor to find out the bare minimum we would need in cash to buy it.

My father loaned us the down payment. The owner, desperate to sell, approved us in spite of our lack of credit. The strange old man living on the farm was now the only obstacle. Dark-skinned and gaunt, with a lined and haunted face, he had signed papers to buy the place several years before. He had not, however, kept up the payments, and the owner had legally repossessed it months ago. His few belongings were still there, and he appeared off and on like a specter, staring with accusing eyes as we made our plans. Our attempts to be friendly fell flat, and he refused our offer to help him move. The court issued an injunction for him to leave and finally, on the day before we were to move in, he appeared with a pickup truck and loaded up his paltry sum of worldly possessions. My eagerness to move in precluded sympathy; greed pre-empted kindness. The look he cast back as he left made me flinch, as if he was putting a curse upon us; and to this day, I can't help wondering if the sad and pitiable circumstances of his departure had somehow tainted our dream.

Any doubts or self-recrimination were soon lost in the joy of our new life. We moved in with our two flop-eared doberman pinschers, Princess and Maybe, and set to work. The neighbors welcomed us with hot casseroles, homemade pies, and offers of help. Verne, who lived at the end of the dirt road, helped Pete haul truckloads of junk to the dump. Verne's wife, Wanda, helped me clean the house. Mildred invited us to a neighborhood May Day celebration.

We scrubbed the rooms, one by one. Rich, a neighbor from down the road, offered to disk our garden, and soon I was on my knees planting vegetable seeds. The progress we were making was palpable; we could see improvements every day. We were cheered on by our new friends and by our families in Virginia, to whom I sent pictures and day-by-day accounts.

We didn't have much money by most people's standards, but Pete had a decent job and I got enough part-time work at nearby dairy farms to pay our bills. We brought back rocks from the Black Hills and completed the unfinished stone fireplace in the living room. We hauled in old bricks and made a firewall for the new woodstove Momma and Daddy gave us for Christmas. We tore out the cheap paneling in the living room, exposing newspapers from nearly a hundred years before, balled up and stuffed in the walls to serve as insulation. We ripped out and nailed up and patched and painted until the house started to feel like home.

Pete and I planted fruit and nut trees in our yard and set out straw-berries, blueberries, and raspberries at one end of the garden. Soon there was an asparagus bed in one corner and a rhubarb patch in another. Corn, potatoes, cauliflower, Swiss chard; we tried everything that anyone said might grow in western Washington, even notoriously difficult celery. I planted an herb garden behind the house. I dried the sage, rosemary, lavender and coriander and hung them on my kitchen walls.

As the months passed, we stocked our barnyard with every kind of animal we could think of. We bought a day-old Holstein calf from a neighboring farmer and bottle-fed Bozo, as we called him, till he grew into a strapping steer. We bought two piglets and fed them scraps from a nearby restaurant, as well as the leavings of our gardens. We brought home baby chickens, ducks, geese, and turkeys, all of whom resided in our bathroom under light bulbs until they were old enough to go outdoors.

Before long, a lovely but mischievous Nubian milk goat, Cocoa, moved into the barn, and one Easter morning Pete presented me with an adorable lamb. I found an ad for Siamese kittens in the local paper and soon Twinkle joined the family. A friend donated a pair of turtledoves, for which we built a dovecote in the back yard. They soon multiplied and we awakened each morning to the sound of their melodious cooing.

One early summer morning we received a phone call from our neighbor, Jim Cordell, who told us he had just found a swarm of honeybees in his yard. He knew we had been hoping to get some bees, and Pete had recently traded some cabinets for a brood box and a couple supers with frames. This was our chance.

We hopped in our truck and drove across the bridge which spanned the Black River and down the lane to Jim's house. He was standing outside, waiting for us, with a ladder and a smoker. He pointed out the swarm, clinging to the branch of a tree about eight feet off the ground. It looked like a basketball--a squiggly basketball! After a few puffs from the smoker Pete climbed the ladder and carefully shook the bees down into a burlap sack held open by Jim and me. We took them home and the next year we had homemade biscuits flavored with our own honey.

Between hauling rocks and sanding sheetrock, I canned vegetables, put up jam and pickles, and experimented with making sauerkraut and green tomato mincemeat. When Pete shot a black-tail deer I helped him butcher it, smoking the tougher cuts to make jerky and putting the rest in the freezer. I borrowed a book on tanning hides and set to work making leather. Pete learned how to snag salmon from our river bank, and before long we were enjoying fresh fish.

When we had our pigs slaughtered (that was a tough one, even though I'd grown up eating home-raised pork) I mixed the pork with the sage I'd grown and stuffed the intestines to make sausage. Pete and I converted the pump house into a smoke-house. We hung hams from our pigs and the older salmon on hooks in the rafters. We built a fire of green cherry and

178

hickory wood, keeping it smoking for days, till we had the most delectable country hams and smoked salmon imaginable. We ate high on the hog, both literally and figuratively, in those days.

Pete's boss needed a truck delivered from the east coast to his office in Washington, so we took a trip back to get it. We used it to bring our furniture and personal items from Virginia, and we furnished our new home with treasures from our childhood, from our early years together, and even from our grandparents.

Pete's mother came to visit. She helped me refinish old furniture, found in thrift shops, and put up vegetables. My parents came. Daddy helped Pete with his carpentry projects and Momma helped me in the garden. My sisters came with their families, and we took them tubing down the Black River and digging for razor clams at the coast. I showed my nieces and nephew how to make candles, dripping hot beeswax onto wicks suspended on a rack.

Everyone loved our farm, and it seemed we'd found us a little bit of heaven. For several years we reveled in our paradise, not realizing that our work of art, our wonderful sand painting, was doomed.

* * * * *

7:00 pm March 10, 2003

I just finished talking to my younger sister, Nancy, on the phone. Her daughter Kristin has returned to college after a long weekend home. We talked about Mom who, she says, is about the same. The same as last time, the same as last year. But different, so very different, from the mother we knew as children. Where did you go, Mom? Are you still in that wasted body, somewhere, or has part of your soul flown far away? You talk to us, you smile and seem to know us, but your mind drifts on a different plane, and you sometimes forget that you are here at all.

Nancy assures me that you are no trouble, but I feel guilty being here, while you are fed and dressed and bathed by her hands. I wonder what you think, or if you think, as you lie there day after day, trapped in a body that can or will do nothing. Do you miss Daddy? Perhaps, when you drift away from us, you are with him, and you are both young and strong and in love again. I hope so.

I miss Daddy. Nancy and I talked, as we often do, about what a different place the world is without him in it. That old cliche, "time heals all," has not worked for us. The wounds left behind by his stroke and

179

subsequent death are still raw and painful. I miss him, and I miss you too, Mom, and I try to remember you in a happier time and place.

3:00 pm March 12, 2003

Eve, Sheryl, and I went ice fishing today! We'd been talking about it for weeks, and a couple days ago we made our plans. Yesterday I stopped by the town offices to get a fishing license, and then Eve and I drove up to Tupper Lake to get bait. Since I knew absolutely nothing about ice fishing, I simply did what Eve said. I was surprised when the bait turned out to be live minnows; even more surprised when it cost $21.00. This looked to be an expensive hobby!

I set my alarm for 5:30 this morning and at 6:15 I took my skis down the hill and set off across Long Lake to Eve's place. It was gorgeous being on skis at that time of morning, the sky a dusky gray, just fringed with pink. Eve's husband Phil had dug out 15 holes for us the day before, using his gasoline-powered auger. We were each allowed five holes, according to our fishing licenses. Carrying everything on a sled, we went to each hole, broke out the ice which had re-frozen during the night, and set what Eve called a tip-up over it. I had no idea what the tip-ups were for, but I soon learned. Each tip-up had a flag, a hook and a line attached. We put a minnow on each hook and placed the tip-up over the hole, then set the flag so that if a fish grabbed the bait, the flag would flip up. We had not yet set all the tip-ups when some of the flags started going up. We ran across the ice to them, but found no fish. Large-mouth bass often nibble the bait and set off the flags, Eve told me.

Sheryl and I arrived and we all brought chairs out on the ice and built a fire. Sheryl and I tried jigging by hand for perch, using earthworms tied to lines. No luck.

Eve and Sheryl cracked open some beer but I stuck with hot coffee. We spent all morning on the ice, cooking hotdogs and watching our tip-ups. It was so cold that the tip-ups were freezing. We pulled them out to check the bait, and Sheryl pulled up a good-sized northern pike, the hook snagged in its gill. It was the only fish we caught, and since this was my first time, they gave it to me.

It was all great fun, though it hardly paid for the fishing licenses and bait! After lunch I skied back across the lake and took a hot shower. I'll fry half the pike, and maybe make chowder with the rest.

11:00 am March 13, 2003

After working at the diner today I made the 22-mile drive up to Tupper Lake to get groceries. Tupper Lake was once a busy logging town with at least four sawmills, and the central point for the railroad that connected it to other villages. It dates back to 1844, I have read, but was almost destroyed by a huge fire in 1899. The people re-built it and now there are a number of businesses there, including the grocery store.

The airwaves are full of the talk of war and George Bush's determination to invade Iraq. When I was in Buffalo, Betsy and I went to see "Lysistrata," the antiwar play written 2,500 years ago by the Greek playwright, Aristophanes. It made one realize how little progress civilization has made in over two millennia. I have written a new song about the horrors of war, which I will sing at my PeopleArt concert later this month.

Life goes on, of course, in spite of this aura of destruction hanging over us. I ski or snowshoe every day, Huck and I walk along our trail. The cold, snowy winter continues. The deer, having eaten all the saplings and bark they can find, begin to slowly starve.

I bought a fifty-pound bag of sunflower seed while in Tupper Lake, which I am told, provides nutrition not only for hungry birds and squir-rels but also for deer, foxes, etc. I smear peanut butter on the tree trunk and put apples and sunflower seeds out for whatever wildlife wants them. The deer come daily to feed, as well as others whose tracks I cannot read. But even as I sit here, watching a red squirrel hang upside down to dine on the peanut butter, the radio continues with its talk of war.

1:00 pm March 15, 2003

There were two red-breasted nuthatches this morning. I don't know if the former one has returned or if this is a new one. They are hanging to-gether on the side of my feeder, plucking out sunflower seeds. I am glad for them. The red squirrels are chasing each other from treetop to snow-drift to treetop, engaged in what must be part of a mating ritual. They run about under the feet of the deer, who ignore them or watch in mild curi-osity. It is warm today and the snow is melting, though I am warned by the native residents that spring is only teasing us. Still, there are rose-colored leaf buds on the beech trees. Spring is surely coming.

I watch the different species sharing the sunflower seeds I put out, showing no signs of animosity. I wonder why we humans can't do the same.

*****

Now I'm back, in my imagination, at our farm in Gate, remembering one very special lady. Some folks say that turkeys are dull and dumb, but I beg to differ.

Buzz

It was Kenny's turn to bat. He stepped up to the scrap of feed sack which served as a batter's plate and swung at the softball the pitcher hurled at him. He missed. Another pitch; another miss. On his third try the bat connected and Kenny took off running. Beside him, making an excited cheeping sound, ran Buzz. Around the bases they darted, both of them crossing home plate together. A home run! Kenny and Buzz reveled in the praise. Kenny smiled, Buzz strutted and flapped her wings, then settled into the lap of one of the other kids. She was ready to run the bases again when the next player came up to bat.

I watched the game from my kitchen window, where I was canning raspberry jam. The ball players were kids who lived in the house at the end of the dirt road; Buzz was a domestic double-breasted roasting turkey who lived in our henhouse at the edge of the field. She was the clown of the neighborhood. She had been bought with Thanksgiving dinner in mind, but she had long ago dispelled all notions we'd had of roasting her for dinner!

Living on a small farm in western Washington could be lots of work, but the joys were worth every minute. Pete's and my family of critters was delightful, all having their own personalities, and none more so than Buzz. Her real name was Turkey Buzzard. She began her life like most domestic turkeys, hatched from a big white egg in an incubator. She was only a day or so old when Pete and I bought her and another hatchling at the feed store and brought them home. They spent the next few weeks in a box in our bathroom; then moved into the henhouse with two Bardrock roosters and eight Rhode Island Red hens.

Pete and I were amateur farmers and did not know that it was unwise to raise chickens and turkeys together. Turkeys, we later learned, are highly susceptible to a disease carried by chickens, which may have been the reason the other turkey died. Buzz, at any rate, was left a lonely orphan in the midst of pigs, ducks, chickens, cows, dogs, cats, and humans. She thrived, making friends with all of her barnyard comrades and especially with Pete and me.

It was not until she laid an enormous egg that we knew that she was a she. Buzz was not pretty, even at her peak, but what she lacked in looks she made up in personality. She loved to talk, but she never learned to gobble like turkeys are supposed to. She always spoke with a high-pitched, rather sweet cheep...cheep. She learned early on that our house was much nicer than hers. Any time she got a chance she strolled in, conversing in her usual cheep...cheep manner, walking through the rooms, looking for someone to visit with.

She helped in the garden, following us as we planted corn kernels or lettuce seedlings, thinking it a great game to have her lunch served in this manner. She trotted behind the rototiller, scooping up the earthworms it dislodged. She watched curiously as I removed the frames from the beehives and harvested the golden honey; then tried to help by snapping up a honeybee or two. She visited the neighbors, standing at their front door to see if the kids wanted to come out and play softball.

She followed us wherever we went; and if we were not around, she followed whoever happened to come by. One day a stranger knocked at the door and asked, in amused exasperation, if we would lock our turkey up; she had followed him all the way to the main road. If there were no humans around she tagged along after our dog Princess.

Every morning, as part of my daily routine, I went to the henhouse to gather eggs. There were nesting boxes built into one wall, where the hens often laid. One day I found only two eggs. The same was true the next day and the next. I was afraid one of the hens was eating eggs, a habit they sometimes develop, curable only by turning them into chicken soup. I loved my hens (they all went by the name of Lucille, since I couldn't tell them apart) so I was dismayed at the prospect. I was also missing my morning omelets!

About the same time, I noticed that Buzz's feathers, particularly on her breast, were getting awfully messy. What on earth was she getting into? I wondered. Then one day I solved both mysteries. I found Buzz sitting in a corner of the henhouse in a nest of wood chips she had made herself. Underneath her were several eggs; but they were not big, thick-shelled turkey eggs. They were chicken eggs, and even as I watched, one of them cracked under her weight and oozed out its yellow yolk onto her feathers! "Buzz!" I cried in dismay. "You've been stealing the eggs!" Buzz cooed at me in a proud maternal manner and reached down to turn an egg.

Buzz had been taking the eggs and sitting on them. When one broke, she simply stole another. I felt sorry for her as I took the remaining unbroken eggs and cleaned up her messy, eggy nest, but this simply wouldn't do. After a few days of my removing the eggs she gave up on her attempts at motherhood and resumed her hobbies of softball and gardening.

In the end, Buzz's destiny as a roasting turkey caught up with her. She started getting weaker, unable to run, and finally unable to stand. I took her to the local veterinarian, who proclaimed her diagnosis. Buzz had been genetically engineered to be eaten at the age of four months. Now three years old, her meaty, tender "double-breasts" had gotten too heavy for her to carry. There was no cure for what ailed her. I took her home and built her a box, which gave her some support. She would have good days, when she could walk around and sometimes even run a little; then she would relapse and have to stay in her box.

Finally her good days ended, and it became obvious that putting her to sleep was the kindest thing to do. We buried her beneath the western cedars that grew next to the driveway. The barnyard was lonely without her piercing cheeps, and softball games were never the same again.

*****

11:30 am March 16, 2003

This is the slowest time of year here, and I don't have many hours at the diner. NPR did a talk this morning on ice fishing. It said that only the hard-core fishermen were out on the ice now, because it so hard to hook the fish. The fish, it turns out, lose their teeth at this time of year and can't grab the hook very well. I guess we were lucky to get the pike! Northern pike, says my guidebook, is the most widely distributed fresh-water fish in the world. It is a popular sport fish and used to be fished commercially. It tasted pretty good, but the numerous thin bones were hard to find and remove.

5:30 pm March 17, 2003

I took a snowshoeing trip with Huck along the Northville-Placid Trail today. Built in the 1930s by Franklin Roosevelt's Civilian Conservation Corps, the trail is the longest in the Adirondacks, traversing 135 miles of wilderness. Huck and I traipsed only a couple miles, as the meltdown made it hard going. The crust which had developed on the snow kept breaking through, plummeting Huck and sometimes even me, in spite of my snowshoes, into three foot drifts. I saw an eastern chipmunk, the first in months, apparently coaxed out of its winter burrow by the warm weather. It was sitting on a shelf mushroom, a foot or so above the snow, as artistically posed as a porcelain Hummel figurine. Huck wanted to chase it but I held him back.

8:00 pm March 18, 2003

After work today I put on snowshoes and visited Doris and Ed, down on Sagamore Road. Doris is gradually getting weaker, and it hurt to see her struggle to breathe. Ed cares for her tenderly.

When I got home I made a pasta dish with chicken and veggies. I added a salad, and as I cut up the cucumber, a picture came to mind.

*****

Now, dinner over, I close my eyes and examine that picture, seeing again the wide fields and gently rolling hills of rural western Washington. This time the woman in the image is driving a big John Deere tractor and pulling a trailer. She's twenty-nine years old and has a great tan. She looks happy and I know for a fact that she is. She loves this part of Washington and the five-acre farm she and her husband Pete bought here a year ago. She had been busy working on it, but she really needed a paying job. Jobs were hard to come by, so when she learned about this one, she accepted eagerly. It is seasonal, as is most farm work, but it will help pay the bills for a while.

Cucumber Boss

I stood up slowly, allowing the muscles in my back to adjust to an upright humanoid position. With the knuckles of my hand I wiped my forehead, displacing the drops of sweat before they ran into my eyes. Then, massaging my sunburned arms as best I could, I surveyed the landscape before me. Long, straight corridors of low-growing, corpuscular green leaves stretched to the horizon, finally disappearing behind the curve of a hill. Beyond them rose the dark silhouettes of low mountains, the Black Hills of western Washington. And farther beyond still, the deep, cloudless blue sky of a Pacific Northwest August.

Scattered in the field before me were an array of strange-looking beings, feeding, it would appear, on the leaves and moving slowly down the rows. It was only through prior knowledge that I recognized them for what they were, fellow human beings bent over in the position that I had held just a few moments before. Like me, they were gathering the succulent fruits that hid beneath the low canopies of leaves.

Cucumbers. They, and I, were picking cucumbers, "Cucumis sativus," members of the gourd family. These were not just any cucumbers; these were highly prized, smooth and perfectly shaped "slicers." They were bound for the aisles of prestigious grocery stores, where shoppers would pick them up (waxed by then to prevent shrinkage,) turn them over and examine them, and then accept or reject them. If accepted, they would end up in tossed salads served all over the northwestern United States.

Across the hill, out of sight, grew the picklers--small, misshapen, warty, and classless; there was no prestige in picking them. They were picked by high school kids who were willing to work for the far lower pay they brought.

I stood for a moment more, stretching my back muscles, before bending down and returning to work. No slouching on the job. I had to set an example, after all, since I was the foreman. I shuffled my feet slowly along, running my hands through the leaves to find the half hidden fruit. I eyed each one, trying to decide if the time was right for picking. The slicers had to be an exact size. If they were too big or too small, they would be rejected by the buyers. Attached to my wrist with a string was a ring, two inches across. Each cucumber must be able to slip through the ring snugly, with no extra space around it. If too many cucumbers missed these specifications, Zap! There went my job. But checking each cucumber with the ring would take too long, so I guessed at most, using the ring just occasionally to keep tabs on myself.

As foreman, I was responsible not only for my own cucumbers but also for those of the whole crew. So in a few minutes I stopped and walked back among them, slipping a ring around several of the cukes in each basket, shaking my head at several of the workers and showing them that this one was too big, this one too small. Our conversations were simple. My year of college Spanish had not produced the language skills necessary for real communication with my crew. Not a one of them spoke English. I didn't know for sure, but I had a feeling they were all illegal immigrants, having slipped past the border patrol and made their way up here to Washington. (My husband and I had enabled a pair ourselves, a few years back, when we were in Tijuana. They had run up to us in a hurry, pursued by the patrol, and begged us to let them hide in the back of our van. We quickly opened the door and slipped a blanket over them, then continued on our way in apparent innocence.)

The Mexicans here on this farm struck me as shadow beings. They came and went without noise--no talking, laughing, or gesticulating, as Mexicans did in other places where I had met them. They seemed almost sullen, but even that was too active a term to describe them. Their faces held no expression that I could discern, and they exchanged themselves from day to day; here and then gone, replaced by another equally indistinct body.

Yet logic told me that for them to be here at all had required courage, ambition, ingenuity, and a deep commitment to something. Each of these almost invisible people had a family, a home, and a story of his own. My inability to read that story made it no less dramatic and noteworthy. I wondered what they thought of me, their boss. Tall, slender, wearing cut-off jeans and a tank top. They never directly addressed me or met my eyes. But they seemed to know how to do the work, and they did it.

I glanced down at my watch. It was almost noon, lunchtime, and the wagon was nearly full. Stepping across the rows, I clambered over to the tractor and started the engine. The bent shapes returned to an upright position and soon all resembled human beings again. Kicking the tractor into gear, I drove down the rows, slowing so that each picker could deposit his basket into the wagon and hop aboard for the ride back. When all the cucumbers had been piled in the wagon and all the pickers had found spots to sit, I turned toward the farmyard and slipped into 3rd gear. We bounced back across the field.

I had started this job a few weeks earlier as a picker, but through tenacity and relative dependability, had a few days before been promoted to the position of foreman, a promotion which included a small raise. My predecessor had also been an English-speaking Anglo, but he had left one day for undetermined reasons. Now I was not only the sole woman on the job, I was the only person who was not Mexican.

For the most part, I enjoyed the work. I liked the feel of the warm sun on my skin, the rich black earth beneath my feet. I felt as if I might be a character in one of John Steinbeck's tragic novels, or in one of Woody Guthrie's poignant depression-era songs about migrant farm workers.

I had time to think, if I felt like it, and would often dream up plans for the small farm I shared with Pete, not far away. "Perhaps," I might say to myself, "we could enlarge the chicken yard, maybe improve the fences and get a horse." More often, I let my mind drift from cucumber to cucumber, lulled by the tedious work and the hypnotic landscape. By the time the workday ended I was exhausted, but it was a good feeling.

Now we had arrived in the farmyard, and the Mexican workers hopped off and went to their lunches. I now faced my biggest challenge; backing the trailer full of cucumbers up to the chute, flipping the lever which would tip it back, and emptying the cucumbers into the storage shed. Sometimes I succeeded, but if, after several tries, it was still not properly aligned, the owner would come over and take over.

Roger, my boss, was a middle-aged, medium-sized man with a sun-burned, work-creased face. His was a small farm, struggling for its survival, threatened by the growth of the huge agri-businesses against which it was almost impossible to compete. The farmhouse was nearby, and his wife Mary sometimes came out to visit as I sat in the grass and ate my lunch. Today, however, she was nowhere in sight, so I took my lunch bag out of my truck, picked up one of the cucumbers which had been rejected for sale--too slender to pass the ring test--and sat down under a tree.

Wiping it off with my sleeve, I took a bite. Scientifically speaking, cucumbers are fruits, since they develop from the flowers of the plant and contain seeds. From a culinary viewpoint they are considered vegetables and are used as such. Whichever you consider them, they are quite tasty. As I chewed the crunchy fruit, I studied the perfect symmetry of its seed pattern. Were I not about to consume them for my lunch, these seeds might one day have grown into new cucumber plants, putting forth big bright yellow flowers which would in turn develop into fruit, continuing a history of more than three millennia. While the origins of the cucumber are hidden in the mists of time, it is believed that they developed in India or Malaysia more than 3,000 years ago. They were introduced into China 2,000 years ago, and were popular with the ancient Egyptians, Greeks, and Hebrews. They were common in England by the 1300s, and would have journeyed to this country with early European settlers. Relatively speaking, they were newcomers to the soils of western Washington.

Raising my eyes, I gazed across the yard to the fields beyond. Now tamed and subdued by the plow, a hundred years ago they were wild lands, visited and hunted by the Chehalis Indians who made this land their home. The Chehalis were not farmers. They lived on the river, using it as a thoroughfare for their cedar canoes and as the source of the all-important salmon. They would have ventured onto these lands to pick berries and nuts and take an occasional deer. Today the Chehalis live on a reservation in nearby Oakville. These lands, divided into neat green rows, would be unrecognizable to their forebears.

I worked for about six weeks, until the last of the good slicers were picked from the vines. My job was finished. I suppose the Mexicans moved on--south most likely--to other jobs, before slipping across the border again to go home. I thought about their shadowed forms a few times during the winter, wondering if they were now in Mexico with children and wives, or if they were among those announced occasionally on the radio, picked up and detained for their illegal presence in our country.

I had another job when cucumber season rolled around the next year, so I did not return to the farm. I hoped that Roger and Mary were able to hang on and not be pushed out of business as so many were by the giant commercial farms. I seldom pass the cucumber bin in a grocery store without remembering the summer I spent in those leafy, fruit-laden corridors, my back bent beneath the warm Washington sun.

✶✶✶✶✶

6 pm March 27, 2003

Today Huck and I drove down past the museum and turned onto Rt. 28, then past the town of Indian Lake to a little road near North River. My friend, Windy, from the museum, has a cabin there with his wife. He had invited me to go maple syruping with him, and I had accepted with enthusiasm. He has taps in 80 sugar maple trees. I took my snowshoes along, expecting to be tramping through the woods to the various trees, but he explained that he does it the easy way. A month ago, when he tapped the trees, (first drilling a small hole and then inserting plastic taps about 2 inches beneath the bark) he attached the taps to plastic piping, and ran all the pipes down into 50 gallon garbage cans beside the road.

When the temperatures began rising, he explained, the sap began to flow. This has been a great syruping year, he said, because of the sudden warm spell we've had, day temperatures climbing high and then dropping below freezing at night. We rode in his pickup truck along the road and ladled out the sap into big cans in the truck bed. I was amazed at the amount we collected, but he reminded me that it took between 25 and 40

189

gallons of sap to produce one gallon of syrup. The sap looked like water. When I tasted it I could barely detect a flavor. It certainly didn't taste anything like maple syrup!

After collecting the sap, Windy, Huck, and I climbed into the front of the truck and drove down to North Creek, following the Hudson River. Windy's boiling equipment was in a shed (often called a sugar shack) at Frank's house. Frank was already in the shack, feeding kindling into a firebox and boiling the sap he had collected that morning from his trees. Sap boils at approximately 219 degrees, depending on the atmospheric pressure, he explained, showing me a thermometer made for the purpose. To get maple cream, sugar, or candy, you need higher temperatures, all marked on the thermometer. As the sap boiled, Frank skimmed off impurities. He scooped up a spoonful of the half-boiled sap and offered it to me. Yep, it was starting to taste like maple syrup, thin enough to drink and delicious.

We brought in the sap Windy and I had collected, ran some of it through a strainer, and then poured it into the boiler. As it cooked, Frank showed me how he had hung a cloth sieve over the container and poured the finished sap into it. It was slowly dripping through as we watched, filling a syrup bottle. He gave me a taste of it. Now it tasted like maple syrup!

They explained how different sugar maples produced syrups with different flavors, depending on the minerals in the soils where the trees grew. The weather conditions and temperatures at which it was harvested also affected the taste, as did the temperatures at which the sap was boiled. It was, as Windy said, an art as well as a hard job.

After we left North Creek, Windy and I drove down to the Glen, to see the ice jam on the Hudson. Frozen solid a few weeks ago, the great river was thawing, and as the ice broke up great slabs of it rushed down the river until it was stopped by the ice ahead of it. It rose up over whatever was in its way, and some of the roads were closed. He showed me a spot where, back in the sixties, a house and car had been swept away by the ice. This had been an unusually cold winter, so the ice jam was worse than usual. We stood at the bridge and watched for a while. A huge slab, maybe twenty by fifteen feet across, four feet thick, broke off as we watched and slid into the river, where it joined the flotilla of ice. I felt like I was watching the last days of a great glacier, broken apart into icebergs.

On the way back, Windy told me about growing up near here, when collecting and boiling sap was a way of making a living for his father and a dreaded job for the kids. His family had been eking a living out of these mountains for nearly a hundred years, but it had never been easy. They hunted and trapped, gardened, logged, and made the guide-boats and chairs for which the Adirondacks are famous.

After saying goodbye to Windy, Huck and I stopped on the way back and snow-shoed the half-mile trail to Rock Lake. The lake was still frozen, but the creek that flowed into it chattered like an angry red squirrel. Miss Kelley was glad to see us return, and is sitting in my lap. Huck and I are beat, and we are all ready for supper.

6:30 pm March 28, 2003

I am leaving tomorrow for Buffalo and plan to stay for a week. I can't wait. It's been pretty lonely here this last month.

Pat Garber

April 2003

Midnight April 4, 2003

I just collapsed here on the couch, exhausted from a harrowing three-hour drive through an unexpected snowstorm, inching along on treacherous winding roads in white-out conditions, followed by four trips up the hill, slipping and sliding with my hands full of guitar, accordion, suitcase, groceries, Miss Kelley's crate, and Huck's leash. That most definitely is a run-on sentence but it's just how I felt, plowing on past exhaustion and good sense to get home. The thermometer inside the cabin read 38 degrees when I walked in, but now a fire is roaring in the woodstove and the temperature is rising. I am sipping a glass of burgundy wine with an immense feeling of relief.

I am grateful for that frightening drive, however, for until the snow began to fall, I was engaged in deep conversation with my old friend, Mr. Blues. Having just left my sister and friends in Buffalo, I was encountering the same old doubts. Why was I coming back here, ensconcing myself in isolation and loneliness?

As I reviewed my desolate options, dreading the days ahead, I realized that the silvery crystals reflected in my headlights were snowflakes. Well into April, when I thought the risk over, I was caught in the dreaded scenario I had avoided all winter; a sixty-mile drive through the mountains, at night, in a snowstorm, with no motels along the way where I could pull over. Mr. Blues fled in the onrush of endorphins, and my depression vanished in the all-consuming challenge of seeing a few feet ahead and staying on the road.

"Just get us safely to Long Lake," I prayed. "That's all I ask!" That was a mistake; I should have asked more. Suddenly, as I climbed a hill doing about 30 mph, a shape flitted into my headlights. It flew straight at my truck and, as I hit the brakes and skidded across the ice, it turned at the last minute. An owl, I was quite sure, but I wasn't sure if it had turned in time. Had I felt an impact? Had I hit it, or it me?

As soon as I regained control of my truck I tried to find a place to pull over. It was hard to be sure, in the deep snow, where the road ended and the steep pitch over the edge began, but I found a safe spot. I pushed Miss Kelley back into her carrier and pulled my flashlight out from under the seat; then uttered a mild oath (is "Shit!" a mild oath?) when I found that the battery was dead. Leaving my blinkers on so that next car would not plow into my truck, I headed back down the road in the dark. I peered anxiously across the pavement and over the edges, praying that I would see nothing resembling a dead or injured bird. A car approached, and I tried to take advantage of its headlights to see farther. Damn. The car had stopped, obviously to check on me. I hurried up to the window and countered the inquiries.

"No I'm not stuck. I'm looking for an owl. I think I may have hit it." The man looked at me a bit strangely. "Well good," he said. "I mean not good about the owl but I'm glad you're not stuck." As he drove away I thought in frustration. "No, it's not good! I'd much rather be stuck!" Several more cars stopped as I searched. A woman said to me, "Well at least it wasn't a deer. That could have messed up your car." Again I wanted to respond, "My car! How does that compare to a life?" But I simply thanked her and continued my search. I found no signs of the owl.

Otherwise it had been a good trip. I played a PeopleArt concert, recorded some songs for the CD I am making with Robb and Tom, and sang at three Head Start centers. My sister Betsy and I went to a Joan Baez concert, its focus on the war. I also read some of my poems at a "Just Buffalo" poetry reading at Crane Library and sang and read at the Screening Room. The War in Iraq--"Operation Freedom?" was a major topic at both.

9:15 pm April 5, 2003

I just got home from the diner, where "Wild Game Night" was hosted tonight. Cathie picked me up at the bottom of the hill and we rode over together. What fun! I tried bear stew, snapping turtle soup, venison tacos, caribou meatballs from Alaska, wild boar soup from Florida, and wild duck quesadillas. There were a number of strange men, all having a rollicking good time, who Cathie identified as the "Woodchucks." I had heard of them, residents of Albany who own a large camp in Long Lake. Cathie, Judy, Jeannie, Kathleen and I (all single women) fended them off as we sampled the food.

I'm not sleepy, so I guess I'll get back to my stories. This one is about fulfilling a life-long dream...

*****

Bareback Bronc

With a thunder of hooves the wild horses galloped by me, rattling the fence I leaned against. I saw ribboned muscles ripple beneath their hides and felt the wind stirred by their passing. I studied each one closely. Mustangs. Wild horses. A thrill of excitement passed through me.

This band was from the badlands of Nevada, captured somewhere east of Reno in a roundup held by the Bureau of Land Management (BLM.) The horses had been examined and vaccinated by a veterinarian, transported up here to Washington, and put up for adoption. My husband Pete and I had applied to adopt two in 1980 and been approved. Now we were here to pick them out.

Mustang has been a sacred word in my vocabulary since I was a child. I had wanted to be a wild horse long before I accepted the inescapable confines of my human body. I had practiced continually as a child, galloping and whinnying and snorting with my cousin Ellen, sure that if I could perfect those equine skills I could transform myself. I had, with my mother's help, at the age of six written a letter to the President of the United States, asking him to protect wild horses out west. I'd read every wild horse book I could get my hands on and watched every horse movie: the Black Stallion, Misty of Chincoteague, Beyond Rope and Fence...

I had learned the history of the horse; how it had originated in this country as dog-sized Eohippus, evolved into the modern Equus, and then disappeared in the extinction (possibly human-caused) that killed off three-toed sloths and mastodons. Its counterparts in the Old World had thrived, and about 5,000 years ago, somewhere in the Ukraine, the horse had been domesticated. Reintroduced by the Spanish into America in the 16th century, horses were revered by many Indian tribes and were instrumental in the settlement of this country. Some had escaped and gone wild again. In the east they lived on barrier islands and were known by names such as Chincoteague and Ocracoke ponies. In the west, they were called by their Spanish name, Mustang. Some still ran wild.

Daddy had gotten me my first horse when I was seven; a brown and white pinto yearling that turned, much to our surprise, into a big feisty stallion. I adored him. Blaze was hard to control, but I loved the way he reared up and pawed the sky with me on his back; the way we thundered across the fields, me clinging tight on his bare back, like a small monkey, with fear and exhilaration. My brother Don, whom we then called Sandy, often rode Blaze, with me following on the calmer pony, Domino. Older and more sedate now, Blaze still lived at my parents' farm in Virginia.

I'd had other horses and loved them dearly, but I had never lost my fascination with wild mustangs. I could imagine no greater thrill than having one of my own, and now it was happening. As of today, Pete and I would adopt not one but two wild horses.

The horses milling before us were not what you'd call beautiful. Life on the range was hard, and beauty was not one of the traits that ensured survival. Mustangs were believed to be a mix of three original breeds of horse: the Arab, Spanish Barb, and Mongolian. Other breeds, which had escaped later horse-owners, had added to the pot. Most wild horses today were small and hardy. The ones before us were thin, with ribs that protruded and heads that seemed too large for their bodies. Many had indelicate Roman noses and some bore scars from fights and, I suspected, from injuries incurred during their capture. Their manes and tails were matted, their coats dull and dirty. Had this band produced any beauties, they would probably have been snatched up before they got here.

I'd known all that ahead of time, however, so I was not unduly disappointed. Once they got cleaned up and put some weight on, they would look a lot better. Appearance was not my main desire, anyway. Mustangs for me personified the spirit of the west, the call of the wild. Pete went along with it, I suppose, for my sake. He liked horses well enough, but I don't think he had the passion for them that I did, especially not for mustangs.

I had another reason for wanting to adopt wild horses instead of buying tame ones. Mustangs had, as the range was tamed and peopled, grown too populous for the amount of available rangeland. At the beginning of the 20th century as many as two million wild horses and burros had roamed the west. They competed for cattle grazing range and as a result were "culled" by cruel and inhumane means and sold to slaughterhouses.

This practice was changed largely due to one woman, Velma Johnston. Born in Nevada and afflicted with a disfiguring case of polio at the age of eleven, she'd devoted much of her life to changing the lot of the wild mustang. Known as "Wild Horse Annie," she was instrumental in getting several laws passed to protect mustangs, the most important being the "Wild Horse and Burro Act of 1971." This act declared wild horses and burros "living symbols of the...pioneer spirit of the West" which "enrich the lives of the American people."

The BLM's Adopt-A-Horse Program was implemented to help end the brutal slaughter of wild horses by finding another option to the over-crowded range. The goal was to reduce to fewer than 40,000 the number of free-roaming wild horses through adoptions. The mustangs were *rounded up and then confined to corrals until adopted. Unfortunately, there were often more horses than there were homes. I wanted to help provide a home for two horses, and I wanted to help support the program.*

In order to have our application approved Pete and I had had to prove that we could provide adequate shelter and pasture, as well as a safe way to transport the horses. Even then, we were not truly adopting them; we would be more like foster parents. We could not obtain full ownership of the horses for five years, after which we had to show that they were well-cared for. This, at least in theory, prevented ruthless horse traders from adopting horses and reselling them to slaughterhouses, and ensured that well-meaning but ignorant adopters did not neglect them.

The bottom three acres of our little farm were fenced pasture, bordering on the Black River. Closer to the house was a barn with three individual stalls and a corral. All had been in need of repair, but we had taken care of that eagerly. We'd made arrangements with our friend, Jim, to pick them up in his horse trailer. We were finally approved.

Now we had to choose which of the frightened, emaciated horses before us would become part of our family. We wanted a stallion and a mare, both young, and we'd hoped for horses big enough for both of us to ride. I watched their frightened eyes, trying to see what they were seeing, to imagine what they thought. One dark red horse caught my eye. He was taller than most, with a proud way of holding his head on a sturdy but graceful neck. He looked at me curiously when I called to him, seeming less frightened than the rest. I pointed him out to Pete, and he agreed that he looked like a good choice.

Selecting a mare was more difficult. All but a few were under fourteen hands, and the taller mares were older than we wanted. We finally settled on a chestnut three-year-old with a diamond-shaped star on her forehead. She was too small to ride now, but we hoped she might grow taller. We paid the adoption fees, called Jim to ready his trailer, and returned home to wait for their arrival.

The horses were scheduled to be delivered the next day. I made sure each stall had what it needed: clean straw on the floor, fresh alfalfa hay in the wooden slatted rack, a salt block in the corner, and buckets for grain and water hanging on two hooks. I had brought my western saddle, bridle, and grooming gear with me from Virginia, and we'd bought new halters and lead ropes. We were ready.

I watched with a mixture of worry and anticipation as Jim drove up with the horses. Pete directed him as he backed the trailer into the barn, and they managed to get the horses into the stalls without any mishaps. We planned to keep them there until they tamed down, neighbors to Cocoa, our Nubian milk goat. I stayed in the barn after Pete and Jim left, talking to the horses and studying them. Pete and I had decided to call the stallion "Nevada," after the state he'd come from. The mare we named for the female outlaw, "Belle Starr."

Nevada soon calmed down and studied me with as much interest as I showed him. When I poured grain into his bucket, he cautiously stepped forward and in a few minutes was munching away. Belle, on the other hand, was terrified of me. She backed into the corner of the stall, watching my every move with distrust. She refused to eat while I was in the barn. Cocoa, meanwhile, was fascinated by everything. She poked her head over and bleated her desire to be included, so I gave her an extra handful of grain and scratched behind her ears.

Over the next few days, Nevada grew more and more trusting, while Belle kept a leery distance. Then disaster struck. Somehow Belle caught her nostril on the water bucket hook, and when I walked into the barn she panicked and ripped it open. Blood spewed onto the straw and terror filled her eyes. Roping and securing her so that the veterinarian could sew it up spawned even more fear. By the time it was over she must have been convinced that we were and always would be the enemy. The scar from her wound healed beautifully, so that you could barely see it. The scar to her spirit never healed. She never came to trust either Pete or me.

In spite of that unfortunate incident both horses thrived. They began filling out and their rough, dull coats became sleek and shiny. Nevada soon learned to take a slice of apple from my hand, his soft muzzle tickling my palm as he gently touched it. He let me stroke him while he ate his hay, flicking his skin at first as if I was a fly, then seeming to enjoy it. Inside the stall I walked around him, talking softly, gently touching him on his side, his neck, a hind leg. I would clip the lead rope to his halter and give it gentle tugs, offering him a carrot or handful of grain at the same time to lure him into following me.

Gradually he learned to come when I pulled on the lead, and soon he was following me around the stall. He seemed to enjoy my company, and would nicker a greeting when he heard the barn door open, his voice blending with Cocoa's plaintive call. Belle would stand in a corner of her stall, watching distrustfully, but she never tried to kick or bite.

After a few weeks, Pete and I decided to turn the horses out into the pasture. They galloped joyously down the hill, then began a dead heat *around the fence line. It was the first time they'd had a chance to run since their capture nearly a year before. They were heartbreakingly beautiful, and it was easy to imagine them running free on the Nevada range. Surprisingly, they seemed to have little inclination to escape. Nevada was becoming quite tame, and Belle seemed happy as long as we left her alone.*

We still fed them in the stalls, which made it easy for me to catch and work with Nevada. I attached a lunge line to his halter and got him used to moving around me in the corral. I stood in the center and gave him signals, letting him know what I wanted him to do. Finally I decided it was time for him to learn about riding. I had ridden my other horses bareback; preferred it, in fact, but had decided that mounting a wild horse would be safer if I had something to hold on to. So one day I took my saddle into the stall. It was a roping saddle crafted of dark tooled leather, bought for me by Daddy at a rodeo we'd gone to in the Shenandoah Valley when I was nine years old. I was very fond of it, but Nevada had no such feeling. He snorted in fear, stomped his front foot, and refused to get near it. "It's okay, boy." I soothed him, "It won't hurt you." But he was buying none of it. Finally I decided to hang it over the fence where he would see it and hopefully get used to it.

The next day when I tried to lead him near it he shied away, dancing around as if it had tried to bite him. Again I tried the reassurance role, but with no success. I set it next to his grain bucket, so that if he wanted grain he would have to go near it. He gradually got used to having it next to him on the ground, but when I picked it up and walked toward him he pitched a fit. I was quite puzzled. In others ways Nevada seemed calm and sensible. What was there about my saddle that was so threatening?

I decided to try the saddle blanket first. He didn't like it, but after a few days he let me slip it on his back. He eyed me nervously, twitching at each touch, but eventually he got to where I could run it across his back, his legs, even under his belly. Surely he was ready for the saddle now.

No such luck. Pete helped me, holding Nevada while I tried to slip it on his back. He reared and lunged until we gave up. We tried it the other way, with me holding Nevada and Pete trying to put the saddle on. It was no use. I was anxious to start riding, but we were making no progress.

One day I reached a decision. Nevada seemed so gentle, pushing his nose against my chest as I stroked him. Surely he wouldn't hurt me. I tied the loose end of the lead rope to the halter, making a loop, and put it around his neck. Then I led him to the fence. I climbed to the third rail, talking quietly as I did so, and slipped my leg across his bare back. I braced myself for whatever would come, but all Nevada did was turn his head and sniff my foot. Then he looked at me as if to ask "What on earth are you doing up there?"

I stroked him and spoke quietly, telling him what a good boy he was. After a few minutes I gathered the reins I had made and gave him a gently nudge with my knees. It took a while but I finally convinced him to take a step or two. I continued working with him, and within a week I could ride him around the corral quite comfortably.

I tried again to put the saddle on him, thinking that now he would be more amenable, but he fought it as hard as ever. He seemed, however, to enjoy having me ride him bareback.

Meanwhile, I had taken a part-time job at a horse stable in Grand Mound, a small community six miles away. Dan, my boss, was a well-respected horse trainer and riding instructor. My job was to clean the stables and groom the horses; my pay, private lessons in cross-country jumping.

I had as a teenager jumped my horses over logs and had set up two-foot-high pole jumps in Daddy's pasture. Never, however, had I done anything like this. Dan showed me how to use a jumping saddle, smaller than a standard English and much smaller than a western saddle. He taught me the proper way to post, raising and lowering myself in the saddle in rhythm to the horse's trot. He demonstrated how to lean over the horse's withers on approaching a jump and move your weight with the horse. Then he put me on a half-thoroughbred, half-Arab gelding, aimed me at a four-foot stone wall, and gave my horse a good slap on the rump. We were soaring over the wall before I had a chance to yell, "Wait, I'm not ready!" It was one of the most exhilarating experiences of my life. I loved it!

Cross-country jumping is similar to steeplechase, done over a long, rugged course with jumps of various heights, widths, and combinations of the two. It is much more dangerous and therefore more exciting than ring jumping, for the jumps are real obstacles and do not collapse if the horse hits them. Dan made my jumps higher and wider each time, sometimes two or three in a row. Before each jump I'd feel an electrifying thrill of fear, a rush of adrenaline, and then that burst of energy and muscle beneath me as I rose into the air. I never got to the point where I didn't want to scream "Stop!" before each jump, but I never stopped

201

loving it and, fortunately, neither I nor my horse ever had an accident. I asked Dan's advice about working with Nevada and Belle, and he gave me some pointers.

About six months after their arrival, Belle came into heat. Pete came into the house one day and announced, with a grin, that he thought we'd be having a colt in about a year. Sure enough, Belle was pregnant. We had, by now, gotten her to the point where she would let us catch and lead her, though with reservations. She hadn't grown any taller so it didn't look like we'd be able to ride her, anyway. We figured we'd just let her be a momma. She and Cocoa watched as Nevada and I cantered around the field. The foal grew in her belly, and a year after conception a chestnut filly pushed her way into the world.

By the time Nevada turned six he was looking and feeling good, and his hormones were starting to work full-throttle. I wanted to ride him off the property, but keeping him under control was becoming a real challenge. He'd sowed his oats and we had our foal, so we decided it was time to get him gelded. He calmed down a little after that, and I started riding him on the roadsides near our house. He was a great little riding horse.

Pete worked a job that took him out of town frequently, so he didn't have much time to spend with the horses. He would have liked to ride Nevada, but not without a saddle. We tried again, but Nevada fought against us every time he saw that leather contraption come near him. I guess a better horse-breaker would have gotten him past it, but neither Pete nor I pushed him too hard. If he wanted to be a bareback bronc it was okay by me. He was, after all, a wild horse, and that's why I loved him.

*****

10:00 am April 6, 2003

I'm watching an amazing little drama going on outside my window. Amid the juncos, chickadees, and nuthatches eating at my feeder is a blue jay. At least, it is trying to eat. Every time it lands, a red squirrel comes at it like a little kamikaze. Once he literally dove off of a branch to land on top of the jay, and both became entangled in a flash of fur and feathers. Had the jay, I wondered, once raided the nest of the squirrel, dragging off one of its babies to have for breakfast? Or was this a preventive measure, a little like our attack on Iraq? I hope neither squirrel nor blue jay gets hurt, whatever the reason.

8:30 am April 8, 2003

Juncos are everywhere this morning, their plump, slate-colored presence turning my yard into a dining room full of busy little gentlemen in gray suits. They perch in the branches around the cabin, balance on the feeder, and pick up the sunflower seeds that have fallen onto the fresh blanket of snow. I watch one as it scoops up beakfuls of snow, its method of drinking, I guess, in winter. The juncos are returning from the south. Also known as snowbirds, they are apt models for the retirees, also known by this nickname, who motor back and forth each year between Florida or Arizona and colder climates to the north.

For me they are symbols of my childhood winters. They appeared in our yard in Virginia as if by magic whenever snow covered the ground. My mother prepared sumptuous banquets of bread and birdseed for them, which my father, dressed in heavy jacket and boots, delivered. One winter I found an injured one and brought it inside. I kept it in the basement laundry room and nursed it, with my mother's help, until it could fly again. My father and I set it free in the back yard.

I don't have to work at the diner today, so I have time for another visit to the past.

*****

My mind drifts back again, to Gate, and to two delightful animals who shared our home for a while.

Goblin and Thumper

It was springtime on the farm in Gate. The apple trees were fragrant with blossoms and violets sprinkled the grass like amethysts. A chestnut foal, born of the mustangs Pete and I had adopted, frolicked in the pasture. There were two newly-born Holstein calves, obtained by bartering with a dairy farm owner and hand-fed by me with a baby bottle, in one of the barn stalls. There were mallard ducklings on the river bank, newborn turtledoves in the dovecote, and swallow hatchlings in the barn rafters. Pete and I had bought thirty Rhode Island Red chicks, now huddled together under heat lamps in the henhouse. In a basket in our utility room were three new kittens, the offspring of Spooky, a tortoise-shell cat

Pat Garber

Pete had found not long before. In a box in our bathroom were four baby turkeys and, in the bathtub, a little black rabbit, given us by a friend who raised them for food.

It was a busy time of year but one which I loved. Pete had plowed the garden and I'd sprinkled it with lime. I'd hauled wheelbarrow loads of rocks out of it and wheelbarrow loads of horse manure in, spreading it into the soil with a rake. I'd measured and hammered in wooden stakes and run strings between them to make straight rows and rectangles. The lettuce seeds I'd planted had already formed bright green corridors, and the tips of potato leaves were pushing up through the cool earth into view. I'd put in peas and Swiss chard and was anxiously waiting for them to sprout. It was still too early for tomatoes, broccoli or cauliflower; but the plants, grown in a cold frame Pete had built in the back yard, were ready and waiting.

The honeybees, which I had coddled through the winter with feedings of sugar water, were busy gathering nectar and spreading pollen. I loved the fuzzy, golden-striped little insects, even though I had to be careful when I walked through the flower-strewn grass around our house. The strawberry patch buzzed with the music of their labor; each delicate blossom a honeybee restaurant offering their favorite repast.

Pete and I had been working hard all winter, remodeling the old farmhouse we'd bought three years before. Now we were going away for the weekend, so we had made arrangements with our neighbors, Joan and David, to feed everyone. We made one last check to be sure all was in place; called our dogs, Princess and Maybe, to hop in the truck, and drove away.

Upon returning we found all well, just as we had left it. Almost, that is. Upon entering the bathroom, we saw that one of the turkeys had escaped from its box and had somehow gotten into the bathtub. It was snuggled up with the rabbit and seemed quite content.

Over the next few weeks we allowed Thumper, as we named the rabbit, to run free in the house. He used the kitty litter and sometimes joined Spooky and her family in their basket, curling up with them like a long-eared, short-tailed kitten. Quite often he jumped into the box with the four turkeys. His bathtub friend, whom we were calling Goblin, would immediately leave the other three and snuggle up with Thumper. Pete and I decided to let Goblin have more freedom, and he and Thumper became inseparable. Thumper was the leader. Wherever he went, Goblin followed. They curled up together in a tight ball to sleep, Goblin tucking his head into Thumper's fur.

When they grew older we turned the turkeys outside in the barnyard. Sometimes I'd let Thumper out and he would frolic with Goblin in the grass, both searching for good things to eat. I'd bring them greens from the garden or young carrots that needed thinning. Goblin was growing too big now to curl up on top of Thumper, but he still tried his best. Thumper would sometimes kick him with his strong, still-growing hind legs, then would turn around and nuzzle his twitching nose into his pal's feathers.

One day, however, their strange liaison came to an end. Perhaps it was a hawk, swooping out of the sky; perhaps a coyote, slinking down from the hills. One day Thumper was gone. Goblin died soon thereafter, of causes unknown. He joined our little animal graveyard in the cedars.

The other turkeys grew big and fat, showing promise of a fine Thanksgiving dinner. The foal grew tall. The kittens found new homes. The calves learned to eat grain and grass. The swallows fledged and flew away; the ducklings, those not caught by muskrats and hawks, grew into hens and drakes. The peas grew and formed pods, which I picked and cooked and canned. The tomatoes grew bright red fruit and the strawberries ripened. The bees magically turned their nectar into honey.

Life on the farm continued. If the little rabbit and turkey were remembered at all, it was in the collective memory of continuing life and in a few pictures snapped by me and tucked away in an old photo album, and in a story I sometimes recall and tell to friends.

*****

5:30 pm April 10, 2003

A new and very wet snow has taken us back to winter, or so it seems. Peter came over for a bowl of bean soup left over from work yesterday. I played some of my new songs for him on my guitar.

Afterward, I realized that this was a great snow for sculpting, so I put on warm gloves and a jacket and created a life-size self-portrait sitting in the Adirondack chair in front of the cabin. I modeled it on a picture Betsy and I took when she was here, me sitting on my deck in my bathing suit in three feet of snow, with my legs crossed and my arms behind my head. The photo turned out pretty well, the sculpture even better. I hope it doesn't melt too fast. My sister Nancy and cousin Ellen will be here soon and I'd like them to see it. I took some pictures of the snow sculpture.

You can create anything out of anything, I guess, if you use your imagination.

11:00 pm April 14, 2003

Nancy and Ellen just went up to the loft to bed. I can hear them puttering around, getting settled in their beds. They arrived two days ago, driving up from Virginia together. I think this is the first time the three of us have been together, alone, since high school. Back then Ellen, who is my age, seemed to have more in common with my little sister Nancy, who is five years younger, than with me. When Ellen's parents, my Uncle Bill and Aunt Jean, split up, leaving Ellen confused and distraught, Momma invited her to live with us. Ellen moved into Nancy's room. I, dealing with my own adolescent hang-ups, was jealous of both of them. Ellen had been my closest friend years before, and even though we had drifted apart, her subsequent closeness to Nancy made me feel left out. The fact that both of them had boyfriends and I didn't, didn't help.

Any feelings of cousinly or sisterly animosity have dissipated now, and we are all quite close. It's great to have time to talk about those times and to re-form new ties. We went maple syruping with my friend Windy today, then had lunch in North Creek and rode the gondola up Gore Mountain. On the way home we stopped at the VIC Nature Center in Newcomb and went snow-shoeing along the shores of Rich Lake. They both seemed to really enjoy their North Woods experiences. Nancy saw a black squirrel at my feeder, and was excited when I told her I had not seen it before.

7:30 am April 16, 2003

Nancy and Ellen left a little while ago, leaving the cabin with a feeling of emptiness. Huck and I walked down to the road to see them off, and Huck stared with dismay as the car rolled away. I have been putting things back in order, trying to ready myself for my old routine. Glancing out the window a few moments ago, I saw the black squirrel Nancy told me about, perched on the feeder. Black squirrels, a color phase of the eastern gray squirrel, are fairly common in the northern woods, particularly across the border in Canada. Huck saw it too and commenced barking. The squirrel was nervous but it didn't run away. It is enjoying the sunflower seeds, no doubt, after spending the winter eating buried seeds from conifers.

I decided to climb up Mt. Sabattis to the power line trail and, with Huck at my side, followed it to a wonderful view of the surrounding mountains. Now I am back in time, thinking about another mountain range I knew and loved.

*****

The Cascade Mountains of Washington overlooked Pete's and my farm, though distantly. A much younger range than the Adirondacks, they were formed by violent volcanic eruptions. The nearest peak, Mount Rainier, was clearly visible from the town of Centralia, Washington, where I was working in 1980, and Mt. St. Helens was just beyond. Pete and I had hiked Mt. Rainier several times and explored the ice caves there.

Work was scarce in this part of Washington, especially for a young woman with no job training, college degree, or self-confidence. She has started taking classes at Evergreen College, hoping to complete her degree, but that does not bring in needed cash. The woman I see has had part-time jobs but, needing steady, full-time employment, she has now taken a job as a nurse's aide.

Closing my eyes, I look back, seeing the single-story, sprawling gray building, a few shrubs planted around it in a half-hearted attempt to make it appear attractive. On one side of the building is a sign which reads, "Welcome to the Good Cheer Nursing Home." On the other side is a window, and if you look carefully, you can see through it an old man lying in a hospital bed. Bending over him is a woman, 30 years old, wearing white slacks and shirt, with her long hair pulled back in a bun.

Ashes and Dreams

The slight figure barely made a wrinkle in the cold white sheets, tucked tight in hospital style around him. He was still, but occasionally a low moan gave proof that he was not asleep. It was 5:30 am, and I had just arrived for the morning shift at the Good Cheer Nursing Home where I worked as a nurse's aide. It was time to start getting the patients up so that they would be ready for breakfast. I bent over him, speaking his name as I touched his shoulder. "Jed, it's time to get up. How are you today?" I jumped back as his fist came slugging out of the sheets, grazing my arm with a strong but misguided punch. "Jed!" I called softly "Don't hit me!"

He turned his head slowly, blinking as he opened dark brown eyes. He seemed to come from a long way away as he slowly brought me into focus. His voice was low, with a crackly edge. "Is that you Pat? Did I hit you? I'm sorry, I didn't mean to. It's just that... my back...it hurts so damned bad."

"I'm gonna have to turn you, Jed; raise you up to change your gown. It's gonna hurt some more..." As I spoke I dodged back, evading the fist that slammed toward me, synchronized with the gasp of pain that escaped his lips as I moved the wasted, pain-wracked body. I intercepted the apology as he began to whisper it. "It's alright Jed. I understand."

He was one of my favorite patients. He'd had a stroke several years before, and now, at eighty-two, his once strong, brawny body lay shrunken and twisted in the nursing home bed. His wife was long dead, and if he had other friends or family they must have forgotten him. I never knew him to have a visitor.

I had been working at the nursing home for eight months. It had been a shock at first, seeing the twisted bodies and empty stares of many of the residents; remnants of human beings who, if they knew I was here, didn't acknowledge it. Smelling the stale odor of dried urine and putrefying flesh which the disinfectants and deodorizers couldn't completely disguise. Looking at the artificial smiles of nurses who always spoke in the first person plural: "How are we today, Bertha?" Did we take our medicine this morning?"

It wasn't a job that I had wanted, but we needed the money. I scanned the classified section of the newspaper and saw the ad for nurse's aide. I'd had no training or experience, but it seemed to be the only job you could get around these parts.

I found out why. Minimum wage, a 5:00 am shift, hard, messy work. But that wasn't what I hated. What bothered me were the expressions of pain, confusion, and hopelessness on the faces of the residents. Faces that had lost all dignity. Faces that were waiting to die. I wanted to make things better for them, and I couldn't. I took them home with me when my shift ended at 2:00 pm and I slept with them through restless nights.

But each morning before the sun came up I dragged myself out of bed, gulped down a cup of instant coffee, and drove back to the Good Cheer Nursing Home. And by the time I walked in the door, I was ready to put

208

on a smile and do my job. The staff always seemed to be in a hurry here, trying to finish one patient and move on to another. But I tried to squeeze in a little extra time for the ones who seemed to need it most. Jed was one of them.

I would stop by his room for a few minutes whenever I had a chance-- bring him a chocolate bar and tell him the latest news. It didn't really matter what--a little gossip about a man I'd met at the store last night, a story about a kitten I'd found underneath the dumpster in the back alley, some incident my mother had written about in a letter. His eyes would brighten above his hawk-like nose, made bigger by the thinness of his face, and he would break into a tremulous smile. He loved chocolate and was grateful for the chance to listen and talk. Unless, that is, the pain was too bad. At those times I would try to re-position him and quietly walk away.

One morning the news I brought was momentous. Geologists had detected rumblings deep in the belly of Mount St. Helens, the snow-capped volcanic peak that towered above the Cascade mountain range forty miles to the south. The majestic mountain was threatening to transform itself into a frothing volcano, and in the process turn the bucolic land around it into a scene out of Edgar Rice Burroughs' "Land Before Time."

I was thrilled and a little frightened, as were most of the people I knew here. Volcanoes did not seem like a real part of life in the twentieth century United States. I was from Virginia, where the gentle Appalachians were folded and pushed into existence over millions of years. The chance of a mountain exploding into a fuming mass of fire seemed beyond the realm of possibility.

Showing Jed the headlines in the "Seattle Times," I spouted out the news, eager to bring some excitement into his life. I was not prepared for his reaction. "I spent most of my younger days on Mount St. Helen's," he told me. "I logged that mountain. Hiked every damned foot of it. Hunted and fished there too; I caught trout up in Spirit Lake with my friend Harry. Harry had the lodge up there, you know. I wonder if he's still alive. God, I'd like to see Harry again."

For the next week Jed's room was always my first stop when I arrived at work. "You can see the steam coming out of her, Jed." "The radio says they're evacuating all around there, and no camping or anything is allowed now. And they're talking about your friend, Harry Truman. He's alive. They say he still lives up there; still has his lodge!"

209

Some days if the pain was bad he'd just lie there and listen. But if it was one of his good times, he'd tell me stories about his logging days, using the colorful, descriptive language of men who worked hard and cussed hard. He'd talk about some huge old cedar he'd topped, almost slipping out of when the wrong branch broke. About being caught in a snowstorm so bad "it made Hell look good!" About an elk he and Harry had shot and trailed for two days, following it deep into the hidden, cedar-draped recesses of Mount St. Helens.

I looked forward to my early morning talks with Jed. I scanned the newspapers eagerly, storing in my mind any bits of news I could find about Mount St. Helens, and particularly about the burly old man on the mountain, Harry Truman.

"Harry's giving them quite a time," I announced one morning to Jed. "They tried to make him leave, but he refused. They said he cussed them out, up one side and down the other. Said Mount St. Helens was his mountain and his home--where his wife died--and he wasn't going to leave. He said that if Mount St. Helens went, he was going with her."

Days passed. "They've got everybody out of there now, Jed, all except Harry. They say she's ready to blow. They tried to take him out by force, but that old man--they say he's eighty years old—he stood them off. It's too dangerous to go back in again, so I guess they'll let him stay."

It was Sunday morning May 18, 1980--Pete's and my anniversary, when Mount St. Helens erupted. I didn't have to work that day, so I was sitting out on the porch steps chatting with Pete when Verne, a friend from down the road, pulled up in his pickup truck and told us the news. We couldn't see the mountain from where we were, so we all piled into Verne's truck and headed for a peak in the Black Hills, a few miles away. From there we watched the steam and ash pouring out of the mountain. It was too far to see where Spirit Lake Lodge had stood, and way too smoky, but I knew it must be gone now, blown apart by the earth-shattering explosion which destroyed every sign of life for twenty square miles. And I knew that Jed's friend Harry would be gone now, too.

"Did you hear the news, Jed?" I asked softly, watching as he slowly, painfully turned his head to look at me. "Noo...I haven't heard anything recently." He was lying on his side, positioned between two pillows, his head propped against a third one. His eyes sought my face as I searched for the right words to tell him. "She blew yesterday, Jed. Mount St. Helens erupted. Blew her top right off."

He was silent for a few moments. "Harry?" He finally asked, in a voice I could barely hear.

"He never left. I guess he died in the eruption. It's what he wanted to do." I didn't say anything else, just watched the tears squeeze from his eyes, slowly wind their way down the tortuous creases in his weathered face. I tried to find words to console him over the death of his friend, but as I started to speak, he interrupted.

"Lucky bastard," he whispered. "I wish I'd been with you, Harry. You lucky son-of-a-bitch."

I didn't keep my nursing home job much longer. I'd saved up enough money to take a bus trip back to Virginia, and I was anxious to go.

The day before I left I stopped by the nursing home to tell Jed good-bye. He was having one of his bad days, the nurse said. I bent over him as he lay on his side with his eyes closed. I spoke softly. "I'm going home, Jed, back to Virginia. I won't be coming in to see you for a while." He didn't answer, didn't move at all. But when I reached out to touch his hand, I saw that his dark eyes were open now, glistening with tears. Turning quickly away, I left the room.

The bus route back to Virginia went east along Route 12, passing not far from Mount St. Helens. As I drew near the mountain, I pressed my face against the window, staring through the glass at the aborted peak which only a few months before had frothed with violence. It was peaceful now. A cloud of steam rose above the volcano's crater, drifting skyward, enticed by a gentle updraft of warm air. As I gazed at the softly swirling cloud, I imagined that I saw a pair of dark, familiar eyes, a lined and craggy face. Then, as we drove onward, it dissipated into the endless blue of the Cascade sky.

*****

7:30 pm April 17, 2003

I saw a robin today, pecking through the trampled snow on the hill near the cabin. Spring is truly coming, despite the 22 degree temperature reading on the thermometer this morning. Most of the snow has melted, but there is still ice, and walking is more treacherous than ever. The melt-off freezes into a sheet of solid ice during the night, and the yak-traks don't work on ice. I slipped twice this week while walking Huck, landing solidly on my behind. Too bad I haven't kept track of how many times I've slid down this hill!

10:00 am April 20, 2003

Today is Easter. I had planned to attend the town's sunrise service and a breakfast provided by the Methodist Church, but I changed my mind. Instead I am spending the morning with Huck, Miss Kelley, my pair of red-breasted nuthatches, several red squirrels and a flock of chickadees.

Work was so slow yesterday that Eve left early. As might be expected, it got busy as soon as she left! At least I made a little money. Before she went home she told me about how river otters had been using our leftover ice-fishing holes, scooting down one and coming out another with fish in their mouths! Cool!

Later, from the window behind the diner, we watched a common merganser, first of the season, transform itself from a chunk of white ice (which is what it resembled with its head tucked under its wing) into a living bird, paddling across the pond. In spite of its name this bird does not look a bit common, with its flashy white on black patches and its crest. They'll be breeding soon.

A man sat down at the counter for breakfast and, noting that his hat had upon it an animal track, I asked him if he was interested in tracking. He said he was; in fact he belongs to a group that tracks and studies wildlife. Dan, as he introduced himself, was injured in Vietnam and has been on disability ever since, but he builds boats and tracks wildlife as a hobby. An interesting man.

6:15 pm April 21, 2003

Spring is surely here! I wore a tee-shirt and got a slight sunburn today when Huck and I followed the trail toward Raquette Lake. I was on a quest, searching for shelf mushrooms to carve for my niece's graduation and my nephew's wedding presents. I found two birch polypores and a thin-maze flat polypore, all of which looked like they would work. I carefully wrapped them and tucked them in my backpack before continuing on.

The creek that cascades along the trail for a ways was like a small river, bursting with exuberance, anxious to hurry the melting snow on its way to the lake and make way for the blossoms of spring. There was still ice on the tree-covered slopes, and I slipped on one hill; but it won't be long now before the earth is warm and brown with last autumn's fallen leaves.

8:20 am April 23 2003

I woke up abruptly at 4:00 am this morning when Miss Kelley jumped on my belly. Lying in the darkness, I tried to pray, as I often do when I find myself awake at this ghost-laden hour. I prayed to the earth gods of the Indians who once hunted here, to the Christian god and to the pagan gods of my Celtic ancestors. As I was praying I fell asleep, and I dreamed that they told me to paint a picture. I began painting it, using great crude slashes of black paint for the ground. Then, in shades of red and brown, I painted myself, life-size, lying prone on the dark ground, dead. I woke up before the painting was finished. I wonder what it meant. I'll be glad when the season picks up and I have more days of work. I think I am spending too much time alone.

8:00 pm April 25, 2003

I stopped this afternoon to peek into the Smiling Pool and I saw a number of blue-tinted, gelatinous globs, each filled with tiny suspended dots which I recognized as frog eggs. It has been years since I found frog eggs in a pond, but there was a time that they were part of my every spring. My friend Donna, my sister Nancy, and I would scoop them out of the murky waters of Kooger's Pond and carry them home in jars to watch hatch into squiggly black tadpoles. We would watch the tadpoles' tails slowly vanish and four legs appear, a form of magic as bewitching as anything performed by Merlin or Houdini. Then we would carry the young frogs back to the pond, where they would float for a moment on the surface, then dive down to the murky bottom and out of sight.

Now it's back to the farm in Washington, another day in May, just a week after Mount St. Helens erupted.

*****

Ashes Ashes We All Fall Down

The morning of May 25, 1980, broke bright and blue-skied above the small farm where my husband Pete and I lived in Gate, Washington. The rays of early morning sunlight peeked through the blinds of our bedroom window, beckoning us to arise on this lovely spring day. I felt lazy, however, as I glanced at the clock. The hands pointed to 5:45. The pigs and chickens could wait another hour. When I next awoke it was dark; coal-dark; midnight-dark; death-dark. I lay still in confusion, question-

213

ing my memory. I looked at the dial on the clock's face. It said 7:00. Was it seven at night? Had I slept through the entire day? The truth hit me like the proverbial ton of bricks. I knew without question what was wrong. Mount St. Helens had erupted again!

Yelling to Pete, still asleep on the other side of the bed, I threw off the covers. Wrapping my bathrobe around me, I opened the front door. Sure enough, drifting down from the sky was a blizzard of gray flakes. It looked like someone living in the clouds above us had just cleaned out their woodstove and dumped the entire contents on our farmyard. I stared in fascination, then called out again to Pete, who was stumbling out of bed by now. The farm animals! We had to protect them!

I grabbed a flashlight and flew out the back door, making sure the cats and dogs stayed inside. I ran down to the barnyard and shoved our two Holstein calves into a stall, then closed the big outer door. I carried the boxes of Rhode Island Red chicks and mallard ducklings from the chicken house into our bathroom. Most of the hens had gone back into the chicken house to roost, no doubt thinking nighttime had come mighty early. Buzz, our pet turkey, was pecking around outside the henhouse in confusion. I grabbed her and hustled her in the door. The Grey Toulouse geese were still outside, under the cedar trees. I chased them around the barnyard, swallowing mouthfuls of ash as I tried futilely to drive them into the chicken house. Finally I gave up and went searching for the horses. Pete was outside too, helping to corral and secure Nevada and Belle. When we finally finished and stumbled back inside, we looked like chimney sweeps after a busy day's work. We stared wide-eyed at one another, peering through the gray masks of our faces, wondering what the rest of the day would bring.

We turned on the radio. It confirmed that at 6:15 am Mt. St. Helens, the Cascade volcanic peak which lay to the southwest of us, had erupted for the second time and was currently spewing ash across this half of the state. The announcer was warning everyone to stay indoors and absolutely NOT to go outside without a mask. Pete and I grinned at each other sardonically. A little late for that!

I made a pot of hot coffee while Pete washed the ash off his arms, legs, and face. Then I took my turn. By now the phone was beginning to ring, and we shared our astonished chagrin with neighbors and friends, asking and giving advice. No one could believe it could be so dark out, and even the old-timers, who always knew what to do, had no answers. No one had *ever been through this before. Then the phone lines, weighted down by the heavy ash, ceased to work.*

This was not, of course, entirely a surprise. We'd been hearing for months about the pressure building up inside the mountain, about the rumblings detected by geologists and the predictions made by seismologists. We'd read about David Johnston, the young geologist who'd been killed in the eruption the previous week, and about old Harry Truman, the man on the mountain who'd chosen to die there. We'd driven into the Black Hills the Sunday before, and we'd sat on a hilltop, drinking beer and watching the spectacular eruption in awe. We'd been lucky that day. The winds had blown the volcanic ash to the east. Now it was our turn.

The ash fall ended in an hour, and by 9:00 AM we could see. But what a sight! The lovely emerald-green cedars were no longer green. The azaleas and rhododendrons blooming outside the house had lost their brilliant shades of rose and red. The young vegetables, just pushing through the black earth in our garden, lay limp and lifeless. The black earth itself was no longer black. Everything, everywhere we looked, was gray.

Lorraine and Jack, the owners of Gate Store, put up new letters on their sign to read "Gate Ash Hole," and gave out free facemasks. Pete went out for beer later that day and came back home with masks for each of us to wear when we went outside. But it was the animals I was worried about. Pneumonia was one of the main concerns, especially among newborn calves. We began dosing ours with penicillin immediately, not waiting for symptoms to appear. We kept everyone inside for several days, but there was no way to keep the ash out. It filtered through the windows and under the doorsills, permeating the water and settling on fur and feathers like a coat of lead paint. Only time would tell how much internal damage it was doing.

Gradually the excitement of having a volcano erupt in one's back yard eroded away and a feeling of moroseness settled over the community of Gate. Gardens had to be replanted. Most of the apples and cherries were lost, the young blossoms and fruit too fragile to survive the heavy ash coating. One of our calves weakened and died. Farmers began realizing the destructive impact of the ash on equipment. Machinery stopped running and chain saws grew dull within minutes of cutting the ash-coated logs.

Inside the house, polishing the furniture became a lesson in futility. Within minutes of dusting, the tops of end tables and desks were covered again. Floor finishes were ruined by the abrasive volcanic ash which was ground in by boot heels and could not be mopped or waxed away. Children sang the old nursery rhyme, "Ring around the rosie," ending with the adage, "Ashes, ashes, we all fall down," but there was little joy in the game. Depression ran high, and doctors and counselors had record-breaking numbers of patients. Living in a gray world was grim, and our moods matched the color of our world.

There were a few more mild eruptions from Mount St. Helens, but none that came close to the May 18th and 25th events. Gradually, life on the volcano began to return; a lichen here, a wildflower there; a hemlock sapling reappearing from a cone seed that somehow, miraculously, survived. The colors of Washington began to re-emerge, and the gray melted into greens, yellows, and reds. In the long run, the nutrients scattered over the earth by the mighty volcano would prove beneficial, replenishing the soil and revitalizing the landscape. If breathing and living in the ash did us permanent harm, there is no evidence. A jar of ash and a few pieces of pumice, tucked away in a box, are all that remain to prove the terror and wonder of that early Sunday dawn, when ash rained out of the sky and turned morning to darkest night.

I visited Mount St. Helen's three years later. We were not allowed to go near the rim, but a park ranger led us along a small trail on the aborted mountainside. He pointed to new saplings and other plants that were already forcing their up way through the ash, promising that life on the mountain would return once more and continue on...

*****

9:30 April 27, 2003

When I turned on the radio this morning the NPR host was talking about a new book on happiness; who is happy, why they are happy, how we can attain happiness. I think a lot about happiness, too, especially when I am not. I am not exactly sure what it is. Is it contentment, acceptance, joy, or bliss? Is it like pain, which scientists say people feel at different levels, or have different tolerances for? Is it a permanent condition, or is it transient?

How, I sometimes wonder, can one be happy in the face of so much suffering in the world around us? How does one ignore or forget or accept the personal sorrows which, if we live long enough, all of us face? Can the feelings induced by anti-depressants be called happiness, or are they simply a way of repressing our true feelings?

I had awakened in a relatively happy mood yesterday until, upon walking down to the highway, I saw the town truck stop to haul away a deer just hit by a car. As I watched the driver drag the corpse up onto the tailgate, I saw in my mind the lovely flash of white, a signal for danger, which I often see when Huck and I surprise a deer up on the snowmobile trail. I heard the indignant huff it makes at having its peace disturbed as it bounds away, and I wondered if this might be one of those deer. Even if not, I couldn't escape a feeling of deep sadness which stayed with me the rest of the day.

5:30 pm April 30, 2003

There is a seasonal, or vernal, pool not far from the cabin, fed by melting snow high up on Mt. Sabattis. It is always wet, but now, with the spring run-off, it is deep and clear and lovely. I am intrigued by this clear sparkling pool, so like the spring pools described in Robert Frost's poem:

These pools that, though in forests,
Still reflect the total sky almost without defect,
And like the flowers beside them, chill and shiver,
Will like the flowers beside them soon be gone,
And yet not out by any brook or river
But up by roots to bring dark foliage on.

I leave tomorrow to go to Buffalo, where I will leave Miss Kelley and pick up Betsy. We will then head south to Virginia for our nephew Sandy's wedding. Huck will go with us. I have not met Sandy's bride, Elaine, and I am looking forward to doing so. Also seeing Momma and everyone. Momma is not well enough to go to the wedding, which makes me sad. Now I need to finish packing.

May 2003

9:15 pm May 6, 2003

I just got back from Buffalo, where I dropped off Betsy, taught two days of Head Start music, and picked up Miss Kelley before heading home. Sandy's wedding went well; a real "big fat Greek wedding!" Actually, I didn't go to the wedding itself, a private ceremony held in a Greek Orthodox church, but the reception was great fun. Betsy and I went to the battlefield at Gettysburg on the way back, and stood on the spot where our great-grandfather, a Confederate soldier, had fought over a hundred years ago.

On the way home I missed the turn for the route I usually take, through Old Forge and Blue Mountain Lake. I found myself on Route 8, which led through Lake Pleasant and Speculator to Route 30.

Just north of Speculator I saw a moose-crossing sign on the roadside, and not a hundred yards further I saw the real thing. There on my right, fifteen feet from the road, were two moose, what I guessed to be a cow and last year's calf. I stopped and backed up so I could see them better, and they seemed only mildly interested in me. I held Huck's mouth shut with my hand, so he wouldn't bark, and watched them for a few minutes. They were eating tree bark, pulling it off the trees in smooth strips, chewing them slowly and methodically. It was dusk, too dark for a photograph, but light enough to paint an exquisite picture on my memory.

My mammal guide says that moose cows calve in late May or early June, and they chase off their last year's offspring just before the new one is born. I'm guessing that, perhaps, unbeknownst to it, this was one of the last times this young moose would be hanging out with Mama Moose. It looked plenty big enough to take care of itself, but I wonder how it will feel, cast out into the world on its own--lonely? afraid? uncertain? Or am I anthropomorphizing--attributing my own feelings to a creature that doesn't need them.

I should go to bed, but I am not sleepy. I think I'll pull out my memories again...

*****

There was one thread that tied together the five years which followed my move to Washington state. Soon after I arrived, I began thinking about returning to college, completing the degree I had begun ten years before. My studies at Evergreen College provided structure through the best and the worst of the time I was there, and left me with a glimmer of hope.

Native American Studies

"What do you want to be for Halloween?" I asked one of my young pupils as we stood outside of the Head Start classroom. He responded with enthusiasm. "I want to be an Indian!" The lead teacher turned and looked at him with raised eyebrow. "You can't BE an Indian for Halloween," she told him. "You ARE an Indian!" Glancing at me, the teacher shook her head and grinned.

I was doing a three-month-long internship with the Chehalis Indian Tribe, part of my Native American Studies program at Evergreen College. It included working with pre-K children in the Head Start program and learning to weave on a loom with a native weaver at the reservation near Oakville. This was my second year of study, and I was enjoying the program immensely.

I was thirty years old when, in 1980, I went back to college in western Washington. I had previously taken classes in North Carolina, Virginia, and Arizona, so I already had two years worth of credits. Evergreen College, located in Olympia, was a half-hour drive from the 5-acre farm I shared with my husband. It was a state school with a non-traditional curriculum. I was thrilled when I learned that they offered a degree in Native American Studies, and I began making plans to enroll. My husband Pete was dubious. "What on earth are you going to do with a degree like that?" he asked. I was undaunted. Short of becoming a "Native American" myself, I couldn't think of anything I would rather do. Evergreen was affordable, so I applied.

Why did I (obviously a "paleface") want to study about Indians, was one of the questions I was asked. I took my time as I answered, explaining that I admired the values and beliefs that most American Indians held; reverence for Mother Earth and her creatures; a belief that all things in nature have a spirit; their connection to the natural world. I admired their artwork and craftsmanship and the deep respect they felt for the traditions of their people. They knew many things that I would like to learn, and I hoped that I would have something to offer back. I also, of course, felt great remorse and guilt for the way my European ancestors had treated them, and would like to try in some small way to make amends.

I talked about my grandfather, Benjamin Garber, who had been chief clerk of the Bureau of Indian Affairs in Washington DC in the early 1900s. My father had, as a child, accompanied him to various Indian reservations and later regaled me with the stories. Daddy also had a deep interest in and admiration for our country's native people, which he had taught to me.

I was accepted into the program, where I was among the oldest and only non-native students. My advisors were Gail Tremblay, an Onondaga/Mikmac Indian artist and poet from western New York, and Lloyd Colfax, a Makah elder from coastal Washington. They helped me create my own study plan, which included learning about various tribes around the country.

I spent my first quarter studying the people of the Pacific Northwest in a module called "Clash of Cultures." I read books such as "Exploring Washington Archaeology" and visited museums in the area. I incorporated into my studies what I had learned from attending workshops at the Lelooska Foundation near Woodland, dedicated to preserving and promoting the art and culture of the indigenous Pacific Northwest people.

I set out to find out more about the historic and current interactions between the people of Gate, where I lived, and our closest Indian neighbors, the Chehalis. I interviewed long-time residents of Gate and visited the Chehalis Reservation, near Oakville, where I talked to tribal members.

The Indians of the Pacific Northwest have a unique culture built around the great cedar trees which dominate the forests and the salmon that run up the rivers to spawn. In former days, I learned, Chehalis men, women, and children had lived in a village called "Sacel't" or "Made Lake," located on the banks of the Black River which passed behind our farm. Sitting on its lush, verdant banks, I tried to picture them, spearing or trapping salmon and gathering berries. They hunted the black-tail deer that flourished here, taking the meat and hides home to longhouses made of cedar planks. They traded with other tribes and gathered together for ceremonies known as potlatches, which included dance and song, feasts, and gift-giving.

The blankets of blue flowers which burst through the ground in spring in our pasture, identified as camas by our neighbors, had been an important foodstuff for the Chehalis and other tribes. They harvested the bulbs in spring, roasted them in underground pits, and made them into loaves or added them to stews. (I roasted some myself and tried them in my vegetable beef soup. Not bad.)

The Chehalis encountered white men in trading ships in 1792, after which they began trapping and trading beaver. The white man's diseases, which they contracted thereafter, soon led to the demise of whole villages. Those who survived were forced onto smaller and smaller plots of land, eventually settling on a reservation of just over 4,000 acres. I thought about the old Indian man, most likely Chehalis, who had been living in our house before we bought it. I tried to imagine how he must have felt, watching us move in and push him out, using "legal" papers, just as had happened to his ancestors.

Today, most of the Chehalis live on the Reservation, working in logging and fishing or in the tribal office. The children go to Head Start on the "res" and then to public school in Oakville.

One year Pete and I found someone to take care of our farm and we headed back east to see our families. I had, as part of my college curriculum, been reading about the Lakota Sioux: such books as "The Road to Wounded Knee," "Lame Deer; Seeker of Visions," and "Black Elk Speaks." On our trip we stopped in Lakota country and visited the Custer Battlefield and the Crow Agency in Montana and the Sioux Indian Museum in Rapid City, South Dakota. Later, based on my studies, I wrote a paper called "Sioux Spiritualism; Does It Still Live?" I concluded that the answer to that question is YES!

After arriving at my parents' house I investigated the culture of the Pamunkey and Mattaponi tribes. As a Virginian, I had grown up hearing about Chief Powhatan, his daughter Pocahontas, and their stories--some true, some not. I had gone with my fourth grade class to Jamestown, where the English had first encountered Virginia's native inhabitants. Now, as part of my degree studies, I visited the Pamunkey Museum, located on the banks of the river bearing their name. I spent time talking to the leaders of both tribes, Chief "Little Eagle" Custalow of the Mattaponi and Chief Tecumsah Deerfoot Cook of the Pamunkey. I tried to re-learn history from their perspective.

On another trip I went to see my sister Betsy, in Buffalo, and while there spent a month learning about the Haudenosaunee, or Six Nations, also known as the Iroquois. I visited the Seneca reservation, speaking with their leaders and exploring their museum and tribal center. Betsy and I attended a powwow there.

Upon returning to Washington, I turned in a report on my various experiences to my advisor. My internship with the Chehalis Head Start followed, a wonderful experience which I enjoyed immensely. I now had just one more quarter to complete; a quarter which coincided with the last days of my marriage.

* * * * *

6:30 pm May 7, 2003

Just after dawn this morning I was awakened by the lilting notes of a white-throated sparrow, so I took a cup of coffee out to the deck to enjoy the music. It is harder to see the lake now, as the branches of birch and beech trees don their new wardrobes of crisp leaves, shimmering with the glow of freshly minted chlorophyll. I heard the cry of a loon echo across the forest from the waters of Long Lake. Around me the treetops were alive with the voices of a hundred songbirds, each staking its territorial claim in melodious song. White throated sparrows are my favorite. The air felt so alive that it almost hurt to breathe.

Joy coursed through my veins, and I felt like my blood was singing, and I was awake today as, according to Henry David Thoreau, some of us never are. I likened my blood to the sap of sugar maples, bursting through the bark and flowing into pails in great gluts of exuberance, unaware that it will be boiled down by the heat of human-fed fires into a thick mire of dark syrup.

  Later I sat in my Adirondack chair, now placed at the entrance to my new log wood shed, and watched a pileated woodpecker searching for dinner in the pile of logs near the cabin. Huck began barking. It flew away and, to my surprise, a pair of boys with bicycles appeared on the trail, an unexpected sight up here.

9:30 am May 8, 2003

I woke up with two welts on my neck this morning. Blackfly season has arrived. They seem to be worse up here on the mountainside than down in the village. I have not been here for a bad black fly year yet, but the natives predict that this will be one. That is the test, I guess. If you still love the Adirondacks after surviving the blackflies, you are accepted!

Carl, my landlord, has been building me a woodshed. He is sure I will be staying another winter, although I did not answer him when he asked. It is made of logs, and he says he'll help me build a fire pit beside it. My

Adirondack chair is already sitting at its entrance, and I envision evenings of roasting hot dogs and marshmallows at the fire.

I checked the Smiling Pool this morning and found that most of the eggs had hatched during the week I was gone. The water was full of tiny tadpoles, not more than a half inch in length. Water striders flitted across the pool's surface, and I wondered if they were hoping to dine on the tiny metamorphosing amphibians.

6:30 pm Sunday, May 11, 2003

Work at the diner was exhausting today. It is Mother's Day, and we were as busy as if it was summer. Evy, Julie, and I rushed through the diner with orders and plates of food as fast as we could go. It's different now, of course, since I am no longer the distrusted outsider. All the staff treat me nicely, and I am becoming good friends with Sheryl and Eve. Still, I am worn out. The walk I took with Huck was short, and I apologized to him, promising him a long run tomorrow. I'll be glad when tomorrow comes.

Mother's Day brings too many thoughts to mind. I've been thinking about my mother, lying in the bed she shared with Daddy, her making love to him on that worn mattress, creating five healthy babies there. Now barely a wrinkle under the blanket--87 pounds Nancy guesses--there and yet not there. My mother, yet not my mother.

I've been thinking about myself, too; the mother I almost was. Dan, when he sat down at the counter for a cup of coffee, wished me a "Happy Mother's Day, if you are a mother, that is." I thanked him.

Later Bunny, sitting with his wife, asked me if I was a mother. "No," I answered him, "all my kids are cats and dogs."

I didn't voice the response that went through my mind. "Yes, I am a mother, but my baby died long ago."

*****

My Baby

"Your pregnancy test came back negative," I heard the voice on the phone announce. "Oh. Thanks..." I was confounded. I had been so sure. I had missed my period, something I never did, but it was more than that...a feeling...something I couldn't put into words. I could feel that there was life growing inside me! Guess I was wrong. Well, things would

just continue on the way they were, then. Which wasn't much of a way. My job, milking cows at a nearby dairy, had come to an end recently when Keith, my boss, decided he couldn't afford to pay a second milker. Pete had been fired several months before, as a result of drinking on the job. (He had hit a police car, beer in hand, with the company truck, and had spent a night in jail!)

He had looked for work for a while, but now he was getting un-employment and he didn't seem very anxious to get off of it. He had a few drinking buddies and a bunch of guys he played rock and roll music with. I wasn't quite sure what else he did with his time. It seemed like he'd lost interest in the farm we had been working so hard on, and he'd sure lost interest in me. Though there'd been a night...

We had talked, off and on, over the years, about having a baby. I kept thinking that once we got on our feet, once our marriage was real solid, I would try to get pregnant. I had thought for a while that that time was getting close. Happy on our farm, with the barnyard full of animals, a baby in the nursery seemed like the next step.

But then things started going wrong, just like they always had. We'd been married for nearly seven years but seemed no closer to having a stable marriage than ever. I was thinking maybe we never would. So when my birth control pills ran out, and we didn't have any extra money to buy more, and life seemed to be going out of control anyway, I just let things be. What happened would happen, and I would hope for the best. I wasn't surprised when I missed my period, and when the telephone voice told me I wasn't pregnant after all I was kind of disappointed. Pete seemed like he was, too.

A baby was, for Pete, a different issue, one which no matter how I tried, I would never fully understand. Pete had had a child already, by his first wife. Michael was a Down's syndrome child, and if that wasn't enough, there was something abnormal with his genes--an extra Y chromosome, if I understood properly. I guess Michael was the biggest tragedy in Pete's life, not that he didn't love his son. What Pete would have been like had Michael been born a normal child I would never know. There's a good chance I'd never have met him, since his first marriage might have survived. It breaks my heart, thinking of both of them. Michael never learned to talk, nor was he ever even potty-trained. He died long before he reached adulthood. Michael was a ghost that Pete always carried with him.

Another month passed and I missed my period again. I was waking up with a nauseous feeling in the morning, and I noticed that my jeans were getting tight. I told Pete that I was sure I was pregnant, regardless of what the test had said. He seemed to be glad, and we were both pretty excited when I went back for another test.

I still remember the moment when the doctor told me I was going to have a baby. "Are you glad?" he asked me in a gentle voice. "Yes!" I told him. "Oh yes!" "Good" he said. "So many times it's the other way."

I babbled on in my excitement, asking him questions and getting his advice. "What about cigarette smoke? My husband is a heavy smoker. Could that hurt the baby?" "Yes" he said. "It would be better for him to stop smoking." He reminded me that I should not drink any alcohol, and gave me a list of foods to eat.

I fairly burst out the door and ran out to the van, where Pete was waiting. Those brief moments of joy in the doctor's office were the last I was to know for a long time; years, it seemed.

Pete was furious when I got to the van. I had taken too long, and we would be late in meeting our friends, Dave and Joan, with whom we were going camping. He did not ask me the results of the test, and we rode in silence to our meeting place. Joan and Dave did ask, as soon as we got there, and when I quietly told them that I was pregnant they rejoiced. Pete said nothing. If they noticed his silence they did not comment, chatting with me about babies, talking about having their own two children.

The distance between Pete and me increased over the next few weeks. Maybe my pregnancy brought back too many memories. Maybe he was afraid of what our baby would turn out to be. Things between us hadn't been good to begin with, and now they just kept getting worse.

I suggested that this was a good time for us to make a new start, and for him to get a job. I had quit drinking, maybe he could try to cut down and even stop smoking. He became even angrier.

Joan took me to enroll for WIC, the program designed to provide low-income mothers with a healthy diet and medical services. I was reluctant to accept their help, but my baby's welfare was more important to me than my pride. I scheduled regular check-ups and followed my doctor's advice to the tee. My neighbor, Wanda, who had lost her baby two years before to SIDS, gave me baby clothes and loaned me a book full of names. She and I sat on the cot in the little upstairs bedroom and dreamed up nursery designs. Pete did not seem to care, one way or the other.

The slight nausea I had been having increased. I found myself unable to eat, and when I asked Pete to cook for me he refused in anger, accusing me of pretending. He stayed away from home for longer and longer hours, and the farm work fell to me. I dragged myself out of bed to feed the chickens and geese, to clean the barn and care for the horses. I wrapped myself in blankets, holding Princess close and shivering, too sick to split the firewood with which we heated our house.

Gradually a different feeling began to grow inside me. Something felt wrong. A trip to the clinic confirmed that I had lost weight, not gained. "It's okay," the doctor told me. "That happens sometimes." But I knew better. I wrapped my arms around my belly, trying to hug my baby, protect it from whatever was happening inside me. Pete was lost to me now. I wanted this baby, needed this baby, desperately. I curled up in the double bed Pete's mother had given us, staring at the walls of the bedroom we had remodeled and wallpapered with such hope and enthusiasm. My dog Princess and my cats, Twinkle and Dinky, curled up beside me, but Pete was never there. He came home long after I was asleep, if he came home at all.

We had planned a trip back to Virginia to see our families for the summer. A couple we knew were going to farm-sit for us. We went, making the three thousand mile journey as best we could, not talking much. I spent the long hours wondering what it would be like to raise a child alone. Without ever discussing it, we went our separate ways when we got to Virginia, me to my parents' house, him to his mother's.

I made an appointment with my sister's gynecologist as soon as I arrived. I had lost more weight. She did not reassure me that it was okay. I watched her as she listened to my belly with her stethoscope. She glanced up at me, a puzzled look on her face. "How far along did you say you are? Are you sure?" I was silent as she scheduled me for an ultrasound.

A day later I stood before the machine as she pointed to the images portrayed there. "It's too small, malformed, and it's not moving. There's something wrong."

"What can I do?" I cried. "I'm sorry. There's nothing you can do. Your baby is either dead or dying. The best thing, the only thing, you can do is have it aborted."

She offered to call the hospital and schedule a DNC. "I can't." I told her. "I have no insurance." She suggested another option, which would not be so pleasant. I could go to an abortion clinic. My memory of the *next few days is buried in a fog. I guess I told Pete, but I do not recall his reaction. My brother offered to pay the $1,000 required for the DNC. I was grateful for his generosity, but I refused his offer. This was my baby, my responsibility. My parents supported me, no matter what I did.*

I called the abortion clinic, located in the poorer part of town, and made an appointment. Pete went out to the fields near his mother's house and shot woodchucks the morning I was scheduled to go. My father took me down to the forbidding gray building, and we sat in the waiting room, surrounded by other young women, each with their own demons of remorse and regret. I wanted to scream out loud, "I'm not like you all! I don't want this abortion! I want my baby!" but I sat quietly. Maybe that's what they wanted to scream too. This was my punishment, I told myself grimly. Somehow I had let my baby down. Somehow I had let it die. I deserved to be in this dismal place which reeked of death and shame.

If the weeks preceding and following that day are buried in fog, the moments that I lay on that steel table, my feet rolled into stirrups, are crystal clear. They could have happened yesterday. I kept my eyes closed, my mind empty, answering the doctor's questions in a monotone. I remember the sensation of coldness when he put the instrument inside me, the sound of his voice when he told me it was done. "No," I answered tonelessly, when he asked me if I wanted to know if it was a boy or a girl.

When I returned to the waiting room an eternity later, Pete was sitting beside Daddy. He had a bouquet of flowers in his hand. He handed it to me, his expression unreadable. Each of us was in our own Hell, but it was a Hell we couldn't share. He returned to his mothers' house; I went home with Daddy.

For the next two days I suffered, belatedly, the agonies of childbirth. My mother hovered over me, trying to help. The pain was indescribable, but I suffered it with a grim sense of justice. I had earned this. Every tremor of pain was retribution, revenge for the ultimate sin--betrayal of my child. I was Judas, pining to be nailed to a cross. Hiding behind my sorrow and pain was an unforgivable feeling of relief. I would not have to raise my child alone, after all.

Later the milk came, engorging my breasts, dampening the front of my tee shirt, filling me with a two-fold pain. Salt rubbed into the wound. The child that might have pulled Pete and me together ripped us farther apart than ever. Our time together would not be long now.

But that was a long time ago. I no longer have to leave the room when a newborn is shown on television, or hold back tears when a new mother enters the room with her baby. Now it is just an ache of regret, not only for the baby I never knew, but for the mother I never became; for the joy and love I never had the opportunity to experience.

Yes, I will be glad when Mother's Day is over.

*****

2:30 pm May 14, 2003

It has rained for the past few days, pelting showers accompanied by rolls of thunder which send Huck scurrying to the safety of the bathroom. The dips in the trail where we walk are pools of mud, and water pours down the mountain in miniature rivers, following any small ravine it can find and plummeting over the rocks. Having already soaked two pairs of socks and my sandals, I pulled on rubber boots today. Huck and I splashed through the water quite happily, him examining each new smell, me peering at just about everything we passed. I had with me the small microscopic lens my sister had given me for Christmas, and I used it to examine grass, leaves, puddles, a large boulder with lichens growing on it.

I stood before the boulder, admiring the concentric circular patterns made by the lichen on the rock. I turned on the light and held the magnifying lens against it, trying to single out the individual fungal and blue-green algal particles which I knew jointly made up the lichen. Under the lens I saw what looked like staghorn coral intertwined with colorful crystals, all in minute detail. I was amazed at what I saw, but what struck me most was what I did not see. The bigger patterns were gone, no longer decipherable. It was only by standing back away from the boulder that I could see the lichen in its entirety.

Memory, I told myself, is like standing on the trail and looking back at the boulder. The details may be invisible or distorted, but the pattern, the greater whole, takes meaning. On the way home I saw a monarch butterfly lying dead beside the trail. I brought it back and examined each separate part beneath the lens. Tiny perfect scales came into view, but I had to set the lens down and look at the whole to see the elegant graceful shape of the butterfly itself.

This is what I am trying to do with my life; examine each minute part and then put them together so that I can see the whole. My fear is that

230

once assembled, they will not resemble a lovely butterfly, or even a ring of lichen. My fear is that there will be no pattern...My fear is that there will be no meaning...

7:30 pm May 18, 2003

The meadow below my cabin is carpeted with the delicate blue and yellow petals of bluets, interspersed with the heartier wild strawberries. On my walk with Huck I collected fiddleheads, newly emerging fronds of fern coiled in spirals. I cut them into pieces, slipped the brown fuzz off the stem, and sauteed them in butter for dinner. They tasted a bit like asparagus, and were quite good.

The man I had met a few weeks ago, Dan, came into the diner this morning with a book in hand. "Do you remember me?" he asked. "Sure. How are you?" I responded. He handed me the book, "Tracking and the Art of Seeing," by Paul Rezendes, and I remembered that he had promised to loan it to me.

2:00 pm May 20, 2003

When I took Huck for a walk this morning I saw, in the mud on the side of the trail, what I think were two moose tracks. Using my hand for a ruler, I measured them, and when I got back here, looked them up in the guide book Dan loaned me. I'm not an expert, but I'm pretty sure...

8:00 pm May 28, 2003

I started back at the museum today. I'll be working two days a week. Huck and I climbed up Mt. Sabattis when I got home, following the creek which I have named the Laughing Brook. Leaving the trail and heading up the mountain was like entering another world. Great boulders, left behind by ice age glaciers and called glacial erratics, are scattered along the hillside like lumpy pumpkins on a giant's farm. They are clothed in velvet green with star moss and lichens, and some have delicate flowers growing through their cracks. Side by side with them are the rotting trunks of great old trees, hard maples and hemlocks and white pines, which must have been over a hundred years old when they fell. All manner of mushrooms cling to the bark, their mycelia threading through the trees and turning them to dust as they feed the fungi.

Cinnamon ferns and wood sorrel are everywhere, and here and there are the delicate petals of purple trilliums. These flowers, I've read, are members of the lily family. They are known as Stinkpots or Stinking

Benjamins, due to the odor which attracts their chief pollinator, the carrion fly. What an odd name for such an exquisite flower!

The creek itself, running full from all the rain, is a series of cataracts pouring over boulders into small, still pools which overflow into yet another miniature waterfall. I would have stayed all evening had it not been for the black flies! I have three or four bites, one of which has swollen my eye half shut. It makes me look dreadful. I guess I won't go out to the pub tonight!

June 2003

5:30 pm June 2, 2003

The woods around here are alive with the goings-on of spring! I saw two small frogs, the color of cinnamon, yesterday, and today there was a red eft, about two inches long, in the middle of the trail. I've seen several of them up here. They fascinate me. The color is such a vibrant red-orange that it looks unreal, as if it were rubber toy left behind by a careless child. My nature guide tells me that the eft is the immature stage of a salamander known as a newt. Hatched from eggs in the water, they remain there for about three months during their larval tadpole stage, breathing with gills. Then the young efts develop lungs and climb onto land, where they spend from one to seven years feeding on small insects. Their skins contain a toxin, and their bright coloration is a warning to predators to stay away. Finally their tails flatten, their color turns yellow-green with red spots, and they return to the water, where they mate and lay eggs, beginning the cycle again. Newts may live for over ten years. I have yet to see an adult, but I'm guessing there are some in the pools I see.

*****

Now it's back in time to the farm in Gate. After losing our baby, Pete and I had tried to patch up our marriage. We returned to Washington and I resumed working on my degree in Native American Studies. We both found new jobs and one day we bought some new turkeys. Another turkey tale; another sad story. I don't know how Pete and I ended up with turkeys with such amazing personalities...

Eagle

Benjamin Franklin thought that America's national bird should be a wild turkey instead of a bald eagle. He felt that wild turkeys better personified the qualities Americans should strive for. "Eagle" was a wild turkey, though bred and born in captivity. He earned his name because of his courage and adventurous nature. He exuded the best characteristics of both birds--peaceful yet brave, friendly yet daring. He longed to soar like an eagle, and that may be what led to his downfall.

Eagle was one of several wild turkeys Pete and I bought one spring. We usually kept them in a box in our bathroom, where it was warm, for the first few weeks. This year, however, we were remodeling the bathroom so we set the box in our bedroom. Our cats, Dinky and Twinkle, and our dobermans, Princess and Maybe, were used to having baby animals in the house, so they paid them no mind.

The turkeys grew and thrived in their warm, cozy home. Two of them seemed quite content. One, however, whom we named Eagle, wanted to see the world. While the others ate their turkey mash and curled up to sleep, Eagle continually tried to hop out of the box. Curious to see what he would do, I gave him a hand out. He was ecstatic, and after exploring the bedroom floor he decided he wanted up on the bed, where I was reading, so I gave him a lift up.

He trotted around the bed, pecking at a wrinkle here and there, and then decided to explore the human mountain rising out of the covers. He pecked around for a while, found his way up to my shoulders, and then discovered what must have been his version of Shangri La: my hair. Long and heavy, behind it made a fantastic cave, nice and warm, with hidden treasure inside--my earrings! He was enamored of the shiny metal trinkets which dangled from my earlobes, and did his best to pull them out. He'd seize one, give it a yank, then dart to the back of my neck to hide...then try the other side.

After this adventure there was no keeping Eagle behind bars. He managed to fling himself over the side of the box each morning while Pete and I lay in bed. He'd peck and scratch at the bedspread until I picked him up; then make himself at home inside my hair. When he grew older he learned how to scale the bed by himself, and he'd wake us up as regular as an alarm clock. I was taking classes, trying to complete my bachelor's degree at Evergreen College, so I had lots of bookwork to do. Oftentimes, after feeding the animals and completing my farm chores, I'd climb back into bed with paper, pen, and books and work on my assignments. Eagle would try to wrest the pen from my hand or hustle a bite of paper; then climb contentedly up into his cave. He was as happy as a pig in a poke.

Before long, however, Eagle began to long for greater adventures. His aspirations went beyond the bedroom. He was learning to fly, and he wanted to see the world. One morning, while his box-mates rested safe and boring in their box, Pete and I still asleep in bed, Eagle set out to explore. Where he went that morning and what he did, I never knew. I only know where he finished his journey. It was, sadly, an ignominious ending for such a great-hearted bird. One of us must have left the lid of the toilet up during the night. Perhaps Eagle was trying to reach the window above it, to soar free in the great outdoors. Had he displayed the characteristics of a duck instead of an eagle he might have had a chance. Instead he drowned, and I found his poor, waterlogged and bedraggled body when I got up. Perhaps an eagle heart in a turkey body was never meant to be.

*****

8:30 pm June 3, 2003

We were slow at the diner today and I got away early. I went kayaking with Huck, and when we got back Huck took off down the hill beside my cabin. He flushed a ruffed grouse, which flopped away through the underbrush in a manner that made me think she was intentionally drawing him away. "She must have a nest," I said to myself, and after trying to call him back, to no avail, I peered down over the ridge. At first I saw nothing, but after carefully scanning the ground I found, beneath a small balsam fir, a shallow nest made of grasses. In it were eight buff, lightly speckled eggs, each about an inch and a half long. I scolded Huck when he came back and told him that he would not be allowed to run free now until the grouse chicks were hatched and flown. I went back out, just before dark, and peered into the nest. I was relieved to see that Momma Grouse was back, her mottled brown feathers spread across the eggs.

6:15 pm June 4, 2003

I returned from my walk today with a pocketful of shit. Well, to be more polite, scat. To be specific, two ungulate pellets, either deer or moose. Ever since I found those moose tracks near the cabin I've been looking for other signs, using the book Dan loaned me. These pellets are much larger than most deer pellets, better than an inch; but after looking them up in the book, I'm still not sure. They could be from a large whitetail buck or a small moose. I found several places on the trees that had been stripped off with teeth, but I'm thinking they were made by deer.

I noticed that the Canada mayflowers near my front door were blooming, their blossoms tiny and delicate. I glanced at the grouse nest when I got back and found Momma Grouse still sitting, motionless. I know that Papa Grouse is long gone, not helping her with her motherly duties. I wonder when she eats.

Birchbark Chronicles

7:30 pm June 5, 2003

I worked at the diner today, but my mind kept straying and I couldn't keep it focused on waiting tables. I'm afraid my days there are numbered. When I got home I noticed a raven and two blue jays prowling the treetops and occasionally diving to the ground. I ran to check the grouse nest and found the eggs shells cracked and empty. A sense of despair overwhelmed me. They must have raided the nest! Overcome with frustration and sadness, I stumbled out for my walk with Huck.

As I walked, however, I thought about it some more. Grouse are similar to chickens and turkeys, whose chicks are able to run almost immediately upon hatching. Maybe the grouse eggs had hatched and the chicks had followed Momma Grouse away, while the jays and crows were just cleaning up the leavings. I checked the nest again when I got back. The nest was not torn up, and the eggshells were neatly cracked in half, as if by emerging chicks rather than bombarding birds.

I headed to the library, where I looked up ruffed grouse in a bird guide. I learned that they are indeed precocial, able to run as soon as they hatch. Now I'm quite sure that is what happened. I'll keep Huck in for another week or two and keep an eye out for the little family.

6:30 am June 6, 2003

It's time for my monthly trip to Buffalo. This will finish up the season for Head Start. It's been a nearly a year since I left my teaching job in Buffalo's inner city. There are hardly any black people in the Adirondacks, in spite of a short-lived colonization project headed by Gerrid Smith shortly before the Civil War. A number of black freemen had settled in North Elba in a place they called Timbucktoo. With them was John Brown, the abolitionist who incited a murderous rebellion near Harpers Ferry. Gradually most of the black colonists drifted away. There is a temporary exhibit at the Adirondack Museum on Timbucktoo now.

I miss the diversity, and I miss the straight-forward, humorous, tangy personalities of many of the people I had worked with in Head Start. I hope I will see them again.

9 pm June 12, 2003

I drove back from Buffalo yesterday, and today I met Elizabeth and Jill, two of the guides from the museum, in Tupper Lake. We drove up to Saranac Lake, where we followed the river walk, explored the shops, and went to lunch at the old Hotel Saranac.

Back in Tupper, we walked around Little Wolf Pond, and Jill, who has a degree in Adirondack Studies, helped me identify some ferns I didn't know. I bought some great bumper stickers to put on my guitar case.

When I got home I took Huck for his walk, and was overjoyed to come across a family of ruffed grouse not far from where the nest had been. I'm convinced that they are the ones who had been born near my cabin.

8 pm June 13, 2003

The mountain around my cabin is a garden of wildflowers. Canada mayflowers cluster on the rock ledge, their delicate white blossoms emerging above one dark leaf from the thin layer of soil. Starflowers grow farther down the hill, wild daisies in the meadow. Yellow goats-beard and orange hawkweed are scattered along the trail as if a sky queen had emptied out her jewelry box.

I gave notice at the diner today, telling Jim that I wanted to have July and August to work on my writing. He said that if they need me they'll hire me back for the fall. I hope I have enough money to get by, at least for now. Dan, my wildlife tracker friend, came in and showed me a magazine article about his tracking group in Vermont. I told him about the moose tracks I had seen.

*****

Looking back, I recall a week of tracking, not moose, but elk, in Washington State, twenty years ago. In spite of our efforts, things were never really right again between Pete and me. We did, however, plan one excursion--an exciting interlude from the slow downward spiral of our life together. It was a strange primordial week, an elk hunt, of which I was a part.

Elk Hunt

I am a hunter neither by training nor inclination. I have second thoughts about swatting flies and I once saved the life of a drowning rat. The idea of purposely taking aim at and shooting a living creature with lovely, soulful eyes is alien to me. So it is with amazement that I recall the thrill; the adrenaline-driven, animalistic pleasure I derived from an

238

elk hunt I participated in, in the Cascade Mountains of western Washington in 1982.

"Participated in" is a relative term. I didn't actually carry a gun; the prey I was hunting on this occasion were chanterelle mushrooms, a culinary taste I had developed while living in Washington. The blood lust that coursed through my veins when the elk hunt was on, however, had nothing to do with mycology. My heart, if not my trigger finger, was with the elk hunters.

Part of it, I guess, had to do with anticipation. Our friends had been talking about elk camp all year, and we had been planning for it for months. Neither Pete nor I had grown up around the large, elegant animals known as Roosevelt elk, but we'd been told how delicious their meat was and how exciting the hunt. We were thrilled to have been invited to go along.

We had bought a wrecked cab-over camper and booted it up to our pickup truck, and we'd been getting it in shape so we'd have somewhere comfortable to stay. Pete had applied and paid for his elk tag. He had taken off the first week of November from his job, and I had told the dairy farmer I mucked stalls for that I couldn't make it that week. We'd invited my nephew Bryan to join us, and he'd flown out from Buffalo. There had been food to buy, warm clothes to pack, arrangements to make for our animals. We had certainly primed ourselves for the occasion.

But it was something more than that. Something about sitting up on that mountain on a cold moonlit night; listening to the cries of coyotes; staring into a campfire with a half dozen comrades; passing around a bottle of Black Velvet; imagining the silent passage of shadow-like hoofed beasts in the cedars. Something that felt dangerous; savage, primeval, like we'd stepped a thousand years back in time, left behind the trappings of our civilization, and slipped into the skins of our ancestors. We had more in common, that week, with the howling coyotes than with the people back in Gate.

Pete, Bryan, and I had driven up the day before bull season opened. The camp we were joining was located in the foothills of the Cascade Mountains near Packwood, a little town with a diner, a tavern, and a store where beer and ammo could be purchased. The terrain was rugged, with cedars and hemlocks grown tall and lush on abundant rain and mist, shadowing thickets of blackberries and Oregon grape. Roosevelt elk thrived in this environment, providing food for mountain lions and coyotes. Chehalis and Klickitat Indians had roamed these forests not very long ago, hunting the elk with stone points attached to split cedar arrows. The landscape was little changed since their day. After they were confined to reservations, trappers and loggers took their places, carving out little niches in the wilderness.

The camp itself was a clearing in the woods with a big stone-lined fire pit. Several campers and a tent were already in place when we arrived, and our friends were setting up folding chairs, putting up awnings, and tying clothes lines to trees. We found a flat spot where we could level our cab-over and detach our pickup truck; then arranged our temporary home.

On our first day we explored the area. We looked for elk signs: large, cloven tracks left behind in soft earth, antler rubs on small saplings, and depressions dug into the earth. Pete and Bryan picked out a good "stand" from which they could see passing elk and, hopefully, not be seen by them; where, during the coming week, they would sit, wait, and watch.

Elk move silently through the woods, not thrashing noisily through the underbrush like deer. Mainly nocturnal, they are most active at daybreak and dusk. We saw two cows, their gender made apparent by the lack of antlers and the presence of a half-grown calf. They seemed to know they were safe, watching us with calm eyes. The rut was over and the bulls had withdrawn from the small herds. They would shed their antlers in another couple months, but for now their majestic antlers were both their crowning glory and their markers for death.

Most of our friends here at elk camp were descendants of the mountain men who'd settled this area. They relished this once-a-year chance to return to their feral roots. Beards, already long and thick, were allowed to grow fuller, to collect leaves, uncombed. Normally clean-shaven men let their whiskers grow, giving them a ragged, if not rugged, look. Heavy flannel shirts, hunting vests, hiking boots and woolen hats were the fashion of the day, more stylish if stained with blood and dirt.

There was one other woman in the camp. Gloria and I did some of the cooking and straightening up, but there was no real division of labor. Cooking consisted mainly of throwing a steak or burger on the fire or frying up some eggs in a skillet, feats many of the men prided themselves on. Housekeeping was a low priority. Gloria had brought her own 30-06 Springfield and hunted with the men. I was the only one without a rifle.

Elk camp was a man thing. I was privileged to be allowed to witness and partake of the ancient pagan rituals. Still, I detected a female element; instincts long suppressed. The wolf bitch feeding her young;

prehistoric woman waiting with avid eyes for her man to bring home a kill, thus carrying on life for another winter; Diana, goddess of the hunt, roaming the woods and aiming her mythological arrows in ancient Roman stories. Artemis...

On the first morning of hunting season the hunters set out before daybreak. The deal was that we'd share whatever was shot, with the shooter getting the biggest portion. I started a fire and whipped up some breakfast so they would have something hot to eat when they straggled in. Pete and Bryan were back, warming up at the fire, when John arrived and announced that Bob had gotten a two-pointer. The men rushed to help him, and the better part of the day was spent in finding and bringing in the elk.

By evening they had it strung up in a nearby tree. Bob set about gutting it, and that night we all shared in the ritualistic act of eating its liver. I'm not normally a big fan of liver of any kind, but I'll tell you right now there was nothing on earth quite like the taste of that elk liver, tough and salty and just barely cooked, seared on the hot coals of our campfire, handed out and passed around with the seriousness of a Catholic sacrament. In partaking, we were inducted into a brotherhood; a secret society which no one from outside could join.

That first lucky day was followed by two days of hiking and looking and waiting. In Packwood we talked to a couple of other hunters who'd bagged their elk, but while some of the guys in our camp saw bulls in the distance, no one else got a shot. Camp life was fun, just the same, and I was having a great time on my own private sojourns into the hills. Pete was at his machismotic best in this wilderness setting, and in the privacy of our camper we rekindled the waning embers of our wedding bed.

On the fourth day, shortly after returning to camp with my mushrooms, I heard a crashing sound in the bushes outside the camper. Bryan rushed up, breathless, and announced that Pete had shot a big elk. There was some question, however, about whose bullet had gotten it, since another hunter had shot at it too. They were tracking it now, but it had headed away from the road, down toward the river. It was gonna be a rough one to track, and even harder to bring in. Bryan was supposed to drive the truck up the road to the spot where they hoped to bring it down. John, Bryan, and I jumped into our pickup and headed out into the forest. Leaving the truck, we began bushwhacking our way down the hill, calling occasionally to locate Pete. Finally we heard a distant voice. "Over here!" We followed the sound, the thrill of the chase pounding in our veins, and clambered over logs and through blackberry thorns toward the voice.

We found Pete standing over the beautiful, still-warm body of a large bull elk. Repressing my feelings of sympathy for the elk, I joined with Bryan and John in hugging and congratulating him. It was too perfect a moment to spoil with twinges of humanity. Pete slit the throat to allow the blood to drain. Otherwise, part of the meat would be ruined. We admired the perfect rack, three matched points on each side, and guessed at its weight. It looked to be at least 800 pounds; enough meat, we declared, to feed us for the winter.

In a few minutes, however, we were joined by another unknown hunter. It was his elk, he declared. He'd shot it before Pete. The argument ensued as other hunters gathered round. The only way to decide, it was agreed, was to examine the wounds, cut out the shots, and determine which had killed the elk. Pete was using a 30-06 Springfield, the other hunter a Winchester 270. No one spoke as one of the men sliced through the hide and removed the slugs. There were several 270 slugs in the left hindquarter, but nothing, it was agreed, that would bring down a grown cervid. The fatal shot had gone in the neck, penetrating the right lung. Extracting the slug, the man held it up for all to see. It was a 30-06. It was Pete's elk.

We were a long way from the truck, so it was decided to hang the elk on the spot, skin it, and quarter it before carrying it back. Here is where my work came in. I'd skinned blacktail deer before and I'd helped with Bob's elk, so I knew what to do. I got to work. I hoped to tan the hide with the hair on, so I was careful as I slid the knife beneath the soft golden fur. It was several hours before we were ready to head back, cold, exhausted, and covered in blood. It was Pete's hour of glory but, as his woman, I shared in the residual glow.

One more elk was shot before the week ended. Even after sharing with our campmates we took home plenty of elk meat. We ate well that winter: steaks, elk-burger, roasts, and jerky. I salted the hide and then soaked it in a mixture I made from a local recipe. I let it cure and then spent hours scraping it. It was gorgeous when I finished, but after a few months the hair began falling out, and there was nothing I could do to reverse the process. I salvaged one piece, enough for a small rug, but it in no way retained the beauty of the animal who had worn it.

Pete and Bryan went elk hunting again, but not with me. I returned to my usual Bambi-loving self, the influence of the goddess Diana subdued.

My hunting instincts were once again limited to mushrooms, my shooting lust confined to film and camera. I know now, however, that somewhere beneath my humane and civilized veneer flows the savage blood of my ancestors. I know that I, and perhaps all of us, am capable of the blood lust of the hunter.

*****

8:30 am June 15, 2003

I woke last night to the mesmerizing call of a great horned owl, its deep voice rippling across the woodland like a stone skipping across the water. Owls never seem to call on the same nights as coyotes--I wonder why. Now I'm enjoying a quiet morning at home after a long day at the "Poets and Writers" Conference held at the Minnowbrook Great Camp yesterday. It was good to meet and talk to other writers. I got enough encouragement to convince me that I made the right decision in quitting my diner job and trying to write more.

8:30 am June 22, 2003

The blackberries are in full bloom, their snowy white blossoms filling the thickets, and the blueberries are getting ripe. Cobbler time is on its way!

My sister Betsy called. Her son Bryan surprised her by flying into Buffalo, and she wanted to know if it was all right for them to drive up here tomorrow. I told her, "Sure!" I'd better straighten up the cabin and make some beds!

7:00 am June 26, 2003

Betsy and Bryan are asleep upstairs in the loft, so I have a little time to myself. Later we'll go for a hike up to Castle Rock, if the weather permits. It's been unusually hot here, in the 90s, but today should be cooler. I noticed yesterday that the raspberries are in bloom. So, too, are the tomato plants Windy gave me, now planted in buckets on my deck.

Last night Betsy and I got to reminiscing. Her marriage ended not long before mine did, and just after her divorce she asked me if I wanted to fly to the Hawaiian island of Maui for a week, her treat. We'd had a pretty wild week together...

Then Bryan and I started talking about the "good old days" when he was staying with Pete and me at our farm in Washington. "Do you remember the time we stole the chickens?" he asked me. A vague memory came to mind. "Sort of." I said, "Remind me." Bryan described how Pete, our wild neighbor Dave (who was no doubt the instigator,) and he had taken two crates of newly hatched chicks off a truck and brought them home. We'd raised them in our chicken house and Bryan had had the chore, he recalled, of decapitating them when they were old enough to eat.

"Do you remember the night you and I raided the blueberry farm?" was his next question. Bryan began laughing as he described the incident. "When a car drove up, I yelled 'Run!' and took off down the hill. It was pitch dark and I guess you didn't see me duck under the barbed wire fence." "Oh Lord, yes!" I recalled. "I hit that fence at a full run! I was impaled! I had holes all the way across my belly, not to mention in my clothes. And worst of all, I crushed the blueberries!" Betsy, sat listening as we laughed, an indiscernible expression on her face.

Bryan and I continued to reminisce, and all kinds of forgotten memories emerged. "Remember the night Pete was helping himself to a few railroad ties and he got the truck stuck in the middle of the tracks? The train had to stop and wait for him to get out of the way!"

"How about the time we went to the K-Mart and Dave pretended he had a stiff leg? When we got back to the truck he reached up his pants leg, pulled out a long chain saw blade, and handed it to Pete! 'Here pal,' he said, "I know you need one of these!"

Our neighbor, Dave, had been a born-again Christian," I explained to Betsy, "but he was the worst of all. He'd lead Pete astray and then tell him he was going to hell for it because he hadn't found Jesus, while Dave himself would be forgiven. But he was such a likeable guy, you just couldn't stay mad at him."

I have often wondered how responsible I was for the less-than-honorable acts committed by Pete. I did not actually participate, nor did I approve, but I didn't stop him, nor did I leave for a long time. "Guilty by association" comes to mind. I have, since that time, tried to live by a strict ethical code that precludes guilt.

Pete and I continued on for a while, but things did not improve. I accept my part of the blame for what happened, too. I was determined to make our home perfect, and I kept on pushing Pete to work on the farm after he no longer cared. I know now that there is no such thing as perfect in this world. I should have been happy with what I had, instead of wanting more.

*****

The desolate days in which our marriage finally ended are portrayed in this next story. Bryan had stayed on after the elk hunt, living with us and attending middle school in nearby Rochester. I am still sorry that he was dragged through our anguish.

Four Blind Mice

With a grunt of effort, I hoisted out a bale of alfalfa hay, moved the timbers it had been sitting on, and destroyed a family. I didn't know it at the time. Had I seen it, it might not have been too late. But I continued moving bales, making room for a new delivery of hay. By the time I realized what I had done, an hour later, it was too late. They looked like tiny pink nuggets, lying on the barn floor, and I reached down curiously to see what they were. I jerked my hand back when one moved. I picked them up, warming them in my hand. Baby mice, all of them still alive.

Not all stories have happy endings. Pete's and my little farm in Gate had seemed like a paradise; our life idyllic. Beneath the bucolic surface, however, there stirred the makings of a volcano as wrathful as Mt. St. Helens. A lava of discontent seethed through cracks and hissed up in fumaroles as I tried my best to ignore it. The dogs, chickens, horses, geese, goat and sheep spent their days in ignorant bliss, not knowing of the discord which soon would rip their lives apart.

I took the mice into the house, made them a tissue paper bed in a jewelry box, and mixed them up some warm dried milk. I fed them with an eye dropper, holding each in the cup of my hand, the hairless skin warm against my fingers. Surprisingly, they lived. Down-like hair appeared on their bodies, their blind eyes pushed open, and they became more active, wiggling in my hands.

No use laying blame or pointing fingers; no point in saying "if only you had done this" or "if only I hadn't done that." I suppose Pete and I were equally guilty, equally blameless; just two people who couldn't make life together work. But for me it was devastating. I could not conceive of surviving should this volcano actually erupt. I tried harder and harder to ignore the signs, the rivulets of burning lava that flowed around me. I just kept on trying to create our perfect farm.

Just in case I failed, however, I prepared for the only resolution I could imagine. I practiced running a razor blade down the pale, semi-

245

transparent skin of my wrists, carving designs and watching my blood paint pictures of despair.

I transferred the mice to a shoebox and put them in my closet, where the cats couldn't get them. I began supplementing their diet with cereal, birdseed, anything I could think of. They thrived. Now they looked like tiny replicas of their parents, which I was guessing were deer or harvest mice. They would jump into my hand, climbing on my fingers, when I reached down into the box.

At some point Pete and I reached the point of no return. I'm not sure where or when. Perhaps with the conception of our baby; perhaps with its prenatal death; perhaps in some forgotten moment when hope and forgiveness quietly lay down in defeat and died. At some point I came to realize that all my hoping, all my pretending was useless. I was on a downward spiral which I could only see ending in absolute defeat and, ultimately, death. I had only one goal now--to find good homes for our animals.

My depression became a fog that I could barely navigate through. Accomplishing my goal seemed an impossibility. Each animal that I placed was simultaneously a relief, an achievement, an admission of defeat, and an overwhelming heartbreak. One by one, my darlings left. Most--geese, chickens, doves and sheep--went to friends whom I trusted. The colt we sold to a neighbor who, it soon became clear, had no way to properly care for him. I agonized as he kept breaking out and coming home. "You can't stay here," I cried. "I can't take care of you." Finally another neighbor, angry with the colt's new owner and at us for selling him to him, took him. We agreed to sign over the adoption papers for Nevada and Belle as well, and I sobbed in relief to know they both had a good home. Cocoa went to a small goat farm. I was sure she would have a good home, but it broke my heart to drive away, leaving her behind and listening to her bewildered bleating. Only my cat Twinkle, and our dogs, Princess and Maybe, remained, and of course, the mice.

The mice learned to climb out of their box. They pattered around inside the closet, but always returned to their home to sleep and eat. They were eating on their own, and I knew that soon it would be time to release them. I hesitated, however; they were now one of my only sources of comfort.

The final days of our marriage were no longer an underground rumbling. The lava of our discontent erupted, ripping our lives apart, leaving a field of destruction for all to see. Pete no longer made any *effort to come home at night, and I drowned my loneliness and heartache in bottles of vodka. He partied with friends and girlfriends; I hid in the bedroom, wrapping my arms around Princess and Twinkle. I played with my mice.*

Pete and I agreed to put the farm on the market. I needed to pack up my possessions and put them in storage, a task which seemed insurmountable. Neighborhood friends helped me and offered me a place to stay. But I could not make myself leave. I moved the mice into an old aquarium and put them in the barn. I should set them free, I knew, but somehow they had become symbols...releasing the mice would be closing the final door. On the other side of the door lay a dark abyss through which I was afraid to step.

Every day I lay in bed and told myself I must go out and set the mice free. I tried to make myself get up, but I couldn't bear the thought. Instead I rolled back into my cloak of despair and pulled it tighter about me. "I must get up...I must go out..." Finally, one eternally gray morning, I forced myself up. I dragged myself out the door to the garage. I would set them free today.

I was too late. Three of the mice lay dead. The fourth tottered weakly back and forth against the glass. I took it into the woods, offered it water and a bit of food, and watched it stumble into the underbrush. The door slammed shut. I tumbled into darkness.

*****

8:30 pm June 29, 2003

Unless one stands among the stars and looks down on the Earth, he cannot know the vastness of the seas. Yet unless he kneels and reaches his hands into the water, raises it up and splashes it on his face, tastes it on his lips, he cannot know what the sea is.

How does one describe water? Standing beside one of the pools near my cabin, I am reminded of a day long ago. It was early May and I, at the age of sixteen, had ridden my horse along a woodland trail and come upon a small pond. Gazing down on it, I saw the perfect blue of sky laced with soft tendrils of white cirrus cloud. I saw the underbellies of shimmering leaves, newly emerged from their winter sleep, the color of a luna moth wing. A reflection of black and yellow stripes flitted by, a tiger swallowtail intent on some wildflower blooming at the pond's edge.

247

As I watched, a breeze rippled across the pond, and I saw the colors dance, melt together, and then re-emerge. It was as if God, finding a minute flaw in his artwork, had quickly dipped his brush in and re-painted it to perfection.

Next day, in chemistry class, my teacher told us that water, an inorganic compound composed of hydrogen and oxygen, was colorless.

"Who," I whispered to myself. "Who is lying?"

The lines between science and imagination, truth and deception, meander like a restless river. Truth is a shadow, clearly visible when the sun shines, disappearing when night approaches. Does a shadow cease to exist when darkness falls? Or does it become part of the darkness, like the channel of a river which continues onward, unseen but ever present, till it reaches the sea?

July 2003

8:30 pm July 1, 2003

I wrote for most of the morning, then decided I needed to get out of the cabin. It was too windy to kayak, so I got into the truck with Huck and headed north, not sure where we were going. I turned down Sabattis Road, a few miles north of Long Lake, into the Whitney Wilderness, a 15,000-acre timber park purchased by the state in 1997. Just as we drew alongside Little Tupper Lake I saw movement above my head. A great expanse of wings soared just above the truck, then glided on a gust of wind across the water to the tree line. I slowed down, watching, and saw another huge bird, likewise riding the wind. Eagles!

I pulled my truck onto the roadside, grabbed my binoculars, and got out. I must have stood there ten minutes, watching the young eagles play. Up and down, twirling and gliding on the erratic gusts, occasionally landing in a tree and then floating up again. I trained my binoculars on one of them, its wings spread against the cobalt sky. I followed it, closer and closer, leaning my head back till it was directly above me. filling my lenses. Then all I could see were the splendid feathers of its breast and the powerful curve of its beak. In that magical, frightening moment, seen through the magnifying lens of my binoculars, it seemed to surround and encompass me. Dropping the binoculars, I could see that it was floating eight or ten feet overhead, as curious, no doubt, about me as I was about it. Then it floated effortlessly away and resumed its game, leaving me with the feeling that I had been bestowed a precious gift.

I watched for a few more moments and then continued up the road to the park headquarters, a group of attractive wooden buildings known formerly as the Whitney Headquarters, where I read a little about the history of the area. Once the hub of canoe routes used by the Abenaki and Mohawk Indians and later by European explorers, it had been purchased in the late 1800s by William C. Whitney and his partner Patrick Moynehan. They had had an extensive road system constructed in the 1930s for horse logging. Afterwards, in 1936, a four-mile-long railroad spur, connecting to the New York Central Railroad, was built to carry out the logs.

There is little evidence of that activity today, as nature reclaims the landscape. Huck and I walked for a way along the Stony Pond trail, where we saw a yellow warbler, a flock of cedar waxwings, and a pair of ravens. They raised a huge ruckus, an unearthly metallic screeching, sure to intimidate almost anyone who heard it. I'm guessing they were this year's babies, squawking for their dinner.

Nothing I saw, however, could compare to the wondrous communion I had felt with the young eagle.

10 pm July 4, 2003

Long Lake celebrated the Fourth today, but I missed it since I had to work at the museum. I was in the new Adirondack Camps exhibit, and I spent my time reading all the captions. There have been 323 children's camps in the park since 1885, when the first one was started by Sumner Dudley. Ernest Thompson Seton, author of several books for children which Momma used to love, introduced the Indian theme as a format for camps. His books, "The Book of Woodcraft" and "The Birchbark Roll of the Woodcraft Indians," provided guidelines for having campfire circles, In-dian names, and totem poles (all considered politically incorrect today.)

Daddy always used to talk about his camp days in Connecticut, where he attended camp and later worked. It was where he and my mother spent their honeymoon, and where my brother was conceived. He also worked as a counselor in Virginia's Shenandoah Valley, not far from his grand-father's farm.

One of the visitors asked me if I had gone to camp when I was young, and I told her just for one week, at 4-H Camp. Later, after thinking about it, I realized that I had a history of camp life. I had been conceived at Camp Chinquapin, a day camp my father had built and operated in Hanover County, Virginia. A beautiful log building with a basketball court in the attic and a swimming pool in the yard, set back in the Vir-ginia woods, it was my first home. I grew chubby eating camp meals cooked by my mother--a hot dog and potato dish christened "Chinquapin Special," for example. I was introduced to music in the form of camp songs, such as one written by my sister Sally: "*Put another camper in, take him out and let him swim. Fill him full of life and vim at good old Chinquapin.*"

Later, as a teenager, I taught swimming with my father at our place in Short Pump. While we did not call it a day camp, it served that function each summer. Daddy opened our swimming pool and tennis courts, built by my brother and him, to the public for daily lessons, supplementing his and my mother's school-teacher salaries and allowing my sisters and me to earn our college tuition. If anyone else asks that question, I'll tell them that I am a born camper!

9:30 pm July 6, 2003

I saw my family of ruffed grouse today while walking Huck. They were taking a dust bath on a bare spot on the trail. They flushed as we drew near, the babies well able to fly now but still hanging close to Mom and Dad. Huck tried to chase them, but I held onto his leash.

I went to dinner tonight with Jamie and his friends from New York City, Bill and Pam, who have a camp here in Long Lake. I met Jamie, a wildlife wood carver, last year. A former professional musician and a budding writer, he and I have a lot in common. He is carving a $5,000 door for Bill and Pam. We went to an expensive restaurant in Lake Placid, well out of Jamie's or my budget, but his friends paid. We had a nice evening.

10:30 pm July 8, 2003

I got up at sunrise today, packed a lunch, and took a trip I've been meaning to try all year. It was too far to kayak with Huck, so I left him at home with Miss Kelley. I shoved my kayak onto the top of my truck, tied it down, and headed for Blue Mountain Lake, just a little ways past the museum.

There is a moving diorama at the museum that depicts the late 19th century route taken by people from New York City into the Adirondacks. Having arrived by train at Raquette Lake, they boarded the steamboat "Killoquah," which carried them to a "land bridge" called the Marion River Carry. There, passengers took a short, standard gauge train which carried them 3/4 of a mile to the end, where the steamboat "Utowana" waited to carry them through the Eckford chain of lakes; Utawanna, Eagle, and Blue Mountain Lake. I wanted to paddle the route, only in reverse.

At the public launch I took the kayak down and parked my truck alongside the road. I quickly loaded the kayak with life vest, camera, sunscreen, water and my lunch; then hopped in and was off. I'd paddled in Blue Mountain Lake before, and I knew what a breathtakingly beautiful lake it was, dotted with tiny islands. I scanned the east shore, looking for Crane Point, where Indian guide Mitchell Sabattis once had a camp. But I had miles to travel today, so I didn't stop to explore. The wind was light so paddling was easy, and it took no more than an hour to reach the narrow passage that ran into Eagle Lake. I passed under the Durant Bridge, built of stone by tycoon and entrepreneur William West Durant in 1891 in honor of his father. The Durants had been responsible for most of the development in the central Adirondacks; they had tinkered in great camps and hotels, steamboats and railroads.

I paddled slowly along the shore of Eagle Lake, studying the place where the rather infamous dimestore novelist Ted Buntline had lived from 1856 to 1862. I saw the shoreline where William Durant had built the elaborate Eagle's Nest Country Club and Golf Course in 1900. Four years later, as his mountain empire collapsed, it was bought by a group of New Yorkers and converted into summer homes. The golf course is gone, but many of the buildings remain. I searched for signs of human life as I paddled by but saw none.

Later, I stopped at a big rock island and ate my tuna sandwich, finishing it off with wild raspberries picked along the edge. From Eagle Lake I entered a winding, shallow channel which wound through the woods and opened up into Utowana Lake. It seemed to extend forever--a long expanse of water that had no visible end. I began to wonder if I would make it to Marion River Carry and back again before nightfall, and I stretched my arms in long, hard reaches as I continued to paddle west.

Finally, the lake began to narrow. I stopped at a lean-to on the south bank to rest and eat a banana I had brought. The lake was getting marshy, its surfaced mottled with the round leaves and white blossoms of water lilies. Bright blue spires of pickerel weed rose above arrowhead-shaped leaves. I approached what looked like a pile of sticks in the water; a beaver lodge. I searched for its residents but saw instead, near the shore, a loon. Upon closer observation I realized that it had on its back two chicks. I trembled with excitement as I raised my binoculars to my eyes. The soft tremolo of its warning call then reached my ears. A moment later another loon, presumably the father, surfaced just a few feet away from my kayak and began swimming away from the mother and chicks.

"It's okay, I'm leaving," I announced, hoping that my intentions, if not my words, would be understood. The father was taking no chances, however. He led me far away from his family, raising his voice in a warlike yodel, diving every few moments and then re-surfacing with a loud splash nearby, always a few feet in front of me. Finally, when I was well on my way down the lake, he disappeared. I did not try to take any pictures, which I kind of regret, but I didn't want to further traumatize the loon family. The picture is, however, firmly ensconced in my memory.

The lake narrowed further and I saw the remains of the pier and railroad tracks from what had formerly been known as Bassett's Carry. Here, a hundred years before, Durant's Marion River train had picked up its returning passengers. I dragged my kayak to shore and began walking along what was left of the train tracks, imagining the loud and no doubt smelly coal-burning engine as it pulled its tiny train of three cars. Today the only sound I heard was the trilling of robins in the underbrush. William West Durant had lost his fortune and all his holdings in the Adirondack Mountains. He ended his life washing dishes at the Adirondack Hotel, a job I had held for a week the year before.

I wished I could stay longer, but I had miles to go. I did a marathon paddle back, running on adrenaline as I raced the sun, taking no breaks. I got back just as dusk settled over Blue Mountain Lake. I loaded my kayak in the dark and got back to the cabin as the moon was rising. I don't know how many miles I paddled, but I'm beat and it feels great!

9 pm July 9, 2003
Working at the museum was frustrating today. Being an exhibit attendant is enjoyable, but there is usually not a lot of excitement. It can get boring. I think back to another job I had once had that was anything but boring. When I drove back from Virginia last time, I brought with me the journal I had kept, documenting that job. I open the journal.

*****

I find myself once more in western Washington. I have returned from my unsuccessful foray into long-lining for halibut and have completed the last assignment for my degree at Evergreen College. I have filed for divorce and am waiting, though I'm not sure for what. My stumbling path now has led me to a fascinating job in an amazing setting on the shore of the Strait de San Juan de Fuca.

On Hoko River

There are places where spirits still exist. Where, if you pay attention, you can hear their voices in the wind; see their eyes in the riffles of babbling brooks; feel their breath against your cheek. When you cross the boundary which separates the daily, mundane world from the world of ghosts and gods, the rules set by conventional society cease to apply. The summer of '83, when I lived on the banks of the Hoko River at the northwest tip of Washington, was a season for conversing with spirits, for crossing that boundary. It was a time for coming face to face with death, when it was least expected. It was also a time for seeking life beyond the parameters of death, and finding it.

I arrived at Hoko River via outstretched thumb. I was finishing up my last quarter of college, earning a degree in Native American Studies from Evergreen College. My advisor, Lloyd Colfax, suggested that I spend a few weeks with his people on the Makah reservation at Cape Flattery, the farthest northwest tip of our country.

Together we made out my agenda: studying at the Makah Cultural Center in Neah Bay; taking the ten mile trip to Ozette, an ancient Makah village which had been preserved in a mud slide; talking to the Makah people who lived in Neah Bay; and visiting an archaeological site at Hoko River, where excavations were in progress.

Having filed for divorce, I found this chance to get away from home welcome. My Honda was not running (Pete was supposed to fix it as part of our divorce agreement,) so I hitch-hiked north with a sleeping bag, pup-tent, and small pack. I followed Rt. 101 past Hoquiam and Quinault to Clallam Bay, where I climbed in the back of a pickup truck with three Makah Indians. I gazed in awe as we passed between cliffs and beaches overlooking the Pacific ocean and the verdant, forested mountains of the Olympic National Park. Once in Neah Bay, they dropped me off at a campground at Hobuck Beach.

The Makahs, or Cape People, were a Nootkan-speaking tribe, first described in the writings of the British Captain Cook, with several villages spread through northwestern Washington state. The treaty of 1855, signed with the American government, reduced the number of villages and the Makah territory to the rocky tip of Cape Flattery. They had formerly been a whaling and fishing people, the best on the Northwest Coast, according to 19th century historian J.G. Swan. Whale protection laws had now reduced their whaling to a rare ceremonial killing, but they still fished for their livelihood, with halibut and salmon their main catch. The village at Neah Bay was small. Native cultural beliefs and customs were now combined with the norms of modern American life.

255

I spent several days in Neah Bay, visiting the museum and explaining that I was a student of their respected tribal leader, Lloyd Colfax. I learned about Makah culture and saw the collection of artifacts unearthed at nearby Ozette. I admired the carvings of the well-known young artist, Greg Colfax, a relative of my advisor, and later visited his home.

Jeff, whom I had met at the museum, offered to take me to Ozette the next day. We drove down a narrow, winding road to a haunting stretch of beach where caves riddled the rocky shoreline. The ancestors of the Makahs had lived here, he said, on the shores of the lake they called Kahouk, for over 2,000 years.

The whaling village of Ozette had been buried by a mudslide over 400 years ago, before the intrusion of white people. There were longhouses and all kinds of household and whaling artifacts, recently unearthed and transferred to the Makah Museum. Only a few rock petroglyphs and ghosts remained today. I gazed across the waves at Cannonball Island, upon which sat an ancient graveyard and a midden. I peered at Ozette Island, where early Makah Indians had kept yellow-colored "wool" dogs, their thick fur used for weaving blankets. At the end of a long day we returned to Neah Bay, and I to my campsite.

I wandered through the village, learning more about daily life. The reservation was, I learned, technically "dry," but drinking was still a big problem. There were a lot of "family politics," I was told, and law suits with other tribes related to salmon fishing. Most of the businesses--motels and such--were owned by non-Indians who leased the land. Most Makah men worked in logging and fishing, but work, especially in winter, was scarce.

So also, I realized, was my cash. If I was going to stay longer, I would need to get a job. I began asking around, and before long I found myself hired on as a mate on a fishing boat, long-lining for halibut. I spent five days on the sea, and while I did not make much money, I walked away with a deeper understanding of how hard a fisherman's life could be.

The next day I set out for Hoko River, walking along Rt. 112 with a hand-made sign stating my destination. The road wound through a thick Olympic forest, with branches of hemlock and western cedar hanging overhead. Before long a blue and white pickup truck pulled over. I gladly accepted a ride from the attractive bearded driver, Lonnie, whom I had met a few days before. He didn't know where the turnoff to the dig was, but he said he was sure we could find it.

Lonnie was a commercial fisherman. As we drove along he described some of the problems, particularly the decline in salmon, that threatened his livelihood. I told him about my futile attempt at long-lining for halibut the week before.

We drove by it twice before we located the little rutted lane that cut off down the hill and bumped across rocks and potholes to an abrupt end. A small hand-painted sign indicated that we would have to walk the rest of the way. Lonnie offered to come along and make sure that I got there. When we spotted several big army tents, he gave me his phone number and said to call him if I wanted to go out on his boat. Then he left.

I hiked down the trail to one of the tents, where I saw several people standing. I introduced myself and explained that I was a student and was hoping to observe what they were doing. Barb, one of the main archaeologists, agreed to show me around. Dale Croes, a professor at Washington State University, was in charge of the project, she said. The University was working hand in hand with the Makah Indian Tribe, a new concept, and the artifacts uncovered in the dig would belong to the tribe. There were several paid archaeologists and one volunteer, but most of the crew were part of an archaeology field school. Everyone lived and worked in the tents. One tent held a laboratory for identifying and processing the artifacts.

Hoko River was a 2,800-year-old site, a fishing camp once inhabited by the ancestors of the Makah Indians. It had two archaeological components--a dry site and a wet site. The dry site included a rock shelter and a midden, or trash heap, which contained animal bones, shells, and broken artifacts. The wet site, located on the bank of the river, was thought to be one of the best in the world, producing pieces of basketry, clothing, and other items preserved in the anaerobic (oxygen-free) mud. It was fast being eroded and lost to the actions of the river, so time was of the essence in excavating it.

As I followed Barb around, listening to her explanations, I had an idea. "I'm finishing up my degree next week," I told her. "Is there any chance you might need someone else? "Actually," Barb answered, "we could use one other person in the lab, but we don't have funds to pay you. You could be a volunteer, like Suzanne. She gets free room and board and gets to participate in all the field school activities, in exchange for working."

A thrill of excitement rushed through me. How I would love to be part of this! But could it work? I responded with hesitation, "I have a dog and a cat. Could they come?" Barb would check with Dale that night, she said. The next day she gave me his answer. He agreed that they could come, but said that I would have to find somewhere to stay other than the community tent. I had nothing to lose. I told her I would figure out something and come back next week. I left, feeling for the first time in months that maybe I had something to live for.

I was thrilled to have a plan, but even then I was hoping that, when I got back to Gate, Pete would want to try once more. It didn't happen. He had met someone else.

. *He did agree that, since he had not yet fixed my car, I could take the van, which we had converted into a camper years before. I met with Lloyd Colfax once more and completed the paperwork I needed to graduate. I packed a few personal things and headed back to Hoko River, bringing my nine-year-old doberman, Princess, my three-year-old Siamese cat, Twinkle, and my guitar. Having found a suitable spot near the camp to park the van, I settled into my new life.*

The next two and a half months were full of new experiences. Everything I learned about this ancient camp was exciting, everything I did an adventure. I worked hard in the lab, learning all the techniques required for identifying, cleaning, labeling, sketching, and preserving the artifacts. I attended all the field school classes and field trips, and in my spare time observed or participated in the excavations.

On the day after my arrival an amazing discovery was made. One of the field school students, Ian, found a cedar tool carved with two bird heads in a 2700-year-old layer of the wet site. It was given to me to clean. We wondered what it was and decided (though it was really just a guess) that it could have been used in making the woven mats often found in the wet site. We pronounced it a matt creaser and decided that the birds were kingfishers or woodpeckers.

Dale, the head archaeologist, was sure that it was a significant find, and further analysis determined that the tool was, by a thousand years, the oldest wood carving ever found on America's Pacific coast. Once the news reached the archaeological world, we were visited by numerous reporters and anthropologists and found ourselves being photographed and interviewed constantly.

Hoko River itself was a wild, beautiful stream. We could explore it using one of several rowboats provided by the university. It fed into the Strait de San Juan de Fuca, where tide pools filled with sea anemones, urchins, sea stars, limpets and small fish abounded among the black rocks along the shore. Bald eagles nested on nearby cliffs, and sea lions could be seen resting like huge logs on half-submerged boulders. Gray whales and orcas were sometimes spotted offshore. Just inland of the beach, a sub-tropical rainforest thrived, thick with vegetation of all kinds. Hemlocks and spruce trees formed an arbor overhead. Nearby rose the Olympic Mountains.

Moving through these quiet places, I thought I could sense the presence of the people, long gone now, whose everyday lives we were investigating. I pictured their dwellings, covered with the cedar bark mats I so carefully cleaned, and decorated with legendary images of ravens and thunderbirds, painted with tones of hemlock, ochre, and alder. I imagined the women gathering the berries that grew in abundance, the men carefully baiting their hooks, fashioned of bone and sinew, and attaching them to lines made from twisted kelp. I pictured them joking and laughing as they waded out to meet the cedar-log whaling canoes, bringing in what would be dinner for weeks.

Working at Hoko River was a great way to spend the summer. Yet I was, on a personal level, still devastated by the ruin of my marriage. I missed Pete terribly. Depressed, on the verge of an emotional breakdown, I saw my life as a downward spiral from which this was only a momentary respite. The two elements of my life paralleled each other during those months but never seemed to meet. I participated in all the work and study related activities, but retreated to the van and the company of Princess and Twinkle as soon as work or classes were over. I played my guitar for hours, isolated by the paneled walls of my four-wheeled home. I made no real friends among the other staff. I had convinced myself during the last months of my marriage that I was a no-good, worthless person, deserving of the contempt Pete seemed to feel for me. I convinced myself that my fellow workers at Hoko believed this, too.

The one person with whom I felt at ease was a boy, a Makah youth working at the dig. He too was an outsider; perhaps this was our connection. Vince and I walked on the beach and explored nearby coves when our work was done. He told me about his life on the reservation, and I told him about my travels. He invited me to his mother's home in Neah Bay, and I became friends with her as well. One evening we went to Soos Beach to see his great-grandmother, Isabella, considered to be the best basket maker in the tribe. I bought a small basket, with a design of orca whales and whaling canoes.

Living in a field camp in a northwestern Washington rain forest was not a lesson in comfort. The climate that created such a riotously rich ecosystem was damp and cold, producing a chill which sank right to the bone. Even with the fire we built every morning and evening, the tents where we ate and worked were always cold. I had not brought appropriate clothing, and did not even have a jacket until I found one at a yard sale on one of our trips to Port Angeles. Rain fell almost daily and turned the earth into a mire of mud. The wheels of my van sank deep into the muck until it was thoroughly stuck. I left it that way, having nowhere that I really cared to go, anyway. Twice a week a group of us would hike out to the parking area, climb into the university van, and go to a high school in Port Angeles for showers. On the first such trip I realized what I had forgotten to pack: a towel! After each shower I would surreptitiously grab a handful of paper towels and try to pat my body dry, not wanting anyone to know of my foolishness. I was always still damp when I went back to the van.

On one of these trips I called the phone number Lonnie had given me. He was delighted to hear from me and was willing to come out to the camp to pick me up whenever I wanted. He took me out on his boat and we went out on several dates, but I was still too much in love with Pete to begin another relationship.

One day, while in Port Angeles, I called Pete. I asked him if he wanted to come up, and he said yes. We spent an afternoon wandering along the shoreline of Cape Flattery, watching waves crash on black neolithic rocks. When the day was over, I realized that our marriage was as doomed, as hopelessly bound for destruction, as those profligate waves.

My personal despair grew worse after he left, and I clung desperately to the two beings I knew loved me, Princess and Twinkle. Princess was a hit at the camp, her predisposition to do stunts and act the clown winning her much applause. Twinkle followed her everywhere she went, the two inseparable.

One evening, however, I went to the van after supper to find Twinkle stretched out on the bed, weak and trembling. Within minutes she was wracked with convulsions and vomiting. She had already emptied her stomach while I was gone, and only a fleck of liquid came out. She lay still, barely breathing, then convulsed again. Princess sat beside her with a puzzled expression on her face, gently nosing her from time to time. I don't know how long I sat holding my darling kitty, as she grew weaker and weaker. The lights around camp went out and the voices quieted. I dozed off, and when I woke up I realized that Twinkle had grown cold and stiff. All signs of life were gone. I lay there, cradling her in my arms and rocking her gently, tears streaming down my face, for the rest of the night. I tried to think where I would bury her, how I would bear the next month without her. Perhaps I dozed.

Sometime around dawn I felt the slightest twitch. Surely it was my imagination! Her body seemed less stiff; I detected a hint of warmth. I watched in disbelief as life returned to her. I took some water and dabbed it on her lips. I borrowed a dropper from the lab tent and spent the day slipping water, a few drops at a time, into her mouth. She opened her eyes. Later, she tried to swallow. Slowly, over the next few days, she revived and returned to her old self. I dared not question the miracle or tell anyone. I only gave thanks to whatever god or gods had brought her back to me.

In spite of my personal sorrows, my fascination with the project persisted. I made several trips to Ozette. On one occasion several of us made petroglyph rubbings, similar to ones I had made in British churches, using muslin cloth and crayons. We captured on cloth the carved images of orca whales and god figures created by people who had walked this beach long ago.

We took an overnight trip across the Strait de San Juan de Fuca to Canada's Vancouver Island. We spent a day exploring the Provincial Museum in Victoria and were given a tour of the Research Tower. While there, I went to an antique shop and bought a wonderful old print of a Nootka totem by 19th century artist Emily Carr.

We visited the Mantis Mastodon Site in Sequim, where paleontologist Carl Gustuson had unearthed the fossil bones of giant prehistoric elephants. We drove into the Olympic Mountains and hiked across Hurricane Ridge, where we saw a black tail doe with her fawn.

Back in camp I studied faunal analysis, learning to distinguish the bones of albatross, halibut, gray whale, elephant seal, and deer, all hundreds or thousands of years old. I learned the different kinds of basketry: woven, twined, or wrapped--and the materials, usually cedar bark, used to make them. I came to know the difference between a halibut and a codfish hook. I also learned the proper format for labeling artifacts and the technique of oheking--a method of preserving the items found at the wet site.

In late July, we prepared for a big evening with the Friends of the Humanities and the Makah tribal elders, a feast fashioned after their

*ancestors. We gathered limpets, chitons, sea urchins, and goose bar-
nacles and laid a huge fire. The Makahs brought fresh salmon, which
they cooked on cedar stakes around the fire. We made fish-eye soup, a
Makah tradition, and after dinner watched bald eagles soar above us. A
young gray whale put on a show, breaching, spouting and rolling, as if
hired for the occasion.*

*One day, as Princess and I trotted along the shore at Eagle Point
Beach, scanning the riffles for flotsam, I had a premonition. Princess
stumbled and slowed for a moment, a strange expression on her face,
and I saw, somehow, that she carried within her the seeds of her death.
The spirits of Hoko River swirled around us, and I clung to her, frightened and crying, there on the edge of the water. When we returned to
camp I told someone my fears, but they laughed at me. She seemed fine,
they said.*

*The field school ended on August 14, and the students went home. The
dig would continue for two more weeks, and I was offered a paid position
for that time. I accepted, happy to at last be making some money. On the
last day the crew helped me push the van out of the mud. Barb handed
me my paycheck, and we said goodbye.*

*Vince's mother had invited me to stay with them after the camp closed,
so I drove back to Neah Bay. We attended the Makah Days Festival, held
on the town beach. We shared traditional food and dance and watched
the famous annual canoe races, in which Makahs and other native
people paddled great canoes across the Strait to Canada. The next day I
gave Vince and Mrs. Cook a hug goodbye and drove across the Olympic
Mountains to the heartbreak that awaited me back home in Gate.*

*Once there I took Princess to our vet, explaining to him the feeling
that had come over me on the beach at Hoko River. He examined her
and found nothing wrong. "She's fine," he reassured me. Pete and I were,
meanwhile, dismantling what was left of our farm and closing up the
house. He stayed with his new girlfriend and I went back, with Princess
and Twinkle, to Virginia. I got a job and returned to college, taking post-
graduate courses in education. Twinkle's illness did not return, and she
lived with me until she was struck by a car years later.*

*Later, still worried about Princess, I took her to a veterinarian I knew
in Virginia. My premonition was, much to my sorrow, validated. Tests
proved that her body was riddled with lymphoma cancer. Placed on med-
ication, she lived for three more months, then died in my arms. The
ancient gods of Hoko River had not lied.*

*****

5:00 pm July 10, 2003

The spring rains have let up and the black flies are nearly gone. Strolling along the trail with Huck at my side was pleasant this morning. Now I need to feed Huck and Miss Kelley and pull out my guitar. There's a jam session at the Longview Restaurant tomorrow. I want to participate, and I need to practice first.

9:30 pm July 12, 2003

Huck and I came upon a flock of wild turkeys on the ridge today--two hens, it looked like, and at least a dozen babies, all half grown. We stopped and watched them for a bit before turning around and going the other way. I picked a few blueberries on the trail, but it looks like the bears are getting most of them. I worked with Irene at the museum today and she said she has a sow and two cubs who come to her house every day now. The momma bear runs the cubs up a tree, kind of a daycare center with walls of leaves, and then just hangs out. One day when Irene opened her front door she saw Momma Bear just sprawled out there, like she was taking a siesta! Irene says as long as the bear doesn't turn mean she doesn't mind.

11:00 am July 14, 2003

Kathleen and I went to Elk Lake yesterday, described by National Geographic as the "crown jewel" of the Adirondacks. It certainly is gorgeous, hidden miles off the Blue Ridge Road on a 12,000-acre parcel of private land. There is a lodge and we stopped in for a moment, then drove back to Newcomb to attend an excellent lecture on mosses, liverworts, and lichens at the VIC Center. We learned about the symbiotic relationship of fungi and algae, which together form all kinds of lichens: flat or "crustose" species, leafy or "foliose" species, and stalk-like, or "floriose" species. We learned about the differences between bryophtes, or mosses, and tracheophytes, which include all the flowering plants. These ancient, spore-producing plants are even more interesting than I had thought, and Kathleen was as intrigued as I was. I don't know many women up here who care about such things. I hope we can become better friends.

This morning I looked for some of the mosses and lichens we learned about, and I found a small bog of sphagnum, or peat moss, which supposedly can absorb 100 times as much water as a sponge. I also saw what I think are old man's beard and reindeer moss, as well as several kinds of crustose lichens on trees and rocks.

5:00 pm July 16, 2003

"So now you know my story." Jen and I were working in the museum's Main Building, which houses the art gallery, an exhibit which explains the formation and evolution of the Adirondack Mountains, and another on the history of humans in the Adirondacks. I have worked with Jen for three years, off and on, but I had never spent much time talking to her. I knew that she had been a nurse, that she had a family and grandchildren, /but little else. We spent all day together today, and between questions from visitors, she told me the story of her life.

She'd been born and raised in North River, a little mining town 40 miles from here where industrial garnets have been extracted from the earth for over a hundred years. Her grandfather had been a teamster, driving the teams of horses that hauled the garnets to the railroad station in nearby North Creek. Her father had worked for the mine also, doing just about everything, till he became a carpenter. Jen met her husband, Willard, at a square dance held in North River's old two-room schoolhouse. Willard worked at the mine grinding the rock away from the garnets.

He came home covered in dust every day. They bought an old house, built in the 1850s, and had six children. One day, at the age of 57, Willard came home from work and, as he and Jen made plans to cut firewood, blacked out. Jen sent her son for the doctor who, upon arrival, had them call an ambulance and then left. Willard died in Jen's arms before the ambulance arrived.

Jen was left with six children to raise. She received a pension of $50. a month from the mine and $150 per child per month from Social Security. She paid off her house and car with her husband's life insurance and went to work as a nurse. She raised her children and celebrated the arrival of her ninth grandchild today. She is still single and still lives in the old house she and her husband bought together.

It seems strange that I could have known Jen for so long and yet known nothing about her. Everyone has a story, and every story is worth telling. The world is full of stories walking around in museums, shopping malls, and bars, but we never hear most of them.

6:30 am July 19, 2003

I woke up at 4:00 this morning and couldn't go back to sleep. I am feeling blue this week, and as always when I feel this way, I want to flee. To pack up the truck, load Miss Kelley and Huck, and go somewhere I've never been. Try to start a new life. (I'm very good at it.) But what is the use? Before long it would grow old, and I would be the same old me, and then I would be running again.

*****

I have not worked on my puzzle for days now, and I have missed my journeys into the past. The piece I visit now took place after my job at Hoko River ended, but before I arrived back in Virginia. It shows a woman, aged 33, standing on a ladder with a canvas bag around her waist, embraced by the branches of a pear tree. Her face shows signs of exhaustion and despair, but also an expression of peace.

Picking Pears in Oregon, or This is the Life!

The highway stretched away in front of me, as empty as my life seemed to be on this early autumn afternoon. On both sides of the road were orchards of pear trees, emerald green in the bright sunlight, filled with Mexican migrant workers picking the fruit. I laid my hand on Princess's head. "How would you like to stop here?" I asked her. I took the wet lick she deposited on my cheek as a yes, and eased my foot off the gas pedal.

I had left Washington the day before in my little orange Honda Civic, bound for Virginia with my doberman, Princess, my Siamese cat, Twinkle, and barely enough money in my pockets to make the trip. My divorce papers had been filed, the farm put on the market, and the remnants of my life shoved into a storage unit in Rochester, Washington. I had crossed into Oregon and headed east on I-84, following the Columbia River past Mt. Hood and through the scenic river cliffs known as the Dalles. There I had turned off the interstate and headed down this unknown road. Now, surrounded by a wide panorama of orchards stretching as far as I could see, crisscrossed by straight, grassy, little lanes, I stopped.

I knew something about migrant farm work. I had read John Steinbeck's classic novels describing the social injustices endured by Mexican laborers in the early part of the 20th century. I often played Woody Guthrie's Depression-era song on my guitar, echoing his sad lyrics about rotten peaches and hungry mouths, about Mexican deportees "scattered like dry leaves" after an airplane crash. I had worked in the fields of Washington side by side with illegal Mexican migrants picking cucumbers and blueberries. But I had never worked in the fruit trees. Now, out of work and money, with no plan for the future, I decided to give it a try.

I walked down one of the lanes and, locating the foreman, asked him for a job. I received an unequivocal "No!" for an answer. "This is work for wetbacks. There's no way I'm going to hire a white woman." I stopped at the next orchard and received the same answer. Then again. This time, after locating the foreman and receiving my rejection, I turned around to go back to my car and found myself lost. Panic seized me as I thought of Princess and Twinkle locked in the car's hot interior. I ran back and forth through the endless rows of identical pear trees, my heart pounding with terror, till I finally located them. I drove on.

I got the same answer at the next orchard. "This is no place for a white woman and, besides, you wouldn't be able to do the work." Frustrated, I argued back, accusing the foreman of unfairness and discrimination; telling him how desperately I needed the job, and assuring him that I could do it. But it was no use. As I trudged back to my car, disheartened, I ran into the owner of the orchard. Noticing my despondence, he asked me what was wrong. I told him. "Well, by George," he said, "I don't believe in discrimination. You go back and tell Jim (the foreman) that I said to give you a job!"

Jim was not happy, but he had no choice but to follow his boss's orders. They both agreed, however, that I would not be able to stay in the Mexicans' camp. I would have to find my own quarters. I drove into the nearest town, located an old motel, and rented a tiny room for $40 a week. I introduced Princess and Twinkle to their new, temporary home. There was no television or air conditioner and it reeked of mold and old cigarette smoke. But it was somewhere for them to stay while I worked and a place for me to lay my head when I finished work.

I arrived back at the orchard the next morning at the prescribed time, 6:00 AM. Jim met me at the gate, a sour expression on his face. He gave me a canvas picking basket and led me to a tall, heavily laden pear tree with a ladder leaning into its branches. Nearby was a wooden crate where, he explained, I was to empty the baskets of pears after I picked them. A driver would be around periodically with a tractor to pick up the crates. I would be paid according to how many crates I filled. It was important, he said, not to bruise the pears. And, he added with emphasis, I had to pick the tree clean. Not one pear was to be left on the tree when I was done.

Before leaving he gave me a baleful look. "I don't believe for a moment that you'll be able to do it, and I want it clear that I do not approve of your being here! But I'm not the boss..." As he walked away I pulled the straps of the basket across my shoulders and adjusted it so that it hung at my waist, in front so that I could quickly drop the pears in. Then I headed up the ladder.

I had been climbing trees all my life, and I was an expert tree climber. The branches were full of the ripe golden fruit, the air sweet with the smell of harvest. I picked quickly, and soon my basket grew heavy, the straps pulling on my shoulders. I didn't mind. "What fun!" I thought. "Imagine getting paid to hang out in a tree!" I deposited the fruit into the crate, moved the ladder, and climbed back up. Hearing a voice, I looked down. Jim was standing below, eyeing me. "Ready to quit yet?" he asked. "No way!" I answered him cheerfully.

It was a gorgeous fall day. I could hear the busy voices of birds, stopped briefly on their migration south, chirping in the leaves. When I got to the higher branches I could see the lofty peak of Mt. Hood, ribbons of snow still clinging to a few of its ridges, and the Columbia River, wending its way lazily through the hills. I could also see the other pickers--Mexican men with their families, talking, laughing, and some-times singing in Spanish. I was thoroughly enjoying myself, in spite of the increasing soreness in my shoulders and back. I smiled sweetly when Jim stopped by again. "I'm doing just fine!" I assured him. "This is the life!"

I had almost finished picking the tree. Only three pears remained, clinging to the far ends of the highest branches. I emptied the 40 pounds of pears into my basket, moved the ladder again and climbed to the top, stretching high to reach one. My fingers brushed the smooth surface, but I couldn't get close enough to grasp it. I moved the ladder and tried again. The ladder teetered precariously as I stepped onto the top rung, trying to keep my balance. I reached blindly above me to find the illusive pear. No luck. Shaking, I slithered back down to the ground and moved it again. "Damn!" Time was passing and with it, my profits. I prayed that the foreman, Jim, would not come along and see my predicament.

I heard the sound of a tractor and, peering through the branches, saw the Mexican driver coming to pick up the crate. "Oh No!" I struggled harder to reach the pear, but with no luck. He pulled up and watched me for a minute, then quickly jumped off the tractor and, motioning me down, fairly flew up the ladder and plucked the pear. Quick as a wink he picked the remaining fruit and deposited them in my crate. Then, with a fleeting grin at my repeated cries of "Gracias," he was gone, taking my crate with him. When Jim stopped by a few minutes later he walked around my tree, looking carefully to see if I'd missed any pears. He was impressed to find the tree picked clean as a whistle.

When quitting time came I was tired and sore, but I assured Jim that I would be back the next morning. I was glad to get back to my little room, where Princess and Twinkle awaited me. I took them for a walk, partook of a lukewarm drizzle of a shower, and walked to a nearby restaurant-bar, where I ordered a beer and a hamburger.

While waiting for my burger, I struck up a conversation with the man who occupied the closest barstool. He said that he lived nearby. When I told him that I was picking pears, he frowned. "Don't tell anyone else that!" he warned me. "Migrant workers aren't welcome in the bars here. Or anywhere else, for that matter." I was aghast at his attitude, but too tired to argue with him. I returned to my room and collapsed into bed. Tired though I was, I soon realized that the demons of loneliness and despair, close companions since the breakup of my marriage but left behind in the pear trees, were waiting for me here. That night and the ones that followed were long and filled with tears.

Each morning, however, found me back out in the orchards, where life at the top of a pear tree seemed more cheerful. I worked for the rest of the week and every time I neared the end of my tree, the Mexican driver would quickly and quietly run up the ladder and finish the job. I was impressed by how fast and capable the Mexican workers were, and by how pleasantly and politely they treated me, in spite of the language barrier.

Despite the terrible reputation that migrant farm work has in this country, the people I was working with here seemed to be enjoying themselves. I envied them their camaraderie, wishing that I could join in their laughter.

Then one afternoon Jim stopped by and told me the job was over. The pears had all been picked, and the workers were packing up to move to the next farm. "I have to admit," he said, "you surprised me. I didn't think you could do it!" I tried to keep the smirk off my face, and I never revealed the little secret I shared with the tractor driver!

The next morning I stopped by to pick up my paycheck, which came to around $27.00 per day. As I was leaving, I saw the owner of the farm. He shook my hand and invited me to come back next time I was in the area. Maybe, someday, I will. There are a lot worse places one could spend one's life than in the top of a leafy, fruit-laden tree, with blue sky overhead, cradled by rolling hills and emerald orchards, overlooking the mighty Columbia River.

I have often thought, since that autumn in 1983, that I would like to pick fruit again, follow the harvest, starting in Washington's cherry trees and finishing up in the California vineyards depicted by Steinbeck's "Grapes of Wrath." I know, of course, about the terrible conditions in which "wetbacks" often enter this country--the crowded, unsanitary camps they are often forced to live in. I know how they are taken advantage of and used by greedy fruit growers, and about the dangers of the pesticides with which the trees are sprayed. I know about the cancers and other health problems fruit pickers are exposed to; about the masks and suits which are recommended but seldom used; about the warnings printed in English, but seldom read or understood by the Mexican workers most at risk.

I know about the lives that are put in danger so that we Americans can have perfect fruit, unmarred by worm or blemish. Still, it was by choice that the Mexicans were there. According to the man I met in the bar, 99% were illegal. They came back year after year because the fruit growers offered something they couldn't get at home. They risked capture as well as other dangers because there was no better way for them.

It makes me sad to think that something so lovely and natural as a fresh pear can be the bearer of death and illness. That the idyllic week I spent in those leafy green treetops, overlooking a great river valley, working for a kindly farmer alongside pleasant, good-humored fruit-pickers, could be a synonym for suffering and social injustice. I am reminded of two lines in Arlo Guthrie's poignant song, "Deportee," in which he asks of us,

*"Is this the best way we can grow our good orchards?
Is this the best way we can grow our good fruit?"*

*****

8:35 pm July 20, 2003

Margaret called at 8:30 this morning to tell me there was a flock of wild turkeys coming up the driveway to my cabin. I looked out the window, and sure enough, they were strutting up the hill. "That must be what Huck's been barking at," I told her before we hung up. I watched for a while. There were two hens, their blue heads vibrant in the morning sunlight, and at least a dozen half-grown chicks. They were feeding busily on something in the grasses which grew along the woods. After a while I quietly slipped out the door with my camera, hoping to get a picture, but they just as quietly slipped into the bushes and out of sight.

After work I went by Stewarts to pick up some tomato sauce, and I saw Floyd sitting at one of the tables. I stopped to say hi, and sat down for a visit. I knew Floyd from working at the diner. He came in every morning for breakfast, a meticulous elderly man with a bit of an accent. I knew he was a widower, and I knew he had Parkinson's Disease, but I knew little else about him. Today he told me his story.

Born 80 years ago in Lake Placid, he had quit school in 8th grade to help support his family. He got a job working in the skating arena where the Winter Olympics had been held, keeping the ice smooth, and he did all kinds of other jobs. He married a French girl whose father refused to come to the wedding because he wanted his daughter to stay home.

Floyd loved to ice skate, he said, and he was on a hockey team for a while. Then he began playing baseball, becoming a semi-professional. Meanwhile, he went to Ohio to attend school to learn to be a pipe fitter, and then he got a job at the mine in Tahawus. He worked there until he retired in 1980. He and his wife had adopted a daughter, and now Floyd is a grandfather, but his wife died a few years ago. I knew the rest of the story--how lonely he is, and how much he misses his wife.

He shook as he talked, but it was not as bad as some days. Finally I stood to leave, reminding him that Huck and Miss Kelley would be wondering where I was. As I walked out to my truck I felt his eyes follow me, lonely and lost. Still, he'd had, as I had said to him, an interesting life, and he had had love.

Home again, I am trying to get together some things to take to Virginia. I'll be leaving in a few days, going to stay with Mom while Nancy and her husband Jim take a vacation at Nags Head. I'm not sure when I'll be back.

6:30 pm July 23, 2003

Long Lake can be dangerous. I have heard it said before, and today I found it out for myself. I had been wanting to paddle downstream (it is, after all, really just an enlargement of the Raquette River) to its north end, where it runs into Cold River, home of the famous Adirondack hermit, Noah Rondeau. I had the day off, a beautiful day without a cloud in the sky, so I gave Huck and Kelley extra food and water, donned shorts and a tank top, hiked down the hill to where I keep my kayak, and headed out. Down along the lakeshore past the public beach, past the dam which separates it from Jennings Pond, under the bridge, past the Adirondack Hotel and lots of camps, till it widens into an extension of wilderness where few signs of human life are seen. The wind was behind me, and it was an exhilarating, breathtaking trip. I fairly flew down the lake. About halfway along, I came upon a wooded peninsula jutting into the lake, a boat tied up to the shore, and the figure of a man working on the boat. Behind him was a beautiful house, a seeming anomaly out here in this wilderness. I waved as I paddled by, and we spoke for a minute. "Be careful," he called out, "and stop back by if you need anything." "Sure!" I replied, glancing back as I continued on down the lake.

In the distance the peak of a mountain loomed, and nearer, the silhouettes of white pine and hemlock reached for the sky. Huge dark rocks--glacial till left behind by a long-ago Ice Age glacier, reached out through hobble and blackberry vines. Not a boat did I see, and I felt like I was in a splendid world of my own.

Gradually I realized that the wind had begun to pick up and was pushing me down the lake at an alarming speed. Waves splashed the sides of the kayak. I began to grow nervous, but I was determined to reach my destination. I decided that it would be wise to move closer to the shoreline, so that if I should flip over I could swim to land. Finally, with whitecaps churning all around me, I decided that I was being too foolhardy. What would happen to Huck and Miss Kelley if I didn't make it back?

I pulled over and rested for a spell. Then I turned the kayak around and headed back toward home. Or tried. Facing into the wind now, I found that the lake sputtered like an angry demon driven by fury. The wind spun me around, first to the right and then to the left, refusing to let me paddle back upstream. The waves threatened to toss my normally stable kayak over like it was a toy canoe. Frightened now, I fought my way even closer to the shore. Then I began a slow struggle to make my way home, clinging to the shoreline and stopping frequently to rest, realizing as I did so that I had little chance of making it back before dark.

I was soaking wet now, drenched by the waves which regularly washed over the kayak, grateful for the self-baling design which allowed the water to pass out again. Even in summer the waters of this northern lake were frigid, and during the brief breaks I took from paddling I realized that I was shivering from cold. Before long I was exhausted, the muscles in my arms aching, but I had no alternative but to keep going. As I worked my way back I thought about the only human I had seen that afternoon--the nice-looking man at the camp, and I prayed that he was still there. He had said to stop by if I needed anything, and I would sure need help if I made it that far.

It seemed like forever, and I could see from the sun that evening was fast approaching, when I saw the point in the distance. Yes, it was definitely the peninsula where the camp stood. The wind had backed off some, but I knew I couldn't make it home before dark, so I paddled straight for it. As I drew nearer, I made out the shape of the man, sitting in a beach chair, with binoculars. He watched me paddle up, waved a slow greeting, and walked down to the dock where I was pulling up.

"I see you're back," he said. "Blew up pretty fast out there, huh? You're soaking wet." I suddenly became aware that the wet tank top I wore, braless, was no doubt see-through now. I wanted to wrap my arms across my chest, but couldn't let go of the paddle. He reached down, offered me a hand, and helped me out of the kayak. Then he pulled my boat up onto the dock.

"You're freezing," he said, noticing my shivering and my blue lips. "Come on in and I'll get you a towel. My name's Ed, by the way." Before long I was wrapped in a man's green bathrobe, my clothes spinning around in a dryer, sipping from a glass of pinot noir wine. I studied the man sitting beside me on the peach-colored futon as he told me a little about his camp, accessible only by boat, its electricity provided by a generator. Ed looked to be about my age, with brown hair graying a bit at the temples. He was of medium height and weight, attractive, with polished manners.

He glanced outside. "It's getting pretty dark for you to paddle back to town. I can give you a ride in my boat, or…if you'd like you can spend the night. I have some fresh fish I can grill for supper." My eyes widened.

The offer was tempting; I hadn't had that kind of adventure in quite a while. I reminded myself, however, that Huck and Miss Kelley were waiting for me. Besides, I knew nothing about this man. He was probably married!

Before long my clothes were dry. We tied the kayak to the back of his boat, climbed in, and soon he was dropping me off near the cabin. He declined my invitation to come in and, although he wrote down my phone number when I offered it, I'm pretty sure I won't hear from him.

But that's okay. I'm just glad to be back safe in the cabin, warm and scarfing down a frozen pizza. It was a pretty exciting day!

8:30 pm July 30, 2003

I've been doing some last minute packing, getting ready for the long drive to Richmond. Before heading south, I'll head back one more time into my past.

*****

My memories place me back in Virginia twenty years ago. I am staying with my parents, waiting for my divorce to go through. I've gotten a waitress job in a Greek restaurant and returned to college at Virginia Commonwealth University. Before leaving Washington I had asked my college advisor, Lloyd Colfax, what he thought I should do with my degree in Native American Studies. "Teach." He had replied. "Get a job teaching on an Indian Reservation. Even though it is better for Indian children to have Indian teachers, there are not enough, and you would be the next best thing." So I have been taking eighteen hours of post-grad classes in education and acing them with a 4.0 average.

I'm still missing Pete terribly, however, and my beloved dog Princess has, after a few months' reprieve with medications, died of lymphoma. Fighting an overwhelming depression, I've visited a counselor at VCU. Instead of trying to help, he dismissed me, saying that I couldn't maintain my good grades if I was seriously depressed.

Everything seems wrong, and my solution, once again, is to make a run for it. Momma and Daddy, knowing my anguish, do everything they can to help. Momma offers to take care of Twinkle, my Siamese cat. I make out a will and go to see a lawyer with Daddy, signing over power of attorney to him. I pack a small pack with essentials. I tell my family that I might never come back alive; but that if I do, it will mean I am healed. Then I set out with a one-way ticket to the Bahamas, accompanied by my best friend Sandy. We have reservations at a beach hotel in Nassau, the capital, located on New Providence Island. We spend a week there, relaxing in relative luxury at Cable Beach. Then Sandy leaves, returning to her life in Virginia, and I set out to find a new one.

I have dug out the journal I kept while there. Leafing through it, I find myself in tears again, but then my mood changes. I smile as I read some of the entries and am transported back in time. The year is 1984. At 34 years old, the woman I see is as slim as a rail and brown as gingerbread. Her hair is streaked by weeks in the sub-tropical sun, her denim shorts bleached and ragged. She is wearing a worn, navy tee-shirt with the letters EXUMA stamped across the back, a gift from an elderly Bahamian shop-owner who had given her a lift and a place to stay on the island.

Crewing in the Bahamas

"Hi!" I exclaimed, hopping across the gunwale onto the deck of a sleek blue and tan schooner tied up at a Nassau marina. "Need any crew?" A man with curly brown hair was standing near the bow, sorting through a pile of lines. He glanced up, then looked me over thoughtfully. "Where you aiming to go? he asked me. "Oh, it doesn't matter! Anywhere you're going," I replied.

After a few moments of consideration, "Can you cook?"

"Sure!" I answered with a cocky assurance I don't usually possess. "Can you cook for thirty people in a galley the size of a crackerbox on a rolling sailboat?" "Why not?" I responded breezily (though I had no clue as to how I would do it). "I can't pay you," he added. "Just room and board."

"It's a deal!" I said. "Well, we're leaving in fifteen minutes. Get your stuff!" "I've got it all right here!" I grinned, holding up my worn pack and eagerly looking around at my new home.

I listened with interest as the captain who, introducing himself as Jim, explained that this was a for-hire sailboat, and it had been hired by a dive club, a group of thirty people from the eastern United States.

It was not his boat; he was just the captain. They'd been sailing around the islands for a week, and were now headed back to Miami. We would stop at a couple islands along the way, do some more diving, and should arrive back in the States in a week. They weren't very happy, he added, glancing around to make sure no one could hear us. There was plenty of food on board, but no one to cook it, and none of them wanted to do it. Neither did he, he added; he was a sailor, not a cook. Everyone had been living on peanut butter and jelly sandwiches for a week and, frankly, they were pretty pissed off.

I heard a lot more about their starvation diet before long. As the passengers came on board the captain introduced me as the new cook. There were 25 men, most in their 20s and 30s, and five women. Their eyes lit up with glee as they shook my hand, barraging me with tales about the horrendous meals they'd had thus far. I allowed myself no time for self-doubt as we untied the lines and pulled away from the dock. Within a few minutes the sails were set and we were on our way, plying through the turquoise waters of the subtropics.

No time was wasted. I was shown to the berth where I would be sleeping, and as soon as my pack was stowed I was escorted to the galley. Everyone was starving, it seemed. The captain had just picked up some fresh meat while at dock, so he handed me two ten pound packages of ground beef and several big packages of hamburger rolls. "Have at it!" he said. "Gary here will help you."

With Gary's assistance, I figured out how to light the propane stove. Soon, however, I found out that cooking on an in-progress sailboat was not exactly the same as working in my kitchen. As the "Marybell" heaved up and down across the waves I had trouble standing in one spot. When I opened the cabinet door to get the pans, everything tumbled out onto the floor. When I tried to set the pans on the burners they immediately slid off, splattering raw hamburger everywhere. Using one hand to hold on and one to hold the pan, that left none to flip the burgers. Gary watched helplessly with no concept, apparently, of how to assist me. After a bit, though, we got some sort of system worked out and soon I had burgers rolling off the grill and up the steps to my customers

Sixty hamburgers, however, is a lot of hamburgers. The grease they created produced a most nauseating aroma, and the heat put out by the stove turned the galley into a sauna. The long up-and-down, side to side rolls of the boat started working at me. I tried to ignore it. I pursed my lips and kept flipping burgers. The butterflies in my stomach began to feel more like bats, and then rocks.

Finally, I slammed down my spatula and tore up the steps, announcing to whomever could hear me that if they wanted a bloody hamburger they could go cook it themselves. Looking neither left nor right, I staggered up to the bow and cast myself down, prostrate on the

Pat Garber

cool surface, and lay there, the breeze rippling across me delightfully. Lunch was over and the dishes cleaned up by the time I slipped sheepishly back down and joined the others.

That was the only time I got seasick on that trip. From then on, delicious meals flowed from my fingers like magic. A passenger was always assigned to assist me, and there were lots of volunteers. My name was forgotten and I became known as "Cook." The other women on board must have resented me, or maybe they were just too ticked off by this time to get over it. They had nothing to do with me. But the men adored me (and my food of course.) Lasagna, omelets, pepper steak, brownies and pies. I seemed to have a gourmet's touch, and I could do no wrong.

The captain showered me with praise, saying that I had saved his ship from possible mutiny. My fragile and badly damaged ego healed rapidly in the warmth of the Bahamian sun and the worship of 25 men. The seas were fair and the skies were blue. I snorkeled (I'm not a certified diver) while the passengers dove in scuba gear. Site of the third longest barrier reef in the world, the Bahamian waters were a fairyland of colorful fish, anemones, and sponges.

Staghorn, brain, elkhorn and oscillating corals vied with one a-nother in their awe-inspiring beauty. One time, as I swam deep beneath the waters, exploring by myself, I came face to face with a ten foot long hammerhead shark. I don't know which of us was more frightened, but we both turned and swam in the opposite direction as fast as we could go.

Between meals I had nothing to do, so I lazed on the deck, delighting in my surroundings. The Bahamas are an archipelago consisting of 700 islands and covering 100,000 square miles of the Atlantic Ocean. The name is derived from the Spanish "Baja Mar," which means shallow sea. The early inhabitants, Arawak Indians, greeted Columbus's ships in 1492 with friendliness. They were later enslaved by Spanish explorers led by Juan Ponce de Leon on his search for the Fountain of Youth. By 1520 the natives had been wiped out.

In 1629 King Charles I claimed the Bahamas for England, and settlers moved here from Bermuda. There followed decades of pirating. At the end of the American Revolution a number of loyalists fled to the islands, bringing with them their slaves. Frustrated by the arid soils, many of the slave-owners moved farther south, leaving the slaves behind. These slaves, freed by England in 1834, were the ancestors of most Bahamian citizens today. They, along with the descendants of the English

276

colonists, had received their independence from Great Britain in 1973, though they were still closely connected. I knew little about the history or geography of the Bahamas when I arrived. I had gained a sense of the islands gradually, as I regained a sense of myself.

I also visited with the passengers, and sometimes the captain. The captain was a wiry, sun-browned man in his early forties, not quite handsome but rugged and masculine. He told me stories about his years running sailing cruises out of Miami, and I told him about the adventures I'd had since coming to the Bahamas two months before.

There was the first mate position I'd gotten with a German sailor bound for Spain. His was a small but highly efficient sailing sloop made of steel and fiberglass. Erick seemed to be a nice enough man--a bit arrogant, perhaps, but I could deal with that in exchange for the chance to sail to Europe. The first day went all right, but then things started getting tense. He tried to talk me into visiting him in his sleeping berth and got angry and haughty when I refused.

On the next night we anchored out in a small harbor near Great Exuma Island. As I lay sleeping on my narrow berth with a light blanket, something awakened me. Opening my eyes, I found a huge, ugly penis about two inches from my face! Fear, anger, and indignation swept through my mind as I slapped it, and then the face that it belonged to, away. Quite honestly, I was tempted to bite it, but the thought was too repulsive.

Abandoning my pack, I hopped over the side of the boat and into the water. My last memory of Erick was a cacophony of English and German curse-words resounding across the water as I climbed up the bank to a huge hotel, soaking wet. It was about three in the morning so no one was about. I waited on a porch at the back entrance, shivering, until morning, at which time I explained my dilemma to the desk clerk. He located a big apron and showed me to a restroom. I removed my wet clothes and wrapped the apron around me. The clerk gave my wet shorts and shirt to the laundry lady to dry while I ate a hot breakfast at no charge; (I expect I looked pretty pitiful.) At that point my crewing prospects did not look too encouraging!

That afternoon, however, found me wandering the docks at Elizabeth Harbor in Georgetown, Exuma's largest town. Erick and his boat were gone. and I was looking for work. My next employer, Darren, was a tall, slender, soft-spoken American. He was house-sitting for someone and did not plan to sail right away, but he asked me if I wanted a job doing the brightwork on his boat. "Sure," I agreed, not having the slightest idea what "brightwork" was. I soon learned. The lovely teak woodwork with which his boat was generously trimmed (it was a classic wooden sloop) needed to be sanded and re-varnished. He promised me a fair wage and a place to sleep. I could either stay on board the boat, he said, or have a room at the house where he was staying. After my previous experience I chose to stay on the boat, alone.

The house Darren was caring for had a private beach, a swimming pool, and lovely furnishings. Darren proved to be a perfect gentleman and after my work was done the two of us would go swimming in the warm waters of the sound or sailing among the 365 cays which made up the ninety--mile stretch known as the Exumas. We sailed to Stocking Island and helped ourselves to coconuts from the numerous groves there. We also explored Great Exuma itself. Breadfruit trees, bought by a local preacher from Captain William Bligh in the late 1700s, grew wild. Cotton plants, left behind along with the slaves brought to the island to cultivate it, abounded. An amazing number of the residents bore the last name of Rolle, Darren told me, derived from the former slave owner John Rolle, who had freed his 300 slaves and provided them with land there.

Georgetown was the largest town, but since the population of the entire Exuma chain numbered less than 4,000 people, it was pretty small. The Tropic of Cancer ran right through its center, which made it the northernmost latitude reached by the overhead sun. In stepping across that invisible line you moved from the subtropics to the tropics (not that I could tell any difference!) Georgetown was, compared to the tourist centers on Nassau, a bit rundown and seedy, but I loved it. The people were warm and friendly. Strains of reggae music drifted through the open doorways, along with the aromas of conch stew and over-ripe fruit. One night I danced for hours in a little back street bar, my white skin and blonde hair seeming not the least bit out of place among the muscular, shining black bodies and pulsing Bahamian music. I was having a grand time, but soon I was yearning to move on.

One day, as I was sanding the upper deck of Darren's boat, a new sailboat tied up at the dock. A fluffy young woman with dyed blonde hair and a bikini came over and asked me what I was doing. "I'm working," I explained, thinking to myself that it was pretty obvious. "Well, wouldn't you rather go sailing with us?" she asked. "I'm tired of being the only girl on the boat. "I want a woman to talk to."

"Us" turned out to be Cherie (the blonde,) Fred, her boyfriend (a heavyset, balding man at least twice her age,) and Hank, the captain, a bearded, long-haired charmer who looked like he might well have been a pirate. The older man was paying Hank, or Captain Kidd, as they called him, to sail them around the Bahamas. The boat was small and not nearly as nice as the one I had been working on, but it was going somewhere, and there was an air of excitement that appealed to me. After a quick consultation, it was agreed that I would join them the next morning. I told Darren and we said goodbye.

If it was a wild adventure I was looking for, I had found it. The captain threw off the lines, set the sails, and lit a joint, which he passed around. The older man, Fred, opened a bottle of Jack Daniels and handed it to me. As we glided through the emerald waters they told me their story, each putting in his or her own bit as we passed the joint and the bottle. It was, in fact, something of a pirate boat, operating without a license, and the crew was on the run. I felt like I was joining Edward "Blackbeard" Teache and Calico Jack Rackham, both of whom had frequented these waters. Cherie and I were Anne Bonney and Mary Reed, female pirates of the Caribbean who had, reportedly, gone topless to distract the crew of the ships they attacked.

Fred, I learned, had quit his job at a reputable bank, pulled all the money from his and his wife's joint accounts, brought along all the credit cards he could get his hands on, and run off with a teller (Cherie) from the bank. They had come across Hank (Captain Kidd) and talked him into sailing them for as far as they could get.

By now the cash was gone and all the credit cards had either run over their limits or been canceled by the wife. But credit checks down here didn't work too well, apparently, so they (we, now) were paying for the travels with the cards that didn't get rejected. It was a bizarre though exciting thing to be doing, and I wondered at the degree of desperation which could have sent this ordinary-seeming, middle-class man to embark on this journey of folly. For soon the credit card scam would fail. Neither of them seemed like people who would be able to cope with the reality that awaited them, penniless on some Caribbean island and probably, eventually, found out. I doubted that Cherie had committed any serious transgression, other than being foolish and mindless, but I had a feeling that Fred was in serious trouble. Hank seemed to be one of those guys (not too different from my ex-husband) who constantly balanced on *the edge of hot water without ever really falling in. Whatever trouble he got into, I figured, he would get himself out of.*

The days I spent with Hank, Fred and Cherie are hazy, clothed in a cloud of marijuana smoke, booze, and extravagance. We sailed to Little Exuma and stopped at several other cays along the Great Bahama Banks. Hank told about the time he had found an entire bale of marijuana floating in the sea, thrown overboard, he suspected, by a drug-runner to escape capture. He was always searching the waves for another such find.

Whenever we located a hotel, store, or restaurant that would accept one of Fred's illegal credit cards we spent to the max; elegant dinners of turtle steaks and caviar, White Russians by the dozens, dancing and rubbing shoulders with wealthy people who must have been aghast at our rapscallion ways. Hank was sexy and fun and with all the booze and pot flowing through my blood I didn't give a damn that I wasn't in love with him or he with me. He was supposed to pick up another crew member (a girl friend? I wondered) in a few days, at which point I would leave. When that fell through, he invited me to continue with them on their voyage to who knew where. But Cherie's immature, silly ways were driving me crazy, the tight quarters provided no privacy, and I had had enough of wild living.

When we returned to Georgetown I said goodbye and wished them good luck, for whatever it was worth. At this point I had had enough not only of wild living but of boat life. I spent a few days sleeping on the beach and living off conch fritters and the tropical fruits that grew in abundance throughout the island. One night I slept on a cot in a little grocery. The next morning the old man who owned it fixed me a wonderful breakfast and gave me a slightly damaged shirt, bearing the letters EXUMA, which he said he couldn't sell. I was learning my way around Georgetown and getting to know some of the Bahamians, when one day I noticed everyone heading for the docks. "A big yacht just sailed in!" I was told. "You should go see it."

I joined the crowd, bound for the waterfront. It was indeed a big and extremely luxurious boat. Not a sailboat, I thought to myself, but it wouldn't be too bad working on a boat like that. I could ask anyway. After everybody left I wandered over and waited until I saw a person moving around on board--a stocky, dark-haired American, around 45 years old. "Hello!" I called. "I was wondering if you might be needing any crew." "Hmm," he said, eyeing me. "Come aboard."

David, as he introduced himself, was a wealthy attorney from New York City. He actually had his crew, an Australian woman who'd been with him for a while. Later that day his girlfriend was joining him, and on the next day his son, Dave, just graduated from Harvard Law School, would arrive. In a week they would depart on a six-month voyage throughout the Caribbean. He showed me around the boat. There were three small berths for sleeping, a living room, a galley-dining room, and an outdoor bar, all decked out to the max. There were two jet skis, a small sailboat, diving equipment, the works. He invited me to join him at the bar, where he fixed me a pina colada, himself a gin and tonic. Then he made me a proposal. His son had never had a real girlfriend. If I would be his "er, friend," I could go on the cruise, enjoying all the luxuries, not as a crew member but as a guest

I stared at him, my mouth half open. "You mean, like be a prostitute?"

"Now I wouldn't put it that way," he answered. "You'd be his girlfriend, and you'd have a great time. It's a wonderful opportunity for you."

I shook my head. "I don't think so," I said. "I've done a lot of things in my life, but selling my body, even for a great opportunity, is not one of them." I started to leave, but David stopped me.

"Wait!" he said. "Just give it a chance. Move on board and join us for a few days. Get to know him, no strings attached. Then, if you like him, go with us. If not, stay here at Exuma. You've nothing to lose. He's a great guy and you'll have fun, either way."

"But he must be way younger than me!" I protested.

"That won't matter," he said, "He's tall, good-looking, and smart. You'll like him!"

"Where will I sleep?" I asked doubtfully.

"You can share the berth with Lois. You'll be safe, I promise. It'll be up to you if you want to move in with Dave."

I thought for a few minutes. Why not? I asked myself. So I agreed to get my stuff and come back, warning him that his plan would not be fulfilled.

"One more thing. I don't want him to know anything about our little arrangement. It's just between us, however it works out."

I agreed and moved onto the yacht that night, meeting David's girlfriend and Lois, the Australian girl who was to be my roommate. Lois and I hit it off immediately. She was glad to have someone to talk to. I had almost no clothes now, having left one set behind when I jumped off Erick's boat and worn out the others. She gave me a new wardrobe of attractive Australian hand-me-downs. She also showed me how to ride her unicycle, which she could peddle around the railings of the boat. I got along much better with her than with David's la-de-da girlfriend.

Next day the son, Dave, arrived. He was just as his father described him--tall, well-built, good-looking, intelligent. He was also shy and modest and just plain nice. He and I hit it off, and we did all sorts of things together for the next few days. We snorkeled and spear-fished (I didn't actually spear any fish); we sailed, swam, went out to dinner, talked. We became good friends. But that's all we were; friends. Each morning, when I got up and stumbled out of Lois's bedroom, rubbing my sleep-blinded eyes, David would look at me with disapproval, glancing toward Dave's bedroom and shaking his head. "You're going to regret this." he told me. I would smile and get myself a cup of coffee, shaking my head back at him. Every day, too, I would sit in the kitchen and write in my journal. This apparently made him very nervous, for he kept asking me what I was writing. I told him he could read it if he wanted to. I always left it out. Not only did he read it, he removed the pages I wrote while on his boat! Or at least, they disappeared.

Finally the day came for the cruise to begin. When I came out and sat down with David, (everyone else was still asleep) he looked at me sadly.

"Do you realize what you're giving up?" he asked. "You and Dave get along fine. I just don't understand." I didn't know how to explain.

`"I like Dave a lot," I told him. "But, for better or worse, I like to call my own shots. I'm sorry." I was sad to say goodbye to Lois and to Dave. I stood on the dock and watched as they set out, Dave still an innocent, blissfully unaware of the deal his father had tried to make with me.

As I walked away, I decided it was time to head out again. There were no new boats at the dock, no crewing jobs available. But I had another idea. I had noticed that there was a small airport on Exuma, so I asked directions and hitched a ride to it. A Cessna two-seater was sitting on the runway, its engine running. Perfect! Pulling my pack across my shoulder, I walked out to the runway and stood beside it, my thumb extended. Before long I was up among the clouds, looking down on the blue sea and watching Exuma melt into the horizon. An hour or so later the pilot and I landed in Nassau at a considerably bigger airport. The pilot offered to help me get a ride to the States, but I was not quite ready to leave the Bahamas. I thanked him and headed into town.

A couple days later, I walked up to the "Marybell" and asked Captain Jim for a job. So now, here I was, sitting on his deck, heading for Miami and little aware that my biggest adventure still lay before me. Jim announced that we would be making a short stop at Gun Cay, part of the Berry Islands. The Berrys, Jim said, lie along what is known as the Tongue of the Ocean, a mile deep trench which splits the shallow Great Bahama Bank in half. Everyone hurried ashore, glad to be on land for a bit and stretch our legs.

But when it was time to depart, several of the passengers were not around. By the time they ambled back it was dark and the captain was irritated and anxious to get going. He pushed the boat off the dock and started the engines. Then, with the engines still running, he lifted the mainsail and set the jib. It was a beautiful, starlit night and we were rushing through it at full speed, kicking up waves which glowed with the eerie green light of phosphorescence. I stood at mid-ship, holding onto the mast with my face raised to the warm wind, exulting in the feeling of freedom.

Suddenly, without warning, there was a strange jolting sound. The "Marybell" lunged to a halt, quivering and rolling sideward with tremors which felt like an earthquake. I was thrown to my knees and I saw people flying across the deck in front of me, screaming. Water crashed across the deck and bedlam broke out. The men were shouting, the women crying.

Jim yelled, "Get the life jackets!" and soon someone was handing them out. I put mine on, but oddly, I was not afraid. I watched the scene unfold before me in fascination but without the least bit of fear. It became apparent after a few minutes that while we were listing badly to one side, we were not sinking. Trying to keep my balance, I made my way over to Jim.

"What can I do?" I asked him. He shook his head.

"We've hit a reef." he said. "I don't know where it came from. I thought I knew this bottom. I need to get down below deck and see if there's a hole. If there is, we've got to get the life boats out. I've been trying to reach another boat but I can't get through. Here, take the radio and keep trying. I'm going below."

Jim's initial inspection did not indicate any major leaks. He asked some of the more experienced men to don their diving gear and check the keel. Meanwhile, a strong cold breeze had blown up. Waves splashed across the gunwale, soaking and chilling us. The divers took turns going down, and they came up cold and exhausted. It was 4:00 AM by now, and we still hadn't been able to get hold of anyone to ask for help.

Pat Garber

"Look, Pat," Jim told me, "if you can figure out a way to get down into the galley and make some sandwiches and hot coffee, that would be great!" I was thrilled to have a job, and with help from a couple of the guys I got the door, jammed shut by the impact, to open. There was water on the floorboard and it was dark, but using flashlights and a sense of humor, we did it. I had thought it was hard to cook with the boat moving, but that was nothing compared to trying to heat water and spread mayonnaise at a 90° angle. But soon we were passing cups of hot coffee and tuna sandwiches up through the hatch. I was having a ball!!!

Captain Jim, on the other hand, was not happy. By the time morning arrived it was apparent that the rudder had suffered serious damage. We were not going anywhere that day. Our best chance to get off the reef, he said, was at high tide. If we could shift some of the weight around and get help from a ship, we might be able to slide her off. Coral is sharp, however, so he was still worried about ripping the bottom. Either way, he figured he was going to be in hot water and maybe out of a job.

We finally got hold of a captain on a passing ship who, with the help of the tide, pulled us off the reef. The divers helped Jim get the rudder off and within 24 hours, it had been marginally patched. We set out again, this time limping along slowly so as not to further damage the rudder, bound for the Biminis. We sailed across what Jim said was a strange 300 foot long rectangular rock formation, five to ten thousand years old, believed by some to be the remains of Atlantis. I stared down, unable to see it but imagining an eerie underwater city. We passed by the island of South Bimini, where Ponce do Leon at first believed the Fountain of Youth to lie. These were the islands the rum-runners worked out of during the 1920s, when they pirated illegal booze up to the states.

Finally we made port, pulling up at a dock in Alicetown on North Bimini Island. Ernest Hemingway had hung out here, fishing and drinking and brawling in the nearby "Compleat Angler Hotel." Here is where he wrote "To Have and Have Not" and "Islands in the Stream."Everyone was exhausted and punch-happy when we crowded into the "End of the World" bar, where we were to wait while Jim got some repairs done. "Cook" was the heroine again, having fed everyone from her lop-sided galley, and all the men began buying me drinks.

"One for me and one for Cook!" the bartender was told each time someone ordered himself a drink. Pretty soon we were having a rollicking good time, high not only on booze but on the exhilaration of our adventure. When someone played the theme song from the then popular

movie *"Ghostbusters,"* our crew revised it to *"Reef Busters"* and began to sing it with loud, slightly off-key gusto. They formed a line, scooped me up with a cry of *"Here's to Cook!"* and hoisted me onto their shoulders. They then proceeded to march through Alicetown, carrying me and singing *"Reef Busters"* at the top of their lungs. It was a day to remember, and I was only slightly hung over the next morning.

The rest of our trip was eventless. We sailed through the Straits of Florida and arrived in Miami with no further trouble. Jim and I had become good friends, and I kind of regretted that it went no further than that. He had a girlfriend, he explained; otherwise he would ask me to stay on with him. Another true gentleman.

"Was I going to be all right?" he wanted to know. I assured him that I was. My time in the Bahamas, and in particular on his boat, had done its healing. I was not over my heartache, but I would be able to cope with it now. I would go back to my family. They were renting a cottage at Nags Head, on the Outer Banks of North Carolina, and I thought I would get back in time to join them.

I got a ride north with some of the guys, but then decided to stop and visit my father's sister, Aunt Betty, who lived in Atlanta, Georgia. They let me out at the exit, then continued on. It was almost dark, so I looked for a place to spend the night. I had only a couple dollars to my name, so I asked at a little motel if I could clean rooms in exchange for a room. I stayed there and woke to the sound of meowing. Opening the door, I found a hungry cat standing before me. I asked the maid where the nearest store was and I headed down the road to it, my pack slung across my back. I bought a small package of cat food with my remaining change and was on my way back to the motel when a police car pulled up beside me.

"What are you doing?" the officer asked me, gruffly. I stared at him, not knowing what to say. "I got a report you're hitch-hiking. That's a-gainst the law here." I stared at him innocently.

"No, I just went down to buy this," I said, pulling the cat food out of my pack and explaining about the hungry cat. He stared at me in disbelief and grumbled, "Well I'd better not see you out here hitch-hiking!" before driving off. I fed the cat and gave the rest of the box to the maid, asking her to continue feeding it.

Then I slipped away toward the highway, keeping my eye out for the policeman. Sure enough, there he was, parked behind a little clump of trees, watching for me. I followed the fence line of a field until I was well out of sight, then skipped across to the highway and held out the cardboard sign I had made. "Atlanta Please" it read. It took only a few minutes before I had a ride and was bound for my Aunt Betty's.

What happened next leads me to the conclusion that there IS justice, sometimes, though it may occur by accident. There are occasions when "what goes around, comes around," though it may happen over such a long expanse of time that seeing the pattern takes more time than one has at one's disposal. Still, this was one of those occasions and, looking back, I can see it clearly. I have to backtrack some more, to 1977, to explain.

My husband Pete's and my marriage had been in shambles, though I refused to admit it at the time. It had been obvious, however, to my Aunt Betty, who was staying in a little travel trailer at my parents' house. Pete and I had left California and moved back to Virginia, broke as usual. I was staying with my parents and waitressing at a Chinese restaurant called Gim Din, where my sister Sally also worked. Pete had gotten a job in Myrtle Beach, South Carolina, putting up siding on glitzy condominiums and supposedly making heaps of money. He would come back to Virginia occasionally but, instead of depositing his profits in our account, he would raid the mayonnaise jar where I kept my tips, explaining that he needed it until the big bucks from his job would start pouring in. Then he'd take off again for Myrtle Beach, leaving me alone, broke, and in tears. Aunt Betty had observed all this in silence.

It turned out that the whole Myrtle Beach scheme was a scam and what money they did make, Pete and his buddies partied away, ending up in debt. I finally left, moving west in an anguished state of desperation. Six months later he followed and we reconnected, spending five more years together in Washington, before I came to the irreversible conclusion that Pete and I were never gonna make it as a couple. When I left again in 1983, it was once more in anguish, but this time for good. Now, the late summer of 1984 found me hitchhiking to visit Aunt Betty.

I visited with my aunt for a few days, watching the televised Olympics with her and talking about various things. One of the first things I did was wash my few clothes. When I reached into the washing machine to take them out, I found a hundred dollar bill. It wasn't Aunt Betty's, she assured me. It must have been in the pocket of my jeans! Who had put it there, and how? Jim? One of the guys with the dive club? My last ride? That was a mystery I would never solve.

Two days later Aunt Betty pointed to a door and said: "Go look in that closet." Curious, I obeyed her. On the floor, in neat stacks, were gold bullion blocks, the size of bricks.

When I came out she said, "Do you remember when I was staying at your parents' house and Pete was down in Myrtle Beach? I kept watching the way you'd work so hard and save up your money, and then he'd come and take it. I felt so sorry for you, I decided that one day I would make it up to you. I'm putting all that gold in a trust fund for you, and when you get older it will be yours."

When it was time for me to leave, Aunt Betty, not wanting me to hitchhike, put me on a Greyhound bus, bound for Nags Head, North Carolina. There, I was happily reunited with my family.

I also took a ferry to the little Outer Banks island of Ocracoke. Here, I found what was to be my new life. Ten years later, it was the money from Aunt Betty's gold bullion blocks that allowed me to buy my Ocracoke cottage, Marsh Haven--money I received in restitution, you might say, for the suffering I had endured eighteen years before. What had gone around, had come around. Justice, in a way, had been done. The Exuma tee-shirt is all that I have to show from that journey, but it changed the course of my life in more ways than one.

An interesting aside: Aunt Betty insisted on buying me a bus ticket to North Carolina, feeing that it was safer than hitchhiking. Once on the bus, I realized that I was the only white person, which made not the slightest bit of difference until a black man two seats behind me pulled out a long knife and started yelling in a loud voice about killing all white people! The woman beside me patted my arm reassuringly, but everyone was frightened, and I, being the only white person available, doubly so. The driver, a brave and wise man, talked to the man calmly, "You don't want to do anything like that, Brother, Just enjoy the ride, Man," and so on, while he steered the bus to the front of a police station. He managed to radio a distress call to the station, and a moment after we pulled up two cops ran out and removed him from the bus. I was not hurt, but I found it ironic that riding that bus had turned out to be more dangerous than hitchhiking.

*****

The car is packed, Huck and Miss Kelley loaded, and it is time for us to leave. On such a beautiful day, with the songs of vireos and a winter wren pealing through the treetops, it is hard. My year on this mountain has been a time of peace and purpose. It has been a period of mourning and of closure, of joy and renewal. But there is more I need to do. Soon I will be ready to move on. This work of self-examination, which I describe to myself as a jigsaw puzzle, has for the past year been my purpose, my entertainment, my surcease from loneliness. It is hard to put down the pen which, like a glass of wine, has offered me solace and an excuse to stay.

The pieces of my early life have been pulled out, examined, and connected together in some kind of order. A few are missing, and others may be tainted by misconceptions, misinterpretations, and the tricks memory can play. The picture they present when connected is, nonetheless, me. Who I might be in the future and what lies ahead, I'm not certain.

.

I'll be returning to this cabin, this mountain, someday, I am sure.

Afterword

Eighteen years have passed since I moved to the cabin in Long Lake and began keeping a birchbark journal; thirty-five since I left my husband Pete for the final time and set out to find a new beginning. The stories recorded during my stay at the cabin span half of my life, beginning with the girl who grew up as Patsy Garber, ending with the last days of the woman who became Pat Barret. Changing my name back to Garber, I have since built a new life.

Too much has happened in the interim years to mention here, but I do want to relate several things.

When, upon leaving my husband, I shoved all of my earthly possessions into a storage unit in Grand Mound, Washington, it was with the belief that I would, before long, return and retrieve them. There was even a tiny piece of hope that Pete and I would get back together one last time and maybe this time get it right. Neither happened.

Years passed, and each January started with a resolution that this would be the year I would go back for my "stuff." It was very important to me, and not only because of the sentimental value (many of the items came from my childhood, some from the happy times I had spent with Pete, some heirlooms from my grandparents.) I had never found closure after the loss of my marriage and my beloved farm and friends in Gate, and I still suffered from the grief and loss. I believed that going back one last time, saying my final goodbyes and picking up the pieces, so to speak, so that all would not seem lost, would help me close that door and move on for good. But the idea of returning to the site of such joy and sorrow, not to mention driving nearly 3,000 miles, was overwhelming.

Meanwhile, I tried to keep up with the payments for the storage unit. Often, however, I found that months had passed without my thinking about it. I would hastily write a check for a month or two and send it off, then forget it again.

The owner called and said someone had broken into the unit, though he didn't know if anything had been stolen. Then later, the storage facility was sold to new owners. More years passed. I still clung to the hope that I would someday return and reclaim the vestiges of the first 33 years of my life, but it seemed less and less likely as time went on.

Then, in 2009, while in northern Arizona, I bit the bullet. I made the decision. I might never be this close to Washington again. It was now or never. I was going back to try and get my things.

"Foolish," I told myself. "Everything has probably been thrown out or sold long ago. Or if not, it's probably worthless, having sat for 26 years in a non-climate-controlled unit in damp, rainy Washington state." I recalled that I had stored jars of home-canned vegetables, venison, and elk meat--sure I would be back to use them in no time. They had probably exploded long ago, I told myself, filling the unit with noxious toxins. Or, should my belongings still be there, I might be handed a bill for thousands of dollars, owed for the many months' rent I had missed.

Still, I needed to go. I needed to say one last farewell to the person I had been there, the life I had so loved. I made a reservation at a motel that allowed pets and set out with my two border collies and cat.

I arrived in Washington after a long but uneventful trip and, following a restless night, I faced the day. I picked up the phone and, trembling with trepidation, called the phone number of the storage facility. I half expected to hear a "no longer a working number" recording, signaling that it was closed down. Instead I heard a pleasant woman's voice say "Grand Mound Storage." When I hesitantly told her who I was she seemed unsurprised to hear from me, as if I had put my things in storage just a few months before, not 26 years ago. No expression of shock, no chastisement for not keeping up with the payments. She simply told me to stop by the office to get the key.

Hardly believing my ears, I called my pets to join me, climbed into my pickup truck, and headed over. Holding my breath, I turned the key and opened the door. Everything was just as I had left it; no smell of rotten meat, not even of mold!

For the next three days I went through the unit, thrilled to rediscover my long-lost treasures. I only planned to take back whatever would fit in or on my pickup, so I gave the furniture to a church that would share them with folks in need. Having no room for all my books, I tried to donate some of them to schools or libraries, but some had to go to the Salvation Army, where I had no idea what would happen to them. When the owners of Grand Mound Storage offered to buy a few things, I was only too happy to give them whatever they wanted.

One day, taking a break from my work, I drove down to Gate. Following the little dirt lane, now paved, I saw that Pete's and my house was gone, replaced by a mobile home which, I'm sure, Pete had put there. I called on some of my old friends and neighbors. A few, I learned, had passed away, and others had moved. Several were still there, however, and we hugged and chatted together, recalling old times. I left with tears in my eyes.

Then I returned to my packing, filling every single space in the camper shell, leaving room only for my cat's carrier. Cutting up several sheets, I made straps to tie other items on top, piling them as high as I dared. Once finished, I eyed the whole affair. It looked like a gypsy caravan! I loaded up my pets, thanked the owners of Grand Mound Storage profusely, and set out for Virginia.

Today, I look with gratitude at the reminders of my past--things I had thought to never see again. There is Dickie, a multi-colored cement horse that my father had won for me at the Virginia State Fair when I was six. There is the woven duck basket, bought on the Papago Indian Reservation for my 16th birthday by my parents on a train trip to California. A photograph of Mr. and Mrs. Hunt in front of their 14th century stone house in the Cotswolds of England. The bronze mining burro I had been so taken with in Manitou Springs, Colorado. The water-color I had painted while hiding away on St. John's Island. The captain's wheel retrieved from a sunken boat in the James River at Claremont, Virginia. The Mayan jade wall hanging Pete and I had bought in Mexico. My "Westward," print, which I had worked so hard to buy in Bend, Oregon. The walnut shelves Daddy had built in his workshop, the tablecloth Momma had hand-stitched. Here are beloved books of my childhood, many of them gifts from my parents. There will be a time, I know, when all will be dust, but for now I am happy to have them.

There is one other story I want to tell. In 2006, while living with my nephew Bryan in what is now my home on Ocracoke Island, North Carolina, I received an unexpected phone call. It was Pete. I had not heard from him in several years. His wife had died the year before, he said, and he was now working in South Carolina. He wanted, after the passage of 23 years, to come to Ocracoke and see Bryan and me. I agreed.

I did not know what to expect, or how I would feel, but I soon realized that the magic--the irresistible attraction that had ruled my life for so many years--was gone. I don't know how he felt, but we both realized that there would be no new beginnings this time, and he left after two days. Before he went I told him that I might publish this book, and that it would not always paint a complimentary picture of him. I asked him how he would feel about that, and he said to go ahead. He said that whatever I had written was probably true.

Pete had had a sore throat when he arrived. He was still smoking heavily, and the unspoken truth lay upon him like a cloud. His father, also a heavy smoker, had died of throat cancer. Not long after he left, Pete received a similar diagnosis. We stayed in touch by phone. Near the end, he could no longer talk but would listen as I spoke, trying to think of items of interest to relay, words of kindness to console. One day I got a call from his sister, who had found my number on his phone. She told me that Pete had died, a sad kind of closure.

I continue to spend time in Long Lake, and still work at the Adirondack Museum during summers. I rented the cabin on Mt. Sabattis until Carl, the owner, died and it was sold. Three years ago I bought a camp on the other side of Long Lake, on Kickerville Road, which I call Spruce Hollow. Very different from the cabin, it is nonetheless a lovely place to call home.

I am thrilled, as I do the final editing of this manuscript, to know that I am finally publishing "Birchbark Chronicles." It brings to life, at least in my mind, the people, animals, and places I have loved, and I hope that it will do the same for those who read it.

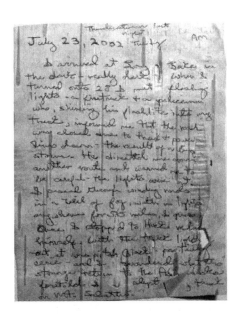

my original birch bark chronicle

Birchbark Chronicles

My Adirondack Cabin

These mountains lay beneath the sea a billion years or so.
They pushed up through the molten earth five million years ago.
Glaciers carved the valleys out where crystal lakes would form
And left behind this slab of stone my cabin sits upon.

There's splendor in the forests where the pines and hemlocks grow,
Beauty in the valleys where alpine rivers flow.
There's music in the treetops where white-throated sparrows sing
And peace within the walls of this little log cabin.

When the glaciers melted, lichens sprouted forth.
Maidenferns and clubmosses spread out across the earth.
The valleys turned to meadows with flowers of every hue.
Tiny seedlings sprouted and majestic forests grew.

And as the rivers filled the lakes, fish and frogs appeared.
The meadows became home to moose and white-tailed deer.
Brawny bears and red wolves came to hunt among the trees.
Porcupines and martens built their homes up in the leaves.

There came a bronze-skinned people who lived upon the land.
They hunted with their bows and gathered berries with their hands.
They touched the earth so gently, they left no trace behind;
Just spirits that breath softly like voices in the wind.

Then settlers and trappers came and harvested the earth.
They dug the soil and worked the stone for what they thought it worth.
They cut the mighty forests till they came to understand
That the greatest wealth these mountains have is that which can't be tamed.

It's the splendor in the forests where the pines and hemlocks grow,
The beauty in the valleys where alpine rivers flow.
It's the music in the treetops where white-throated sparrows sing
And the peace that can be found in a little log cabin.

But I am just a wayfarer along this rocky trail
Seeking solace and a moment of peace from life's travail,
And I can never claim this land, it is not mine to own
But for a little while I'll make this mountaintop my home.

Where there's splendor in the forests and the pines and hemlocks grow,
Beauty in the valleys where alpine rivers flow.
Music in the treetops where white-throated sparrows sing
And peace within the walls of this little log cabin.

A Song by Pat Garber

Pat Garber

Birchbark Chronicles

Made in the USA
Columbia, SC
24 October 2021